Destination of the Species

The Riddle of Human Existence

First published by O Books, 2010
O Books is an imprint of John Hunt Publishing Ltd., The Bothy, Deershot Lodge, Park Lane, Ropley,
Hants, SO24 0BE, UK
office1@o-books.net
www.o-books.net

Distribution in:

UK and Europe
Orca Book Services
orders@orcabookservices.co.uk
Tel: 01202 665432 Fax: 01202 666219
Int. code (44)

USA and Canada
NBN
custserv@nbnbooks.com
Tel: 1 800 462 6420 Fax: 1 800 338 4550

Australia and New Zealand
Brumby Books
sales@brumbybooks.com.au
Tel: 61 3 9761 5535 Fax: 61 3 9761 7095

Far East (offices in Singapore, Thailand,
Hong Kong, Taiwan)
Pansing Distribution Pte Ltd
kemal@pansing.com
Tel: 65 6319 9939 Fax: 65 6462 5761

South Africa
Stephan Phillips (pty) Ltd
Email: orders@stephanphillips.com
Tel: 27 21 4489839 Telefax: 27 21 4479879

Text copyright Michael Meacher 2009

Design: Stuart Davies

ISBN: 978 1 84694 263 1

A CIP catalogue record for this book is available
from the British Library.

Printed by Digital Book Print

Destination of the Species

The Riddle of Human Existence

Michael Meacher

BOOKS

Winchester, UK
Washington, USA

CONTENTS

INTRODUCTION

This book has been a long time in the making as I have struggled, often desultorily but sometimes intensively, with the fundamental question which has long perplexed me, but which I felt I could not satisfactorily answer, yet I couldn't get out of my mind.What do I really believe about human existence, why we're here, what is the universe for?

The credo ('I believe') that I was brought up on was the Nicene Creed, but that was written a millennium and a half ago, focused on repudiating the long-forgotten heresies of the day, and with little guidance for today's very different world. If we were trying to understand the ultimates about existence in the universe as we know it today, what would we write?

I have never been one of the lucky ones whose experience has given them an inner and unalterable certainty for answering these fundamental questions. Indeed I have always been struck by the fact that most people seem to have quite a clear and fixed view about the world and their place in it, even if when pressed it seemed based on rather fragmentary evidence. So confronted by this farrago of often mutually exclusive and even contradictory options (atheism versus religion, scientific rationalism versus ideological belief, predestination versus pointlessness, humans at the centre of the universe or an irrelevant scum at the margins, to mention just a few of the jarring antitheses), what did I really believe?

This book is the result of more than a decade of musing on this question. I selected each of the nodal issues, from the beginnings of the universe through to the present day, which I believed were most likely to yield the relevant evidence on which a systematic answer to my question could be based. This is of course a very well-explored area, but nevertheless I believe my approach is entirely novel and has not previously been

deployed in this form across the whole spectrum of interconnected disciplines. Drawing on the latest data from the fields of
physics, chemistry, geology, biology, philosophy and theology,
the book aims to set out as tightly, systematically and dispassion-
ately as I can (within the span of a shortish book) all of the main
components that need to be brought together to underpin the
answer to the central question – Who are? Where did we come
from? Where are we going to?

The quest has been remarkably revealing. The systematic
review of all the scientific evidence strongly suggests that the
Dawkins and neo-Darwinian view that the universe is driven by
pitiless, directionless chance is seriously wrong and misleading.
Rather the evidence indicates: astronomically precise fine-tuning
in the construction of the universe; early life driven for billions of
years by symbiotic and co-operative networking, not blindly by
mutations; and the spontaneous transposition of matter and
energy into new higher organisational states at certain thresholds
of complexity both in biological and cosmological systems.

All this, and so much else, suggests an utterly different, far
more complex, much more meaningful picture. Instead of an
analytic, reductionist and arbitrary model of the universe, it
uncovers a dramatically different subjective, holistic and
purposeful one.

The book is not parti pris, not written from the propagandistic
viewpoint either of science or religion. It is written as a sceptical
searching after how all the component parts of human experience
fit together within a single indivisible reality, and what that
totality means. Whether the issue is the origin and development
of the universe, the origin and evolution of life forms on Earth,
the absurdly unlikely but probably inevitable evolution of the
human species, or the intellectual, cultural and spiritual
uniqueness of humans, the survey of all the evidence repeatedly
returns to the central question: what does all this <u>mean</u>?

Is it also compatible with other dimensions of human

experience, including religious experience which is ratified, not by scientific verification, but by its own different (though equally demanding) paradigm of validity? What the evidence again indicates is that religion and science, so far from being incompatible, are in fact mutually complementary. The book spells out how the latest scientific findings about a designed and purposeful organisation of the universe and of life forms within it point to an ultimate reality, not of the human race as the summit of evolution, but of an overarching cosmic plan of which we are a key part.

The narrative is in two parts. The first, chapters 2-9, systematically examines the range of the key sources of evidence, while the second part, chapters 10-13, assesses the status of the evidence and aims to bring together the summation of the evidence in a single consolidated new theory. Unsurprisingly, it rejects a number of widely held current views on grounds of ideological or doctrinal bias which no longer fits the evidence as currently accumulated. The book ends with a new perspective based firmly within the parameters of the whole range of available evidence.

Inevitably the thread may in places not be easy to follow, though in general that simply reflects how complex and technical the evidence base of scientific discovery can sometimes be. It seemed preferable to lay out the full weight of the scientific case rather than to simplify or abbreviate the necessary information at the risk of undermining the full force of the argument. However, each chapter ends with an Implications section which tries to draw out the meaning behind the evidence just presented. In addition, a glossary is provided of all the main scientific terms.

The bringing together of all the tributaries of argument begins in chapter 11 and runs through to chapter 13. The significance of the scientific, religious and philosophical material is then assessed in conjunction (provided statements of non-scientific experience meet acceptable criteria of reliability), and the cross-readings between the insights of these very different aspects of human experience are pulled together to point the way to reach a new synthesis and a new vision.

Chapter 1

The Model's Wrong

The framework of inquiry

Que sommes nous? D'ou venons nous? Ou allons nous? There is really only one question for human beings that in the end matters. That is, what, if any, is the purpose of existence, and what are we here for? It is a question that has underlain religious conviction and philosophic inquiry throughout human history, and to which scientific rationalism in recent centuries has added some important insights. It highlights two contesting views of the nature of reality: is there a purpose behind the universe, and if so, is the evolution of man somehow related to that purpose, or is it a mechanistic universe driven by blind natural forces in which there is no ultimate purpose and no meaning of life? Or is there indeed some alternative third explanation? These questions will recur throughout this book and in every case, as each dimension of human understanding and experience is analysed, the question is posed: what does this tell us? What does this mean?

These are also clearly questions to which there is no final and absolute answer. Each generation, drawing on its inheritance of understanding, builds on its own experiences, new discoveries and fresh insights to construct its own special approach to ultimate meaning. For centuries until the Enlightenment, religion seemed to offer an authoritative repository of final truth, until the rise of empirical scientific method removed its mantle of certitude. But just as religion survived the onslaught of rationalism by adopting a more pragmatic and flexible approach to religious phenomena, in the same way scientific propositions have come to be seen, so far from being fixed and invariable descriptions of the world around us, rather as constantly shifting approximations to an endlessly elusive underlying reality. 'Truth' is not an objective element out there; as preached by scientists it often turns out to be no more than prejudice inspired by prevailing social and political beliefs[1].

What then is one to believe about the ultimates of human existence? Regretfully, too many start from an a priori position. Either that is a religious standpoint which is taken as fundamental based on experience or faith, and all other observations of human affairs and of the universe are fitted to this pattern and its presuppositions. Or it is a starkly material framework which precludes all non-cognitive evidence as at best fantasy or at worst fraudulent. In either case the starting point is usually preconceived, and judgements are adopted about the world to rationalise pre-existing attitudes. What this book seeks to do is rather to assess the evidence – the whole range of it – without a predetermined worldview as a premise, and to decide, as objectively as possible, what the evidence on balance points to.

In one sense, such objectivity is a chimera. We all approach matters of judgement with a set of values acquired throughout life which propels us to one particular interpretation or another. All that one can do, by being conscious of this, is to try to resist the impulse and to remain open to the widest range of interpretation of phenomena. For the questions to be answered are almost metaphysical in form – not so much what is the evidence, but what is the relevant evidence, and what does it mean? And how do all the relevant strands of human experience – physical, psychological, aesthetic, moral and spiritual – connect together, as they must in some way since reality is indivisible?

But the question goes a great deal wider than the centuries-old disputes between religion and science. It requires at the outset a determination of the total framework of eligible evidence. For any final conclusions will clearly depend heavily on what categories of data are regarded as admissible, what weight is attached to different kinds of evidence, and how the relationship between them is assessed. Furthermore, the 'meaning' of things is not a mono-dimensional concept, to be ascertained and verified by experiment. It is a matter of interpretation, values and above all perspective, and there can be no certainty that what seems to offer an intellectually satisfying insight in one generation will not be superseded by deeper understanding of the same phenomena in the next.

Plan of the book

The framework adopted for exploring these issues is as follows. First, alternative theoretical models to explain the existence of the universe need to be identified. These need to be assessed on the basis of several fundamental dimensions. These include the time dimension (infinite/created in time), causative agency (chance/necessity/God), mechanism of creation (quantum fluctuation within the vacuum/singularity), and rationale (created for a purpose/mechanistic and purposeless).

Next, the most up-to-date empirical data, and the theories derived from them, need to be analysed according to a range of major criteria. What empirically, or by deduction, do we know about the origins of the universe, the fine tuning of its formation, the generation of life forms, the development of the biodiversity of life, the uniqueness of the human species, the complexity of design of the material world, and the virtual universality of religious experience? And in each case what does this tell us about the validity of each of the models or the need for another different model? The argument of this book is that there is indeed a need for a new theory and a new model, and this is gradually developed throughout the course of the analysis, concluding with a new presentation of the likely destination of the human species.

Part I

The Factual Evidence

Chapter 2

Origins of the Universe

There are several cross-cutting dimensions by which competing theories about the nature of existence can be categorised. Either the universe (all that there is) always existed and is infinite, and was therefore never created, or it (the universe we know, or pre-existing universes traceable back to an initial point of origin) is finite, and was therefore created in time. If it was created, another dimension concerns the dynamic of that creation. Either it was created without a purpose, whether by chance or by necessity, or it was created for a purpose. And again, if it was created, another dimension concerns how it originated. Either it arose out of nothing, or it was generated by means outside and beyond the physical universe we know – generally taken to refer to some ultimately existent being (God). All these theories have had their adherents.

Against that background, there are basically five prevailing theories about the origin of the universe. One, associated with Bondi and Gold, claims that the universe had no origin because it is infinite in time and extent. A second, a version of which was propounded by Hawking and Hartle, asserts that the universe is finite, but not bounded in time, in that its space-time boundary is rounded and cannot therefore be shown to have its origin at any one particular point in time. Other versions philosophise about whether the universe came into existence out of necessity or by chance. The third, advocated by Atkins, hypothesizes a universe that came into existence ex nihilo, as a result of a quantum fluctuation within the vacuum whose expansion was then colossally accelerated by a postulated process known as inflation. The fourth, the standard model of physics, argues that the universe arose out of a singularity, a point of infinite density subject to infinite compression where the laws of physics break down. The fifth, which is not incompatible with the others but equally not limited to them, believes that the universe was created by God. This framework of alternatives does not of course exclude the postulation of other models. But it is important to bear in mind that all these models are speculative and not susceptible of proof, since ipso facto the initial conditions at the beginning of the universe cannot be reproduced or tested.

Model 1 - A universe without beginning or end

The theory of an infinite universe was postulated in the 1940s by Bondi and Gold. They envisaged that the rate of expansion of the universe remained constant, with matter being created at a rate just sufficient to maintain a constant average density. This 'steady state' universe had no beginning and no end. However, this left several questions unanswered. How was matter created, and at the right rate? A colleague, Fred Hoyle, proposed a 'creation field' that would produce new particles of matter, though without violating the law of conservation of energy because the creation field carried negative energy which matched the positive energy of the created matter. But even if this postulate were true, it does not adequately explain how or why the universe happens to exist as it does, as opposed to its equilibral state once created, or why it has the form it does. Nor does it explain why the universe has relevant fields such as the creation field, or how the physical principles originate that generate the steady-state condition.

What however falsified the steady-state theory was the observation by radio telescopes probing billions of light years into deep space that the universe looked very different in much earlier epochs, contrary to the steady-state hypothesis. This was confirmed by the finding in 1965 that the universe is immersed in heat radiation at a temperature of about three degrees above absolute zero. This was seen as the fading glow from the primeval heat at the explosive creation of the universe, and was incompatible with the steady-state thesis.

Model 2 - A finite universe without a beginning

An alternative cosmology proposed by Hartle and Hawking does not assume a background space-time in which the universe is created. Instead of the universe springing into existence from a point singularity, they depict its origin as the smooth hemispherical base of a cone so that there is no abrupt beginning at any point. This would have remarkable implications if it could be validated (it is purely speculative): it would abolish the Big Bang singularity, it would remove the conventional dualism between laws and initial conditions, and it would end the distinction between space and time – in this model time emerges slowly from space as the hemisphere curves gradually into the cone. Also if the universe has no boundary and no beginning, it would remove the need to posit a supernatural act of creation at the outset.

Their model depends on a theory of quantum gravity, though this is at present only a hypothesis. The idea of external time, as a dynamic reality implying passage and development, is replaced by the concept of internal time associated with the curvature or temperature of a particular 3-dimensional space. As an explanation of the origins of the universe, however, the Hartle-Hawking model falls short on several counts. In effect it transforms the phenomenological reality of time into a mathematical variable and then treats it as a pure abstraction, which can hardly then be rightly understood as time at all. In addition, deriving an origin from a quantum mechanical state function does not avoid the concept of a beginning. It requires pre-existent Hilbert spaces, quantum operators, Hamiltonians, imaginary numbers, and other abstract mathematical entities. Further, if external time does not exist, no state can follow any other, which would seem to imply a wholly static domain where fluctuations, entailing change in time, cannot take place.

Model 3 - A finite universe with contingent causation

If then the universe is finite and was created in time, was it created for a reason, or irrationally whether by chance or necessity? Some philosophers like David Hume have claimed the universe came into existence for no reason at all. It is simply there as a brute fact, the bottom line of any available explanation. But this is wholly unsatisfactory as a rationale. If, as almost all scientists now believe, the universe sprang from the Big Bang singularity, it is necessary to explain why it did so, not in a random or chaotic manner, but according to discoverable mathematical constants and scientific laws which have governed its development to the state seen today. There must have been already a complex set of quantum laws determining the interactions of elementary particles, and indeed some have postulated that the universe originated from fluctuations in a quantum field governed by those laws. It is disingenuous to describe such a comprehensive and integrated array of basic laws as a brute fact, defying further analysis.

If then the origin of the universe cannot be treated as a chance event, did it happen by necessity? Some physicists like Steven Weinberg reject the irrationality of the 'mere chance' hypothesis, and posit a universe by necessity so that it can be wholly intelligible. It is suggested that there is only one logically consistent set of quantum laws which of necessity produces a universe like ours. However, it is impossible to prove that no other systems than the ones we can imagine could possibly exist. The claim that the existence of this particular universe is necessary implies that no other universe could come into existence, and in order to know that, we would need to know every conceivable contingency possible. In fact, it is perfectly feasible to postulate a universe built on different physical laws or different initial conditions which would generate many finite space-times and many different forms of existence than those in this particular space-time. And even if the universe did come into being through mathematical necessity, how could it give rise to the contingent world we know today?

If then the universe did not come into existence either by chance or by necessity, how did it arise? Did it come into being out of nothing? This thesis, advanced by Peter Atkins[2], and drawing on quantum cosmology, proposes that fluctuations may occur in nothing, and eventually produce a physical universe. It can be claimed that gravitational energy, which is negative, and rest mass and kinetic energy, which are positive, could balance out leading to a state of zero net energy. If in that state quantum fluctuations take place, it might be said that the universe has arisen out of nothing, i.e. come into being by chance out of a vacuum (quantum fields in their lowest energy state). But it is quite false to suggest this represents a universe coming into existence out of absolutely nothing. For quantum fluctuations to occur, there must be a background space-time, and there have to be quantum fields with precise properties of energy and mass. Moreover there would also have to be in place probabilistic laws governing quantum fluctuations. Pre-existing entities and structures are therefore necessary for this theory, and creation out of nothing is not tenable.

But even if the universe were to have arisen out of nothing, it still has to be asked why such an event should have happened. The mathematician Roger Penrose has estimated that the probability of our universe, fine-tuned as it is to such extraordinary precision is about 1 in 10^{123} out of the array in 'phase space' of possible universes [3]. Even though the odds against this universe coming into existence by chance are so astronomically colossal, what Atkins seems to suggest is that this absurdly improbable universe would, given the infinity of time, come into being sooner or later through a process of purposeless chance.

However, since the issue is the origin of space-time, it isn't clear what is meant by his concept of 'before' the existence of space-time, let alone the pre-existence of infinity of time. Also it is not explained how or why every potential universe is apparently actualised, or what mechanism is driving this process, and where that derived from.

Model 4 - Origin from a singularity, the standard model of physics

Whilst the idea that the universe began as an explosion was first put forward by Georges Lemaitre in 1910, the evidence for the Big Bang theory was originally produced in 1922 by the Russian physicist, Alexander Friedmann, by reworking Einstein's general theory of relativity which predicted a non-static universe. Either the universe starts out from a singularity (a point of infinite compression where the entire cosmos would have been squeezed into a single point, and the gravitational force and density of material were infinite), and then goes on expanding forever if there is insufficient matter for gravity eventually to bring the cosmic dispersion to a halt. Or it burst forth from an initial Big Bang, expands over several billion years at an ever-diminishing rate, and then begins to contract again until it finally disappears at a Big Crunch. Or the cycle is continually repeated (the oscillating universe model), perhaps with cycles growing larger over successive multi-billion year periods.

Several subsequent discoveries seemed to confirm this theoretical prediction of an expanding universe. Edwin Hubble found in 1929 that galactic light was red-shifted, which implied that the galaxies were rushing apart from each other as from an explosion. In 1965 two American radio astronomers Penzias and Wilson detected a weak hiss of radio noise coming from all directions, which was explained as the fading afterglow of the fireball birth of the cosmos. Then in 1992 NASA's Cosmic Background Explorer (COBE) satellite confirmed that ripples in the background radiation of exactly the right size needed to explain the existence of galaxies had indeed been found. It detected the colder and denser spots of the early universe from which, some 300,000 years after the Big Bang singularity itself, wispy clouds of matter began to form and stretch across vast distances – clouds which later collapsed in on themselves under the force of their own gravity and then broke up into clusters of galaxies. Yet another finding which seemed to lend support to the Big Bang thesis was the discovery that about 25% of the mass of the universe is in the form of the element helium. Whilst most elements, such as carbon and iron, are known to be made from hydrogen by nuclear reaction inside stars, the universe has simply not existed long enough for stars to have made such a large quantity of helium. This suggests that at one time in the past the entire universe passed through an ultra-hot dense phase in which nuclear reactions forged most of its helium from hydrogen. Calculations show that such a phase – a Big Bang fireball – would have turned about 25% of the mass of the universe into helium, exactly as observed.

Yet doubts are accumulating about the validity of Big Bang theory. First, it relies on a growing number of hypothetical entities which have never been observed, of which inflation, dark energy and dark matter are the most prominent, in order to align the predictions of the theory with the actual observations of astronomers. Without the speculative inflation field, Big Bang does not predict the smooth, isotropic cosmic background radiation that is observed. Without so-called dark matter, Big Bang theory makes contradictory predictions for the density of matter in the universe, since inflation requires a density twenty times larger than that implied by Big Bang nucleosynthesis, the theory's explanation of the origin of the light elements. And without dark energy, the theory predicts that the universe is only some eight billion years old, which is billions of years younger than many stars in our galaxy. Also, the Big Bang theory has not been able to make any quantitative predictions which have later been validated by observation. And discordant data on red shifts, lithium and helium abundances, and galaxy distribution, among other issues, are too often ignored. Moreover the latest evidence from the Wilkinson Microwave Anisotropy Probe, the jewel in the crown of cosmology instruments, suggests that the hot and cold regions in the cosmic background radiation are not randomly distributed, but seem to line up along the same direction, indicating that the universe is not the same in all places and in all directions, which would flout a fundamental assumption of all Big Bang models.

Thus the standard model which has been used to deduce the age and make-up of the universe is disputed. The standard model predicts that the universe is 13.7 million years old (based on the most widely accepted estimate of the Hubble constant) and that its contents comprise just 4% ordinary matter (half unseen), 23% dark matter (nature unknown) and 73% dark energy (also nature unknown). In other words, in order to fix the problem of the extra tug needed to speed up galaxy formation, the standard model calls into existence a vast amount of invisible dark matter for which no independent evidence has ever been adduced. Moreover, dark energy is hard to square with theories of quantum gravity and its observed density is so small that it may be quantum mechanically unstable.

In recent years however several alternative models have been formulated that dispense with these hypothetical constructs and hence with the Big Bang itself. Lerner's plasma cosmology[4], for example, noting that almost all observed matter in the universe is in the form of plasma, explains the cosmic microwave background, not as the afterglow of the Big Bang, but as jets of plasma squirted into intergalactic space by highly energetic quasar galaxies which then as plasma filaments continually fragmented until they filled the universe like fog, and that this fog then scattered the infrared light radiated by dust that had in turn absorbed starlight so that the infrared radiation became uniform in all directions. Another theorist, Scarpa[5], noting that dark matter turns up in places where the standard model says it shouldn't exist – for example in globular clusters, tight knots of stars that orbit the Milky Way and many other galaxies – argues that the phenomenon which dark matter is posited to explain may be explained rather by a breakdown of Newton's law of gravity, in that his inverse square law holds true only above some critical threshold of acceleration. The evidence for this is that the same effect has been observed in spiral galaxies and galaxy-rich clusters, which led Milgrom[6] to propose a theory known as modified Newtonian dynamics (MOND) to explain it. Counter-arguments that MOND is not compatible with Einstein's theory of relativity, so it is not valid for objects travelling close to the speed of light or in very strong gravitational fields, and so is powerless to make predictions about pulsars, black holes and above all Big Bang, have been refuted by Bekenstein's relativistic version of the theory. Researchers at the University of Oxford have shown that relativistic MOND can indeed make cosmo-logical predictions, and researchers have reproduced both the observed properties of the cosmic microwave background and the distribution of galaxies throughout the universe.

If MOND is right, then the law of gravity from which Big Bang is derived is wrong, in which case a new cosmological model based on MOND is needed. This process, whereby a standard theory which has stood the test of time and has been almost universally accepted, is finally overthrown because it is shown to be based on insupportable premises, is not uncommon in the history of thought. The old Earth-centred cosmology of Ptolemy needed layer upon layer of epicycles to sustain it, until it was finally discredited by Copernicus, Brahe and Galileo. Newtonian dynamics reigned supreme based on the implicit premise of an absolute space and time, till this was disproved by Einstein's theory of general relativity. Einstein in 1917 invented a 'cosmological constant' in order to make general relativity compatible with a static eternal universe, until Hubble's discovery in 1929 of expansion of the real universe made this fudge factor redundant. In the same way it may be that the current standard model's dependence on observations retrospectively fitted with a steadily increasing array of adjustable parameters has reached the point where there must be serious questions about the validity of the underlying theory.

Model 5 - Creation by God

This uncertainty must inhibit any final religious conclusions being drawn from the Big Bang scenario, though that did not prevent the Vatican triumphantly, but rather naively, proclaiming that Big Bang confirmed the Genesis story of creation. Whatever the scientific explanation of the origin of the universe, which is likely to undergo several revisions yet, the theistic hypothesis is that the universe emerged out of the unrestricted actuality of the mind of God, by an intentional act of creation[7]. The strongest force behind this claim is that the universe – the totality of things which are contingent or not self-explanatory – requires an explanation for the existence of every-thing that is external to itself, and that sufficient First Cause is what people understand as God. This is in effect a restatement of Aquinas' cosmological argument and a reformulation of Leibniz' Principle of Sufficient Reason. It is dependent on the concept of an uncaused cause, the unmoved mover, the Being having of itself its own necessity. It is a rejection of the atheistic argument that 'the universe is a brute fact, it just is, and that is all there is to it'.

There are two reasons however why this might seem an unsatisfactory position. First, it might appear as another example, for which there are many historical precedents, of resort to 'the God of the gaps' – the invocation of God to fill a gap in scientific knowledge, only to be dispensed with later as science extends the boundaries of its understanding. However, that should be rejected as an argument here when what is at issue is not a missing link in a skein of scientific knowledge, but rather the much more profound philosophical question of whether it makes sense to think of a world of causality without an originating cause. The second point is more fundamental. It could be argued that what the Cosmological Argument arrives at is not the God whom religious believers worship. In this Argument, God is portrayed as a metaphysical causal entity, far removed from the personalised being in the world's religions. However, that too may be countered on the grounds that God (assuming he exists) is by his very nature systematically unknowable by human beings, and that any portrayal of him in any context is inevitably a fragmentary and selective glimpse of the unknowable totality of his being. It may also be argued that the whole purpose of religious revelation, whether through prophets or a messiah-figure, is precisely to enable the unknowable to be seen in the only (very limited) form that humans can comprehend. If – and this is a central if – God exists, then by the very nature of his God-ness there can be no constraint on the full range of manifestation of his being in any context or any purpose that he chooses.

Implications

The evidence presented here is not decisive in answering the question about the nature and origin of the universe and therefore of man's role within it. The philosophical views are not tenable; the scientific theory is uncertain and in any event can only answer the question 'how', not 'why', while religion provides an ulterior explanation which is dependent on an a priori assumption about the existence and nature of God and the application of causality beyond the material universe. Philosophers like Atkins or scientists like Hawking who seek to explain the origin of the universe mechanistically without reference to God cannot validate their case, while religious believers simply treat the creation of the world as another manifestation of an all-powerful deity whose existence is pre-judged. Disputation about the origins of the universe do not settle the central argument of this book either one way or the other.

Chapter 3

Fine-Tuning

Whatever the precise origins of the universe – exactly how it came into existence, and why – there is one aspect of its creation which is scientifically indubitable and has profound implications for any attempt to explain it. This is that the universe, as steadily uncovered by science, turns out to be spectacularly fine-tuned for life, in the sense that if there had been even very small changes in the basic features of its structure, it would have made the generation of life and the evolution of life forms impossible. This does not automatically mean that the fine-tuning must be the work of a designer God. The explanation needs to be assessed on the merits of the evidence.

The evidence

In several ways the development of the cosmos at or shortly after Big Bang (as formulated by the standard model, even if that will require modification for reasons set out in chapter 2) is astonishing almost to the point of incredulity. That conclusion applies to several different categories of evidence.

First, the construction of the Big Bang event itself is extraordinary. The nature of the explosion reveals a balance between centrifugal and centripetal forces which is mind-blowingly exact. If the former had been even a fraction too strong, then the cosmos would have expanded so fast as to preclude galaxy formation. If the latter had been ever so slightly too strong, the cosmos could have re-collapsed almost immediately. To prevent both these scenarios, the rate of expansion in the early instants had to be fine-tuned to perhaps one part in 10^{55} – that is a precision with a deviation of only 1/10000000000000000000000000000000000

00000000000000000000th, equivalent to hitting a dartboard on the other side of the universe billions of trillions of miles away. Secondly, a universe as smooth as this one, allowing all regions to expand in a carefully orchestrated manner, also requires amazingly accurate fine-tuning. Large regions extruded from Big Bang might be expected to be uncoordinated, and when they made contact enormous turbulence would be generated, leading to a cosmos of black holes or of temperatures which prevented galaxies from forming for billions of years, after which matter would be far too dissipated for them to form at all.

Third, the phenomenon hypothesized to solve these two problems, known respectively as the flatness problem and the smoothness problem, is 'inflation', but this itself requires extraordinary fine-tuning. The hypothesis – which is purely speculative, and simply designed to get round Big Bang's two main problems – is that within the first second after Big Bang, after initial deceleration, a short burst of enormously accelerating expansion occurred which could have increased the size of the universe by a factor of as much as $10^{1,000,000}$. It has been estimated that within a miniscule period of time between 10^{-35} and 10^{-33} (i.e. between 0.000000000000000000000000000000001% and 0.000000000000000000000000000001% of a second) the universe expanded from a radius of 10^{-25} cm to the scale of our visible universe today (with a radius of 3×10^{27} cm). This could mean that the world we now see had developed from a region whose component parts were well coordinated at the outset, which would provide the observed smoothness. In addition, a space suddenly colossally expanded might be very flat like the surface of a hugely inflated balloon. However this expedient itself needs almost fantastically accurate fine-tuning for it to happen at all and for it to generate irregularities that are not even fractionally too great or too small for galaxies to form. In fact, the two components of an expansion-driving cosmological constant cancel each other out with an accuracy better than one part in

10^{50} (i.e. less than 1/100000000000000000000000000000000000 00000000000000000th inaccurate). Even that minutest inaccuracy may not represent a shortfall in perfection. If the balance had been completely perfect, inflation might well not have occurred. This is all absolutely staggering in its precision.

But it is only the start of a long series of extremely finely balanced phenomena in almost every aspect of the universe's structure, particularly the four fundamental forces and the particle masses. First, the strengths of the nuclear weak force and of gravity are calibrated so precisely that a difference of even such an utterly miniscule amount as one part in 10^{100} (i.e.1/1000000000000000000000000000000000000000000000000000000 0000000000000000000000000000000000000000000000000000th, or one thousandth trillionth trillionth trillionth trillionth trillionth trillionth trillionth trillionth) in their present strengths could destroy the cancelling out between the two most fundamental forces holding the universe on its present course. Equally, if the nuclear weak force had been significantly stronger, Big Bang would have burned all hydrogen to helium, and then there could be no water or long-lived stable stars. If on the other hand it had been significantly weaker, it would again have destroyed the hydrogen, and in addition neutrons formed in the early stages of the universe would not have decayed into protons. Again, if the nuclear weak force did not have precisely the strength it does, neutrinos would not have been able to interact with stars both weakly enough to escape from the core of a collapsing supernova and strongly enough to blast its outer layers into space so as to provide the building blocks for planets such as ours.

If carbon, the essential component of all living creatures, is to be created in sufficient amounts inside stars, the nuclear strong force needs to be neither 1% stronger or weaker than its present strength. If it were as little as 2% stronger, protons would not be formed, and hence there would be no atoms. On the other hand, if its strength were around 5% less, the deuteron would not bind together, which would make it impossible for stars to burn, and hence the material for life would not be created.

The third force, electromagnetism, also needs to be very fine-tuned if stars are not to be either too cold or too hot for life to evolve as it has. If it were only very slightly stronger, main sequence stars would then all become red stars, unable to explode as the supernovae needed to create elements heavier than iron. Even a strength as little as 1% greater could have doubled the time necessary for intelligent life to evolve, because it would make chemical changes more difficult. If however its strength were very slightly weaker, all main sequence stars would be very hot and short-lived blue stars, rather than burning in stable form over billions of years to produce the conditions necessary for life. Equally, the ratio between electromagnetism and gravity, the fourth force, is crucial, and gravity also needs to be extremely fine-tuned for stars and planets to form. Gravity is about 10^{39} times weaker than electromagnetism, but if it had been only 10^{33} times weaker, stars would be a billion times less massive and would burn a million times faster, making the evolution of life much more unlikely if not impossible.

Particle masses also have to have very precise values if life is to emerge. If the difference in mass between neutrons and protons – as little as one part in 1,000 – had not been almost exactly twice the mass of the electron, either all neutrons would have decayed into protons or all protons would have changed irreversibly into neutrons, and if either of these had happened there would not be the 200 or so stable types of atom on which the chemistry and biology of life depend. If the super-heavy particles operating shortly after Big Bang had had small changes in their masses, it could have led to profound alterations in the ratio of matter particles to photons, yielding a universe full of black holes or of matter too dissipated to form galaxies. Further, the masses of a whole set of scalar particles might affect the value of the cosmological constant in relation to its capacity to allow inflation to occur and whether it was later tiny enough to allow space to be very flat. Otherwise there would be very violent expansion or contraction. But the margin of appropriateness here is again utterly miniscule – the constant today is between zero and 10^{120}, a value of almost unimaginably precise dimensions.

This evidence, and much more, has been set out comprehensively in several sources[8]. Even if some of the particular details need to be modified slightly in the light of future scientific knowledge, the impact of the broad picture is overwhelming. The chances against several of these phenomena being mere coincidences are stupendous. The chances against all of them being mere coincidences must be virtually infinite. So how then are they to be explained? How does one explain, according to the calculations of Roger Penrose, the English mathematician[9], that in the absence of new principles guaranteeing a smooth beginning, the accuracy required in selecting our highly ordered universe from the range of physically possible ones would have been of the order of 1 part in 10^{123} (one in a hundred trillion trillion trillion trillion trillion trillion trillion trillion trillion)? How does one explain, as Dicke calculated[10], that a speed decrease of only one part in a million at one second after Big Bang would have led to the re-collapse of the universe before temperatures fell below 10,000º, while an equally miniscule speed increase would have made the gases so dilute that minor density irregularities could not have arisen for the formation of stars? Or how does one explain that the cosmic density at Planck time, 10^{-43} of a second after Big Bang, must have been within one part in 10^{60} (i.e. within a trillionth trillionth trillionth trillionth trillionth) of the critical density required to place it exactly on the line between collapse and unstoppable expansion? If inflation did get started, how did it end without great turbulence (the graceful exit problem), and how did it produce irregularities neither too little nor too large for the later formation of galaxies? And if then some Grand Unified Theory were cunningly formulated to construct laws offering the necessary explanation, is that not re-introducing the fine-tuning which inflation was designed to avoid?

The key point in assessing the importance of fine-tuning to near-incredible precision is that even the tiniest changes in the fundamental constants would have meant that no nuclei, atoms, stars or galaxies would have been created, and hence of course no life. If there were a change even as tiny as one part in 10^{100} (a change smaller than a trillionth trillionth trillionth trillionth trillionth trillionth trillionth trillionth) in the adjustment of gravity to the weak nuclear force, the cosmos would suffer either swift collapse or explosion. Equally, changing by as little as one part in 10^{40} (a change of less than a billionth billionth billionth billionth) in the balance between gravity and electromagnetism would have catastrophic effects on stars. If electromagnetism were ever so slightly stronger, stars would burn too slowly and be unable to produce the supernovae explosions needed to spread heavy elements as the source of life (our solar system for example being triggered, it seems very likely, by such a supernova explosion). On the other hand, if electromagnetism were only very slightly weaker, stars would burn too fast to support the evolution of life on their planets.

Similar considerations apply to particle masses. John Barrow and Frank Tipler have shown that if the electromagnetic fine structure constant were not as small as it is – about 1/137 – the difference between material things and waves could not be maintained[11]. If the fraction had been much larger, atoms and molecules would be rendered very unstable. Again, it has been indicated that if space did not have its present topology (the way its points are connected) and metrical properties, long-lasting material particles could not exist. Thus space need not be three-dimensional; current theory suggests that space-time has at least ten dimensions, though only four can now be detected because the others became 'compactified' or very tightly rolled up in the process of Big Bang. But Ehrenfest long ago argued[12] that such crucial conditions as the stability of atoms and planetary orbits, the complexity of living organisms, and the ability of waves to propagate without distortion (vital for example in nervous systems) are only available in three dimensions.

The list of elaborate checks and balances that have kept the material universe developing smoothly over billions of years is a long one (and no doubt many further discoveries remain to be made). As further additions to the evidence, the nuclear strong force repels at extremely short ranges and thus prevents the protons and neutrons in a complex atom from collapsing into each other, but at slightly longer ranges it attracts and thus holds them tightly together, giving the atom a very accurately located centre; otherwise all matter would be fluid. At ranges somewhat longer (though still very short) the nuclear strong force falls to zero; if it did not and acted at long range, it would rapidly collapse the universe. Then there are principles like 'baryon conservation' which, though mediated by no force field, prevents the entire material contents of the universe from being consumed in a fireball of gamma radiation, as protons decayed to positrons and annihilated all the electrons. And, to give one final example, as Rozenthal has commented, if particles had no spin (measured as the angular momentum of a rotating system), there would be neither electromagnetism nor gravity; and equally, if hadrons (particles which feel the strong nuclear force) did not have isotopic spin, complex stable nuclei could not exist.

The nature of scientific laws

Yet however compelling cosmological fine-tuning is as a series of staggering facts to be explained, it is still not by itself a sufficient explanation for the complex intricacy of the world we see. For the precise measurement of the fundamental constants often seems to be over-determined, i.e. force strengths and particle masses often seem to be required to be what they are, not just for one overriding reason, but for several. Yet clearly they would not be able to satisfy several different requirements if these were in conflict, because obviously they cannot take on several different values at once. It requires some explanation therefore why these requirements are in practice not in conflict. One widely accepted theory is that the forces were originally all equal, part of a single unified force, and that there was just one species of particle. As the universe cooled in the first few seconds, this unity was destroyed by a process of symmetry-breaking. A series of scalar fields (fields characterised by intensity, not by direction) were set up, and interactions with these fields caused the particles to take on mass, and particle masses underlie the differences between the four main force strengths in the cosmos. But what established the values of the scalar fields? Were they random or were they deterministic, and if the latter, how were they caused? This is an instance of a recurring problem as scientific theory pushes the process of explanation further and further back. If there were special initial conditions which started the evolution of the universe on the course leading to the present, what selected those rather than any other initial conditions?

The traditional classical view is that initial conditions are independent of the laws of physics. If on this view the initial conditions of the universe can be freely specified, their status would then be secondary to the laws of physics and the values of fundamental constants. An alternative view is that there is some meta-law governing initial conditions which is fundamentally linked to the notion of scientific laws in a manner that transcends our normal experience of classical physics. If such a link exists, it would entail a situation with some probabilistic element about possible forms of evolution, and that is precisely the current focus of quantum cosmology (the theory developed from Planck's quantum principle and Heisenberg's uncertainty principle). Thus the equation proposed by the American physicists John Wheeler and Bryce De Witt sets out the probabilities that the observed universe will be found to possess certain large-scale features, hopefully with values that correspond with the way that large everyday objects have definite properties. However, that still requires some initial conditions for the Wheeler-De Witt equation that is an initial form for the wave function of the universe.

This leads to the question of whether there exists a 'law' of initial conditions. If so, it would seem to imply that the laws of nature are transcendent. They are universal, absolute, eternal, and omnipotent (i.e. nothing escapes them). Yet since they are only manifested in physical phenomena, in what sense do they have an independent existence? One answer, by analogy, is that the laws of physics correspond to 'cosmic software', a sort of computer programme for the universe, while physical states are the hardware. For, strikingly, all known fundamental laws are found to be mathematical in form. But taking this analogy further, is this software or computer programme a human invention or does it reflect a fundamental reality out there? It is surely clear that the laws of nature are not simply artificial constructs, but it is equally clear that there is no finality in our perception of them. Three-dimensional Euclidean geometry for example was for two millennia regarded as a fundamental fact of the world, but we now believe this was only so because we live in a space-time in which gravity is quite weak, so that the curvature of space was not noticed. Thus a given set of data may be able to be explained by more than one or even several different laws, and our choice between them may be arbitrary, based on culture or with a bias towards simplicity (on the principle of Occam's razor – entia non sunt multiplicanda praeter necessitatem). Yet that still leaves the most fundamental question: why these laws rather than some other set? And why laws at all rather than a completely random universe? These questions, valid as they are, confront the logical equivalent of the First Cause – the need for a meta-explanation to begin the whole chain of explanation. To that, science does not at present have, and perhaps never can have, an answer.

So how is fine-tuning to be explained?

One answer to the question as to how or why the universe is so fine-tuned is that if it were not so fine-tuned for life, we would not be here to observe it. Put more formally, the weak anthropic principle states that the conditions necessary for the development of intelligent life will be met only in certain regions of the universe, and intelligent beings in those regions not surprisingly observe that their locality in the universe satisfies the conditions necessary for their existence. But this is a logically necessary truth, not an explanation. The strong anthropic principle however states that our universe must be such as to admit the creation of observers within it at some stage. In effect it posits an ensemble of universes and an observational selection effect. It proposes a multiverse, or set of universes, each perhaps with differing laws, and that only a small sub-set of this total framework of universes possesses the rather special laws for living creatures like us to emerge.

So is it plausible that multiple worlds exist? John Leslie, in his comprehensive and thorough analysis of this theory[12A], sets out the options. One proposal, by GFR Ellis and GB Brundrit[13], suggests that traditional cosmic models, when combined with the low densities suggested by direct observations, provide for a cosmos whose space is 'open' (i.e. its surface edges do not curve round and join up with themselves). An open universe would seem to be infinitely large, and if it is the same in all directions – as seems to be the case – then it contains infinitely many regions. And if these regions are counted as separate universes when they are situated beyond one another's horizons, a collection of infinitely many universes is arrived at. However, an obvious objection is that there seems no simple means for such a universe to come into existence in a Big Bang (and no alternative origin is proposed). From its earliest moments its parts would have been too far separated to achieve concordance on the time they would all spring into existence.

A second possible generator of multiple universes is the currently popular idea of an inflationary cosmos. AD Linde has even suggested that the universe grew by a factor of $10^{1,000,000}$ (an incomprehensibly gigantic figure, i.e. by a trillion x trillion x trillion times.....80,000 times repeated!) before 10^{-30} seconds (less than a billionth billionth billionth of the first second) had passed![14] A figure for the rate of expansion of $10^{1,000,000}$ might seem quite large enough, but Guth, the originator of the theory, has actually suggested $10^{10,000,000,000}$![15] Even on the Linde figures, a region stretching perhaps 10^{-33} cm (a millionth billionth billionth billionth of a centimetre) would have grown within such a miniscule time to a size far greater than the entire visible universe before settling down to billions of years of leisurely Big Bang expansion. If then this inflationary stage is seen as associated with a 'grand unification transition' (GUT) when, at 10^{-35} seconds the nuclear strong force breaks away from the electroweak one, then it would have resulted in a phase transition into many domains of differently broken symmetries. Linde's idea is that several scalar fields switched on in succession as temperatures fell, and each affected particles differently. These domains might then vary according to their number of dimensions, their vacuum energy densities, their metric signatures, their gauge symmetries, and in the strengths of their forces and the masses of their particles. On this basis Linde has calculated that there might be as many as 10^{83} different regions (nearly a trillion trillion trillion trillion trillion trillion trillion mini-universes) which were causally separated when the symmetries broke. If Linde's probabilistic approach were right, a spectacularly large number of variations would be obtained. If there were many scalar fields each with differential effect on different particles at symmetry breaking, and if the intensity of those fields were settled randomly, there would be a mechanism making it likely there would exist, somewhere within a colossal set of universes, at least one universe whose force strengths and particle masses were tuned to the requirements for life with enormous accuracy.

Several variants have been proposed to this general theory. One is that, prior to the GUT transition at 10^{-35} seconds a first transition had already taken place at fractionally after 10^{-43} seconds from the start of Big Bang, when gravity separated from the other forces, according to what is described as a 'primordial or super-gravitational inflation'[16]. It is also estimated that a further phase transition took place at perhaps 10^{-11} seconds (still only a hundred billionth of a second after Big Bang) when the electroweak force split into the nuclear weak force and electromagnetism. And the desert of time (albeit almost unbelievably minute) between the GUT transition and this latter electroweak transition could itself, according to some theories, have 'flowered with multiple transitions'[17]. The same theme could even be used to revive the Steady State or Continuous Creation Theory of Hoyle and Narlikar, by positing that the cosmos undergoes bursts of creative activity whenever expansion thins out the distribution of matter sufficiently[18]. Yet for all its ingenuity, this theory still leaves unanswered questions. If the strengths and masses were indeed fixed randomly, why should they be fixed in the same way throughout the visible universe? It is true that inflation could solve that difficulty by taking just one region out of an immense number where conditions were fine-tuned to create life and then inflating it far beyond anything now seen by us. However, the problem with that is that inflation itself requires to be very accurately fine-tuned if it is to occur appropriately, indeed at all.

A third proposal as to how multiple universes might have been generated is derived from the view that universes start as quantum vacuum fluctuations. Based on the idea that empty space is a quantum ferment of fleetingly existing particles, and combined with the theme of inflation so that the fluctuation does not have to be extraordinarily gigantic, Tryon postulates our universe as 'a fluctuation of the vacuum, the vacuum of some larger space'[19]. Given many different spaces – open or closed, static or expanding, foam-like in different degrees – it is possible to generate up to infinitely many universes. It has even prompted the idea that our universe was 'quantum-tunnelled' from nothing, though that is a misleading description when what is meant is a space-time foam and a well-structured space characterised by several different fields each in their lowest energy state. However, the problems of this theory have already been discussed, in particular that quantum fluctuations – which is not creation ex nihilo – still require pre-existing entities and structures subject to probabilities and Heisenberg uncertainty for such fluctuations to occur.

A fourth framework for generating multiple universes is the oscillatory cycle of Big Bangs followed by re-collapses. Wheeler has speculated that whenever an oscillating cosmos undergoes a Big Crunch, there may be an ever-fluctuating 'pre-geometry' at the Planck length (10^{-33}cm) at which no point has fixed neighbours so that when a rebound occurs (because it is now accepted that gravity can in certain circumstances act repulsively), there would be no pre-determination of the properties following the Bang and they could be decided in quantum-probabilistic fashion[20]. The number of particles, proportion of matter particles to photons, period of expansion, particle masses, force strengths, and even perhaps the topology of space-time may all undergo reprocessing at each bounce. On this basis it is assumed that all possible combinations of properties would be realised if the cycle of oscillations continues indefinitely. However, this theory is built on several speculative (and unprovable) assumptions, and also the timescale required for this model to generate a sufficient variation of force strengths and particle masses via each bounce to explain the phenomenal fine-tuning observed in the current universe is prodigious. Barrow and Tipler for example predict the extinction of all carbon-based life-forms in the current universe at 10^{34} years ahead (more than a billion trillion trillion years into the future) and the final evaporation of super-cluster mass black holes at 10^{117} years ahead (an almost unimaginable billion trillion trillion trillion trillion trillion trillion trillion trillion trillion years from now) before one bounce in the cycle of our universe comes to an end and another with entirely fresh properties is created.

A fifth, and perhaps most startling, option for the production of multiple universes if the many-worlds quantum theory. This postulates that every change which quantum theory recognises as possible does actually occur in some branch of reality (or mini-universe). Perhaps therefore there are infinitely many branches, for each unstable particle may decay at any moment whatever. The earliest branching would result in worlds greatly different in scale, while later branching might produce worlds in which symmetries had been broken in a whole variety of ways; and the greater the variations, the more justified it would be to classify the branches as multiple universes. However, it is stretching credulity that every single potential change that could happen, at every moment in respect of every creature in the universe (the branch known to us), does actually achieve realisation in another universe which is exactly the same as the immediately preceding one in every respect except the one different possible change that was decided upon. Not only would the number of actual universes is rapidly approach infinity, but the rate of growth in generating such new universes would become exponential. Better to accept that reality is ultimately probabilistic than the de-Ockhamized (multiplying entities beyond what is strictly necessary) ontological extravagance of endless branching!

A sixth proposal for the generation of many and varied

universes is the hypothesis of 'child universes' – regions of an expanding false vacuum which are pinched off once they become surrounded by true vacuum[21]. In quantum mechanical terms, a false vacuum is an apparently empty space which is seething with a ferment of fluctuations in which particles are continually bursting into being and then vanishing. The energy density of the ferment would be enormous, and it would lead to extremely rapid expansion. These children therefore continue to grow, with regions of true vacuum forming inside them and thus pinching off further children, and so on perhaps ad infinitum. As a variant of this idea, child universes might be created simply by quantum-tunnelling from their mothers[22]. Again these are a series of imaginative hypotheses, but there is no direct evidence to substantiate them, and again mere endless randomised propagation of derived universes seems highly unlikely to explain the excessive fine-tuning of a remarkably wide range of interconnected phenomena.

Implications

Having reviewed all the main theories for generating multiple universes, the conclusion must surely be that whilst elements of some of them are clearly plausible, they either depend on generating a virtually infinite set of universes in order to replicate the staggering degree of fine-tuning in such a wide range of variables in our observed universe, or they adopt metaphysical appendages that are more extreme than the alternative theory of design, or they end up implying the same premises they were constructed to avoid. Occam's razor (a simpler explanation is preferable to an unnecessarily complicated one) points to the argument for design. The impressively long list of natural constants which seem spectacularly finely tuned to life's needs, including many constants fine-tuned for several different functions at once, strongly suggests some selection effect. None of this however is to deny that the ensemble of universes theory is quite compatible with the idea of a designer God (assuming no other, third alternative explanation can be put forward) – though whether that is a personal God according to conventional religious doctrine or a more abstract Neo-Platonist divine creative principle is left open for debate (chapter 9-10). But even if the universe (or a world-ensemble) seems clearly to imply some selection effect, did that selection, and in particular the law-like character of the universes, have to be made the way it has been? Many have thought that only this one kind of universe was logically or mathematically or even cognitively possible – including several mediaeval Aristotelians, Albert Einstein, Paul Dirac, Arthur Eddington, JA Wheeler, Roger Penrose, and perhaps Stephen Hawking. Yet that is not really tenable. When physicists argue that physical reality is logically required to be as it is, what they mean is that it is the logically necessary consequence of certain fundamental premises. But those premises are not themselves logically necessary. There is nothing contradictory in our universe obeying wholly different laws, or being so disorderly as not to be described as law-obedient at all. So why is it the way it is, and what deeper meaning, if any, attaches to that? Chapter 4 tries to answer that.

Chapter 4

The Evolution of the Universe

Problems of the standard model

According to the standard model of cosmology, some 13.7 billion years ago (based on the latest estimates of the Hubble constant) the universe erupted from a colossal singularity event which exploded all of space and matter. At 10^{-43} seconds after this Big Bang, the so-called Planck time (the earliest moment which physical theory can meaningfully describe), the temperature of the universe is calculated to have been about 10^{32} Kelvin, about 10 trillion trillion times hotter than the deep interior of the sun. At this point quantum gravitational effects would have been significant, perhaps severely distorting space-time structure, though further analysis is prevented by the lack of a reliable theory of quantum gravity. The density of the universe at this earliest point has been calculated at a scarcely imaginably colossal 10^{97} kg m^{-3} At about a hundredth thousandth of a second after Big Bang the temperature had dropped sufficiently – to about 10,000,000,000,000 degrees Kelvin, about a million times hotter than inside the sun – for quarks to bind together out of the cosmic plasma in groups of three, forming protons and neutrons. About a hundredth of a second later, the nuclei of some of the lightest elements began to congeal out of the particle plasma. Over the next three minutes the universe cooled to about a billion degrees, producing hydrogen and helium as the predominant nuclei, but also traces of deuterium and lithium. Then the rate of cooling slowly diminished with time, so that it took a few hundred thousand years for the temperature to fall to about 10,000 degrees Kelvin, which allowed free protons and electrons to combine together to form atomic hydrogen. At this stage the cosmic material became transparent to light, so that matter and radiation then largely became decoupled. Then about a billion years later, galaxies and stars and finally planets began to emerge as clumps of the primordial material bound together by gravitation.

However, this standard model has major weaknesses. The most important one is that it is dependent on nineteen free parameters which can simply be adjusted to ensure agreement with experimental measurements. To that extent it is clearly not a fundamental theory, since it omits additional principles that are needed to set the values of those parameters. It may also be regarded as a breakdown of the theory rather than a correct description of the universe's earliest condition that the standard and inflationary cosmological models posit an initial state of infinite energy, density and temperature. However, recent scientific advances have suggested modifications to the models on both these counts which not only avoid these dilemmas but also have profound implications for the theme of this book – understanding the meaning and role of life in the universe.

String theory began to be deeply investigated in 1984 as a result of the failure of the proton decay experiments which paved the way for more radical departures from the standard model of elementary particle physics. As opposed to the latter's reductionist strategy, it put forward the idea that all the particles in nature are equally fundamental, and that the properties of each particle are derived from their potential interactions with all the others. This advanced Leibniz's principle two centuries earlier that all properties arise from relations, by combining it with the principles of relativity and quantum theory to explain all of the properties of the elementary particles. On this basis the laws of physics cannot be postulated a priori. What the theory instead seeks to do is to find a self-consistent set of properties and interactions which explains both how each particle contributes to the network and how it is itself determined by the network of interactions. And what the solutions to the equations indicated was that fundamental particles did not fit the traditional concept of a point, but rather behaved more like stretched, one-dimensional objects, akin to rubber bands. They take up no space because their diameters are zero, but they do have length. String theory therefore resolves the paradox of radical atomism by positing that the end of the process of reductionism are fundamental entities that are one-dimensional strings, not points. Enthusiasm cooled however when it was found that one-dimensional objects could only be consistent with quantum mechanics and relativity theory if space had twenty-five dimensions. Nevertheless this problem was partially resolved when an extension of the gauge principle (which underlies the quantum mechanical description of the three non-gravitational forces) was invented which bridged the gulf between particles and forces so that both were different manifestations of the same fundamental entity. This unification, called super-symmetry, when introduced into string theory, enabled it to become a consistent quantum theory of all the interactions including gravity, but only if the world had, not three dimensions, but nine (at least not twenty-five as before).

One suggestion how this final problem for string theory might be resolved is to postulate that our world does indeed have nine dimensions, but that six of them are rolled up so that the diameter of the universe in these directions is only a Planck length. A proposal as to how this might have happened has been put forward by Brandenberger and Vafa[23]. They postulate that at the beginning of the universe all the spatial dimensions of string theory are tightly curled up to their smallest extent at the Planck length. They then draw on the small-radius/large-radius duality of string theory which asserts that when a dimension is curled up like a circle, a string can wrap around it, thus preventing it expanding. However, if a wrapped string and its anti-string partner (i.e. a string that wraps the dimension in the opposite direction) came into contact, they would quickly annihilate each other, leaving an unwrapped string. If then this were to happen sufficiently quickly and efficiently, enough of the band-like constriction would be removed for the dimension to expand. Brandenberger and Vafa then postulate that in the case of three circular spatial dimensions, two wrapped strings will be likely to collide with each other, as happens for two particles moving in one direction. But in four or more spatial dimensions, wrapped strings are increasingly unlikely to collide, as is the case with point particles in two or more dimensions. In their view that could explain why the symmetry reduction singles out precisely a three spatial expansion for expansion and not more, and why therefore we experience three dimensions today.

These are of course only hypotheses, and may well have to be modified or rejected in the light of further investigation. Nevertheless, string theory remains a very attractive thesis on several grounds. It harmoniously unites quantum mechanics and general relativity, the previously known laws of the microscopic world and the macroscopic world of everyday experience, which are otherwise incompatible. It implies that the universe has a size, even to the smallest possible extent and even in the most extreme conditions, which is contrary to the Big Bang of the standard cosmological model which claims that the universe had shrunk completely to zero. Thus the infinity problems of the initial singularity are wholly avoided by string theory. It also thereby opens up the possibility of a pre-Big Bang scenario when the universe may have developed from a very different state from that described in the Big Bang tradition. In addition not only are both quantum mechanics and gravity incorporated by string theory, which is a requirement for any claim to a unified theory, but several other key concepts now regarded as central to analysis of the universe, many of them experimentally confirmed – such as spin, the family structure of matter particles, messenger particles, the equivalence principle, gauge symmetry, symmetry-breaking and super-symmetry – all emerge naturally out of string theory. And finally, and very significantly, while the standard model has to depend on a series of adjustable free parameters, string theory has no such dependence, and its implications should be unambiguously testable.

Yet progress towards a final understanding of the universe may still be in its early stages. Whereas the Newtonian concept of an absolute space and time held sway for centuries and seemed immutable, it has given way to such arcane concepts as wave functions and probabilities, the constant fluctuations of the seething energy of the vacuum, the distortions of the space-time fabric, quantum tunnelling, wormholes, black holes, the smearing together of space and time, and Big Bang itself (though now under challenge). But the process of ever deeper discovery continues, and even superstring theory is now evolving into M-theory which unites the previous five superstring theories into a single overarching framework. Its fundamental ingredient, known as a zero-brane, behaves like a point particle at large distances, but has very different properties over short distances. This geometrical framework reveals a hugely different conceptual landscape where the conventional ideas of space and distance between points simply melt away, though they re-emerge on scales above the Planck length. But current work is still focussed on trying to achieve a mathematical reformulation of string theory without involving a pre-existing notion of space and time.

This evolving picture does have certain profound implications. If quantum effects completely eradicate the singularity, there would be no moment of creation in the manner of Big Bang as envisaged by the standard model. Time would not end in a black hole (an object whose gravitational field is so extreme that it entraps anything, even light), but stretch back indefinitely into the past, to some new region of space-time connected to our universe only at its first instant. Big Bang might then represent a bounce in a black hole that formed in some other region of space and time. The term would no longer refer to a moment of creation, but rather to some dramatic event that generated the enormous expansion of our region of the universe. Two other important considerations then arise. One is that this scenario then opens the way to ask whether there were processes operating before Big Bang which determined the conditions found afterwards in our universe, notably the parameters of elementary particle physics. The second is that the act of creation is not abandoned under this hypothesis, simply pushed back further, perhaps indefinitely, into the past.

Why are the laws of physics as they are?

Even given these modifications (or replacement) of the standard model, how are the parameters governing the elementary particles and their interactions so fine-tuned and balanced as to produce our universe of such variety and complexity? There are really four alternatives. One is that it happened by chance. The unlikelihood of this is astronomical, and some of the large set of almost absurdly unlikely contingencies are summarised in chapter 3. The formation of stars is one of the key perquisites for the emergence of life, and it has been calculated that the probability that a universe created by randomly choosing the parameters will contain stars is about one chance in 10^{229}! This is an unimaginably gigantic number, and even the total number of particles in the entire universe, 10^{80}, is infinitesimal beside it. Chance therefore is no explanation.

A second possibility is that there is only a single unique mathematically consistent theory underpinning the whole universe. As explored in chapter 3, this splits into two alternatives. Either (option 2) this unique formula was used by a designer God who created the universe with staggering precision in order that there would eventually arise rational creatures who would respond to his love – a strong version of the anthropic principle; that then becomes a matter for religious belief. Or (option 3) there exists a colossal proliferation of universes (or separate and inaccessible regions of a universe or large ensemble of universes) such that in the end there is likely to be one at least that generates stars and therefore the possibility of life. The objection to the latter is that it is not so much an explanation as an evasion of an explanation. It is systematically unverifiable and can be used as a device to rationalise virtually anything.

A fourth explanation is that the parameters for the particles and interactions with such unlikely values were not set definitively at any single time, by whatever process, but evolved over time. In particular, Lee Smolin has proposed a kind of cosmological natural selection whereby the laws of nature themselves may not be eternal categories, but constructed over time through natural processes of self-organisation[24]. His hypothesis starts from the assumption that the parameters of the initial universe are selected randomly and hence highly unlikely to be fine-tuned to a series of values as extreme as 10^{-19} and 10^{-60} which generate a big universe full of stars. Instead it is likely that this initial universe will either inflate so rapidly that after a few Planck times of 10^{-43} it is virtually empty, or it will completely collapse. Either way it will contract to a Planck length of 10^{-33} and then bounce back to form a second universe. This process could then develop a series of tiny universes, one after the other, each developing from the previous one. But Smolin inserts a second, crucial, hypothesis which is that the parameters of the second and of each succeeding universe differ from the preceding one by tiny random changes (rather like the DNA of a biological progeny differing from its parents by a mutation in a single gene). In effect a whole range of different possible parameters are picked randomly in succession, and the results of each are tried out. There is no limit in time of how long this process could continue, until a set of parameters is chosen by chance, perhaps after an inordinately lengthy period of time, which specifies universes that produce black holes, and hence leave behind more than one progeny. At this point the population of universes begins to explode. There is then no longer a simple linear progression of 'Phoenix universes', as cosmologists had speculated in the 1930s, which repeatedly expanded and then collapsed and then exploded again each time the re-contraction became sufficiently dense. Instead, to use the biological metaphor again, time branches like a tree, and each black hole becomes a bud that spawns a new universe.

So far as we know, most black holes are produced when a massive star implodes after it has burnt all its nuclear fuel. If the mass of a collapsing star is below an upper mass limit which is somewhere between 1.5 - 4 times the mass of our Sun, it will contract massively into a white dwarf or neutron star. Where however it retains a mass above this limit even after the star has exploded and spewed out most of its mass into the galaxy (a supernova explosion), it collapses into a black hole of almost infinite density where the gravitational field is so overwhelming that nothing, even light, can escape it. Once again however this process will only occur if the parameters are fine-tuned. A supernova only happens if tiny neutrinos take energy away from the inner core of the star and supply it to the outer layers, and this will only happen if the strength of the weak nuclear force governing their interactions is fine-tuned within a narrow range. Equally, it seems likely that the great majority of black holes would not have formed if there had been no carbon since carbon is the key element that enables giant molecular clouds to cool sufficiently to form new stars despite the presence of existing stars all around them which would otherwise heat them up.

If then black holes are very largely produced under certain precise conditions through the implosion of a dying massive star, what are the conditions that favour the birth of such stars in the first place? Such stars are not common, because the circumstances that lead to their birth are even rarer than for ordinary stars. The clouds of gas that contract under the force of gravity to form stars have to be dense enough for gravity to overcome the resistant pressure of the gas, and cold enough because a higher temperature will increase the pressure resisting the force of gravity. It is known that star-creating clouds are exceedingly cold, only some 10° above absolute zero. These locations are found in the discs of spiral galaxies, of which many exist in our universe, so that there are many more stars (and hence many more black holes) than there would be if stars had only formed near the beginning of the universe. We now know that the key element that enables the giant molecular clouds to cool sufficiently to produce stars is carbon, and clearly very large quantities have to be made inside stars for this purpose. This process too again turns out to be remarkably fine-tuned. If large enough amounts of carbon are to be generated inside stars, its nuclei, as Fred Hoyle discovered, must vibrate at almost exactly the same frequency as the nuclei of another element, beryllium, so that a resonant effect is created between them. This appeared highly unlikely since at that time no state of carbon was known with that frequency, though later it was experimentally found.

The implications of cosmological natural selection

Smolin's hypothesis is ingenious, but it still involves serious problems. The most significant is that the theory of natural selection on a random basis through aeons of time of successive sets of a large number of parameters until a wildly improbable set with differentially extreme values is finally encountered is liable to the same objections as options 1 and 3. It is the extension through almost infinite time of the same colossal improbability as generating a ready-made universe at one moment in time (option 1) governed by such spectacular fine-tuning as to produce stars, and later black holes, over subsequent billions of years. Smolin's refinement of the bounce speculation that the extreme conditions of near-singularity cause small random variations in the laws of physics is still driven by blind (i.e. random) forces, so there is no cumulative 'learning' between successive bounces to guide the process. If then the selection of a large set of such stupendously improbable parameters as will produce a viable universe that will generate stars is likely to take a near-infinity of time, Smolin's scenario is really a variant on the multiverse idea (option 3) whereby if a near-infinite number of separate universes (or domains within universes) are – somehow – generated, almost any outcome will in the end be brought about. But that is not a satisfactory scientific explanation.

Once however an initial viable and sustainable universe (which may be quite different from ours) is generated which can produce stars – though no scientific theory is yet able to explain acceptably how this might have happened – Smolin's scheme does open up a dynamic of universe creation which has profound implications. One is that universes with physical parameters suitable for the formation of many stars will also form many black holes which then, via the bounce hypothesis, generate many baby universes with similar (though not necessarily identical) values to these parameters. These universes do not compete on the analogy of biological natural selection, but a sort of Darwinian selection effort operates to favour 'successful' universes that are efficient at making stars. The potential scale of this new universe creation is very large indeed. It is conservatively estimated that there is about one black hole per 10,000 stars. This implies that each galaxy contains at least 100 million black holes, and a universe such as ours produces perhaps 10^{18} (a billion times a billion) black holes. If then we assume, which is reasonable, that each of this enormous progeny of new universes also themselves generate stars and thence large numbers of further black holes leading to new universes, then the number of universes (or at least domains inaccessible to us) rises exponentially. However, the physics of what happens on the other side of a black hole is, unsurprisingly, not well understood. In quantum theory the singularity is somehow smeared out and there is speculation that the sharp space-time boundary may be replaced by a tunnel (or umbilical cord?) connecting the mother universe to a new baby which is eventually severed by quantum effects causing the black hole to evaporate. But whatever the precise mechanism, this picture suggests that life, far from being an extreme rarity as in other many-universes scenarios, may well exist widely across the totality of universes, though very likely not in the form in which human beings have evolved. It does however inevitably raise the question, against the background of a huge ensemble of universes, of how we should now view the role and significance of the human race. We return to this later.

A second profound implication of cosmological Darwinism is that the evolution of universes that are self-organised through a succession of configurations characterised by increasing complexity may itself provide the essential conditions for the development of living systems. Smolin's thesis is that a universe finely tuned to produce stars is a universe in which many of the conditions required for the existence of life are also satisfied – most notably carbon which seems necessary for extensive star formation is also an essential component for life. Thus, without having to postulate life as a special or necessary condition, the increasingly complex self-organisation of universes – the fact that they have to display a rational explanation, consistent with Leibniz's principle of sufficient reason – may largely explain why there is life in the universe. The very conditions that underpin the consistent formulation of a theory of cosmology based on relational concepts of space and time are the same conditions required to explain the existence of living organisms, including us. And the most important implication of this hypothesis is that the world is hospitable to the existence of living beings, not because it was created for mystical or metaphysical reasons or because humans are somehow necessary or significant for the universe, but rather because living systems exist as a by-product of a much larger process of self-structuring without which the world could not be logically understood.

Implications

Whether the standard model survives in some revised form, whether string theory or its associated derivatives turn out to provide a fundamental explanation or merely a milestone towards deeper understanding, and whether quantum effects open up a pre-Big Bang scenario (perhaps of almost near-infinite periods of time in the past) all remain currently uncertain. What is certain is that the universe has evolved in a manner which is amenable to precise rational comprehension, which immediately raises the question of where the laws of nature come from. The laws are universal, absolute, timeless, and omnipotent – nothing escapes them. They are also mathematical in form. The odds against their developing by chance are so incalculably vast that the idea can be dismissed. There are then really only two ultimate explanations. One is that they were devised by a designer Deity; but that cannot of course ever be scientifically proven, and it also extends the revelation of a personal God in the great religious faiths to a role that is neither revealed nor demonstrable. The other is the generation of the multi-universe concept on such an exponentially prodigious scale that in the end a universe with these laws and characteristics will be developed. But that is less a predictive and verifiable explanation than a mere compendium of an indefinitely huge range of contingencies. The theory of cosmological natural selection, which ingeniously seeks to avoid these dilemmas, turns out in fact to be a more complex variant of both these theories. But it does raise new questions as to whether human beings can claim to have a special position in the universe if the passage of near-infinite time in the past or the generation of a huge ensemble of universes or the creation of living creatures (including us) as a by-product of much wider and more powerful cosmological processes are confirmed by future evidence.

Chapter 5

The Origin of Life

Conditions prior to the emergence of life on Earth

According to radiometric dating of rocks, the Earth was formed some 4.55 billion years ago. It is a small part of our solar system which combines the sun, nine major planets and their natural satellites, the asteroids, the comets, and the meteoroids. The sun, in which is concentrated 99% of the mass of the solar system, is a mainstream star which formed some five billion years ago and is located in our spiral galaxy, the Milky Way, about two-thirds out from the centre. The galaxy measures nearly 100,000 light years across (around 575,000 trillion miles), so the sun is around 33,000 light years, or about 191,000 trillion miles, out from the centre of the galactic disc. The galaxy as a whole contains perhaps 100,000,000,000 stars similar to our sun. Beyond the Milky Way there are millions of other galaxies, each of which may contain as many individual stars as our own local galaxy. That puts in perspective the microscopic insignificance of the Earth within the universe as a whole, let alone within the much vaster framework of the enormous ensemble of universes postulated in some theories (chapters 3 and 4).

The nine planets within the solar system formed out of the swirling turmoil of the solar nebula, initially from particles colliding and merging and then gradually forming into ever larger lumps of solid matter. These bigger masses then exerted a gravitation pull on other surrounding masses, leading to more violent collisions and the building up of much more sizeable bodies. After some 10,000 years of this process these objects would have aggregated into planetesimals hundreds of miles across. After a million years scores of planets as large as Mars were orbiting the sun, with the inevitability of further gigantic collisions. At some point the Earth was struck at an oblique angle by another huge body which ripped a path to the centre of this planet, creating its iron core. The lighter mantle towards the surface of the Earth was torn off into space, setting up a mini-disc of orbiting debris which gradually aggregated into our moon. The enormous force of this cataclysm boiled the Earth dry of volatile material like organics. By contrast, in the outer reaches of the solar system the cooler temperatures enabled materials to condense into water and sulphur, and hydrocarbons to survive from the original gaseous cloud. In these colder conditions icy particles were pulled together over lengthy time to form comets a few miles across or icy planetesimals a few hundred miles across. After around ten million years enough of these icy bodies coalesced to form the nucleus of the giant planet Jupiter, followed over much longer time by the formation of Saturn, Uranus and Neptune. Then over long ages a vast number of the remaining small icy bodies were haphazardly either flung out by the planetary gravitational fields into inter-stellar space or inwards into the inner solar system where some crashed into the inner planets of Mercury, Venus, Earth and Mars. These comets played a significant role in preparing the conditions for the emergence aeons later of life on Earth. In this bombardment of the inner planets which lasted several hundred million years, they delivered enormous quantities of water, enough to form the present oceans many times over, together with life-supporting organic material. Also, the hydrogen, helium and other gases from the earlier solar nebula having been blown away by the solar wind leaving the Earth with almost no primary atmosphere at all, the incoming cometary material restored again a dense coverage of gases round the planet. The formation of the Earth had taken about 100 million years, but for the next half billion years the surface remained hot, volcanic eruptions extensive, the atmosphere oppressive, and the tides huge. Only as the planet very slowly cooled and the atmosphere thinned were the conditions ready for life to emerge, and even then the bombardment from outer space continued unabated.

How did life forms then originate?

There are several alternative conflicting (and unresolved) theories about how living organisms first emerged. They could have developed by natural agency – whether seeded from outer space, or originating in the oceans in deep super-heated vents, or on dry land whether by chemical accident or by complex self-organisation beyond a certain threshold, or by some other means – or by supernatural agency. None of these is proven, and perhaps never can be. Nor, despite the successes of molecular biology, is it even certain what exactly constitutes life, what it is that distinguishes a living organism from other physical material. However, it is generally agreed that the properties of living systems include self-determination, nutrition and metabolism (chemical processing and generation of energy), reproduction, organised complexity, and growth and development. But this is not comprehensive, and there is no agreement as to what comprises a complete description. What is agreed however is that traditional notions such as vitalism and the life force have long since been discredited.

The earliest known evidence of primitive life on Earth derives from ancient sedimentary rocks in the Itsaq Gneiss complex in south-western Greenland. Studies reported in 1996[25] reveal that the rocks contain the tell-tale isotopic signature of life, which are dated to 3,850 million years ago, some 300-400 million years before the earliest micro-fossil evidence. This indicates that life forms, however primitive, came into existence only 700 million years after the formation of the Earth itself, and very shortly after the blistering conditions so inhospitable to life for more than 500 million years had finally dissipated, and only 100 million years after the Earth was heavily bombarded by meteorites which would have sterilised its surface. On this evidence there has been life on Earth for 85% of its history, and life evolved almost as soon as environmental conditions allowed.

So how did life come about at this time? There are several plausible theories. The conventional theory dates back to 1929 (or even to Darwin's 'warm little pond' idea in 1871) when JBS Haldane noted experiments in which ultraviolet radiation facilitated the build-up of organic compounds from a mixture of water, CO_2 and ammonia, and then concluded that the right carbon compounds for the chemistry of life must have developed slowly in the oceans over geological time until the complexity of the compounds from the chemical reactions produced the first life molecules. Further controlled experiments from the 1950s have not produced proteins, but they have produced amino acids, composed of chains of carbon atoms, which are themselves the building blocks of proteins. So combining simple molecules with energy to bring about chemical reactions may well produce molecules complex enough to be regarded as precursors to life. But that is insufficient for life forms to emerge. That still requires turning the first living molecule into actual living cells in which all the important chemistry of life is safely protected inside the cell wall. The blueprint for protein construction is provided by RNA (ribonucleic acid) into which DNA (deoxyribonucleic acid) is translated. If then proteins, RNA and DNA are all essential for life, how did they arise simultaneously on an otherwise lifeless planet? One answer was that the first RNA molecules on the pre-biotic Earth were assembled randomly from nucleotides dissolved in rock pools, and that among the trillions of short RNA molecules there would have been a few which could copy themselves – an ability which soon made them the dominant RNA on the planet (the so-called 'RNA world' theory). This combined with the discovery that RNA had a catalytic capability and, it was proposed, could have acquired membranes and taken on additional catalytic tasks needed to run a primitive cell.

However, this RNA scenario would have required a supply of adenine, cytosine, guanine and uracil, the nucleic acid bases that, with sugar and phosphate, make up nucleotides. Moreover the incipient Earth was hydrogen-starved and wholly unsuitable for organic synthesis apart from rare havens such as deep-ocean vents. It was then argued that the organic building blocks could have come from outer space, when it was discovered that a meteoroid crash 2 billion years ago at Sudbury, Ontario, in Canada had left behind about one million tonnes of extra-terrestrial buckyballs (football-sized molecules made of carbon atoms); if complex buckyballs could fall to Earth without being burnt up, so could complex organic molecules. Even if this were not the case, it was also argued that high concentrations of urea, likely to have been found as shallow pools of water on the Earth's surface evaporated, would have produced more than enough quantities of the missing nucleotide bases. One final addition to the RNA world theory was the finding that adding montmorillonite, a positively charged clay believed to be plentiful on the young Earth, enabled the RNA chain to build up to the length of about fifty nucleotides needed to catalyse production of more RNAs.

A contrary view, propounded by Woese and Wachtershauser, claims that it was an energy producing metabolic cycle, not RNA, which triggered life on Earth. They argue that the RNA world scenario is flawed because it fails to explain the source of the energy to fuel the production of the first RNA molecules or the copies needed for replication. What they believe was required was a biochemical machine which transformed energy into a form that was immediately available for the production of organic molecules. Such a machine could have been created by the combination of iron and sulphur in the primordial mix to form iron pyrites. Short negatively charged organic molecules then stuck to its positively charged surface and fed off the energy liberated as more iron and sulphur reacted, which created longer organic molecules. This energy-trapping cycle could then have evolved into life forms when, by chance, one of the enlarging organic molecules turned out eventually to be of the right composition to catalyse its own synthesis. Then, ultimately, cycles of organic molecules would evolve which could trap their own energy, thus dispensing with the inorganic energy cycle. If this account is correct, comparisons of genes may soon reveal the identity of the first energy-producing metabolic cycle. When the genes first appeared, they would have been co-opted into improving the efficiency of the metabolic cycle by producing enzymes to catalyse each step. These genes would then have been subjected more rigorously to selection pressures, and should be present in all modern organisms in a similar state, as whole genome sequences currently being sought should reveal.

Another theory, pioneered by Stuart Kauffman of the Santa Fe Institute of New Mexico[26], drops altogether the model of a single type of molecule, such as RNA, gradually evolving to assume the catalytic burden of self-replication. Instead it draws attention to the principle of complexity theory that when a system reaches some level of complexity, it naturally generates a degree of complex order. This would overcome the otherwise virtually insuperable problem of life originating by chance. Two astronomers, Hoyle and Wickramasinghe, estimated the chances of obtaining, not even an entire bacterium, but merely a functioning enzyme (in the form of a set of twenty amino acids used to construct enzymes) at 1 in 10^{20} - a hugely low probability. However, to duplicate a bacterium, it would be necessary to assemble some 2,000 functioning enzymes. The odds against this would be 1 in $10^{20 \times 2,000}$, or 1 in $10^{40,000}$! This is such an hyper-astronomical unlikelihood that it can be discounted as no more probable than the chances of a tornado sweeping through a junkyard and assembling a Boeing 747. Kauffman's answer to this dilemma is that life emerged as a natural phase transition in complex chemical systems. According to his theory, when the number of catalyzed reactions is about equal to the number of chemical units, a giant catalysed reaction web forms, and a collectively autocatalytic system snaps into existence, and a living metabolism crystallizes. It is thus postulated that the original mix of nucleotides, lipids and amino acids that composed the primordial soup would at some moment have become an integrated system as a natural consequence out of complex and chaotic disorder. To demonstrate his theory, Kauffman used a computer model of the primordial stew to show that when a group of molecules reached a critical level of diversity, they spontaneously formed an 'autocatalytic set' – a molecular co-operative which replicates as a group and evolves to create more complicated members.

Kauffman then develops a theory of the laws of complexity and requirements of order to explain why such autocatalytic networks settle down into stable behaviour and small state cycles and do not veer off into chaos. He illustrates this from the example of the human genome: since each of our cells houses some 100,000 or more genes, the number of possible patterns of gene expression (each gene being either turned on or off) is at least $2^{100,000}$ or $10^{30,000}$. Yet it is found that such a massive network settles down into an orderly state with cycles among only a mere 317 states (i.e. the square root of the number of binary variables, not the square root of the number of states). This is an extremely remarkable finding, since a mere 317 states compared with the entire state space is a minutely tiny fraction of that state space, about 1 in $10^{29,998}$! In other words, in this class of open thermodynamic systems, the spontaneous dynamics drive the system into an infinitesimal corner of its state space and hold it there. He also notes that sparsely connected networks exhibit internal order; densely connected ones tend to chaos. But he also hypothesizes that networks just at the phase transition, just poised between order and chaos, achieve the best mixture between stability and flexibility. And since all systems capable of complex behaviour have a definite survival advantage, he surmises that natural selection tunes the parameters of the autocatalytic networks until they are in the ordered regime near this edge.

In addition to providing an alternative explanation to the RNA world view for the origin of life, Kauffman's theory has other important implications. First, it suggests that any sufficiently diverse mix – whether composed of carbon compounds or particles in a dust cloud in space – will form autocatalytic sets, act as a life form, and evolve. Secondly, it proposes that the orderliness of the cell, previously generally attributed to refinement by Darwinian evolution, more likely derives from the dynamics of the genomic network. Natural selection can only achieve stability after a series of evolutionary experiments; it cannot explain the origin of the very ability to evolve. Third, and perhaps most important, so far from suggesting that the emergence of life is extraordinarily unlikely or an amazing fluke, the theory propounds that the emergence of autocatalytic sets is almost inevitable. Instead of tracing the origins of life to an improbable RNA molecule, life is seen as an emergent phenomenon which automatically arises as the molecular diversity of a pre-biotic chemical system increases beyond a threshold of complexity. Life is not located in the property of a single molecule, but is the collective property of systems of interacting molecules. Life is not a reductionist concept, but rather possesses a fundamental holism as an emergent self-reproducing whole. The collective system contains a stunning property that its constituent parts, which are just chemicals, would never by themselves possess.

The earliest evidence of life

It remains true however that Kauffman's theory, like all scenarios on biogenesis, is speculative. To prove it, it might be necessary to analyse the contents of a pot percolating billions of different organic molecules, identify the autocatalytic entities and isolate them, and subject them to their self-replicating cycles. Such experiments would seek to match the hypothesized origin of living forms to the first surviving evidence of life, but they stretch the limits of the technically feasible. An alternative approach is to examine that earliest surviving data, and assess what that might indicate about ultimate origins. This latest evidence has thrown up very different scenarios from earlier ideas of a primordial terrestrial pool, in particular life originating in super-heated ocean vents or seeded from outer space.

Increasingly the evidence points to the first land organisms living deep underground, buried in geothermally heated rocks in pressure-cooker conditions. The dominant life form on Earth for four billion years, nearly 90% of its history, has been microbes, minutely tiny but collectively a significant force (as seen for example in the spread of infectious diseases, the fermentation of alcohol, and the rotting of food) because of their overwhelming numbers and variety. The mass of microorganisms on this planet might amount to as much as 100 trillion tonnes, exceeding the whole of visible life put together. We live, and all our ancestors have always lived, in the Age of Bacteria. The linkage of today's microbes with their ancient ancestors derives from the biochemical evidence of their genetic composition and metabolic pathways. If they could still be found today in conditions similar to those afflicting the Earth in its earliest existence – bombarded by asteroids, shrouded in gas, and a boiling atmosphere – it might suggest how life could have originated under such extreme circumstances which prevailed for 700 million years till 3.8 billion years ago. Such conditions do in fact hold today in some parts of the deep ocean floor where the Earth's crust stretches and rips to expose molten rock to the icy water above, spewing out a searing chemical-laden fluid and throwing up a maze of fissures and tunnels as the oozing lava cools and cracks.

Some microbes (superbugs) are known to be able to endure extreme conditions, whether in water trapped below the

Antarctic ice sheet, or frozen to liquid nitrogen temperatures, or in excessive alkalinity, or even ingesting plutonium and other radioactive elements. Some also appear extremely ancient and primitive, almost a surviving vestige of the universal ancestor. It is now known since the late 1970s that the regions around the deep-sea volcanic vents teem with life, including microbes living very close to searing effluent as hot as 110°C, and there is even evidence of 'hyperthermophile' microbes living deep under the sea at temperatures as high as 169°C[27]. Moreover it was found that microbes obtain their energy directly from the boiling volcanic chemical streams rather than from light energy or photo-synthesis (and hence were named 'chemoautotrophs' – self-feeders from chemical energy), and were astonishingly fecund, with populations of more than a billion per cubic centimetre near the surface to 10 million deep down).

Given this microbial capacity for survival in these utterly extreme conditions, there are good reasons for believing that life may well have started and developed deep near the ocean floor. First, the catastrophic violence of the meteorite pounding inflicted on the Earth till the first signs of life appear 3.8 billion years ago were on such a scale and intensity that the Earth's surface would have been sterilised repeatedly. Vaporised rock would have boiled the oceans dry and melted the land lethally down to a depth of at least 10 metres. In addition, the lack of an ozone layer would have exposed the surface to deadly ultra-violet radiation. Second, in the depths of the sea the raw materials for life were abundant, since the Earth's crust steadily spews out hydrogen, methane, hydrogen sulphide and other reducing gases, as well as reducing chemicals like ferrous iron, precisely the kinds of chemicals necessary to synthesize bio-molecules efficiently. Third, the energy also required is readily available near deep-sea hydrothermal vents, which one researcher, Everett Shock, has described as an enormous thermo-dynamic drive to form organic compounds as the mixture of seawater and hydrothermal fluid, far from equilibrium, move towards a more stable state[28]. He found that the energy is maximized at around 100-150°C, which is just the range where hyperthermophiles live. He also found that these microorganisms can even gain energy by making simple organic compounds, exploiting the thermodynamic bonanza by generating biomass at an extraordinary rate. Fourth, the gene sequencing technique pioneered by Carl Woese, which can be used to reconstruct the tree of life, strongly suggests that the archaea, one of the three great domains of life, split from the other two, bacteria and eucarya, very early on in Earth's history, perhaps as early as 3.8 billion years ago, and that those species within archaea which are the evolutionary throwbacks and slowest at accumulating genetic change are dominated by the hyperthermophiles. In other words, the genetic evidence points unmistakeably to the microbes of the deep ocean super-heated vents as most closely resembling the universal ancestral organism.

It must be stressed that the mooted universal ancestor, who may well have lived far below the Earth's surface at 100°C or more and ate sulphur, is not the first living form, but was already preceded by a lengthy evolutionary history. Of that history that separated them we know next to nothing. Life may have started there, and evolved in situ; or life may have started at or near the surface, only to be wiped out by massive cosmic bombardments and then rising again successively from the ashes. Whichever is the case, the physicist and cosmologist Paul Davies in his detailed review of the evidence[29] concluded that it was likely that hyperthermophiles were the earliest microbes or at least the only survivors of the constant catastrophic battering from space, and that these early cells were rock-eaters processing iron, sulphur and hydrogen, but without either light or oxygen as part of their metabolism. Since microbes have the capacity to multiply explosively fast, it is likely that they spread out rapidly to invade every accessible niche. But maybe as the cosmic bombardment subsided over millions of years and cooler conditions prevailed, some may have mutated to adapt to the new environment, opening the way for life to develop at or near the surface of the planet. But this can only be conjecture.

Yet another alternative theory is that life did not originate on Earth at all, but was seeded from space. The evidence for this comes from a number of sources. On 27 December 1984 the US Antarctic Search for Meteorites team discovered a green meteorite beside a glacier in the Allan Hills region (thereafter classified as ALH 84001 when later curated first in the 1984 collection), and when chemical analysis found traces of iron disulphide and ferric iron within it, it was concluded that it could only have come from Mars. Radioactive decay indicated it had solidified about 4.5 billion years ago, soon after the formation of Mars. By studying the effect of cosmic radiation in producing new isotopes in the material, scientists were able to estimate that it must have spent some 16 million years in space before landing on Earth, and by also measuring how much the radioactive isotope C^{14} had decayed after the production of this isotope had stopped when it fell, they concluded that ALH 84001 must have hit the Earth about 13,000 years ago. The significance of all this is that the distinctive carbonate material in the rock pointed to living organisms, for several reasons. Layered blobs coated in iron-rich material of iron sulphide and magnetite, produced in combination, could suggest formation by live organisms. More importantly, the scientists discovered tiny traces of polycyclic aromatic hydrocarbons (PAHs), molecules produced by decaying life forms. Thirdly, above all, they detected under an electron microscope thousands of miniscule sausage-shaped blobs attached to the carbonate grains, looking just like terrestrial bacteria, and concluded that these must be the fossilised husks of microbes that lived on Mars around 4 billion years ago. But before this can be taken as proof that life on Earth could have been seeded from space in previous aeons, the evidence is not conclusive, and has indeed been challenged on several grounds – the-called fossils were too small to be remnants of bacteria, the carbonate grains were deposited in temperatures too hot for life, and contamination from terrestrial sources could not be ruled out (though in fact it had been stringently guarded against).

Other meteorite impacts have provided additional evidence. The Murchison meteorite, which fell in south-eastern Australia in 1969 and exploded in mid-air scattering its fragments, was a carbonaceous chondrite rich in organics. It proved that there are rocky lumps in space containing precisely the kind of organic compounds necessary to produce life, ready-made. The Alais meteorite that fell in France in 1834 contained carbon compounds, and the Orgueil meteorite in 1864 held organic matter which a mass spectrometer in the 1960s indicated was very likely biological in origin. The Giotto spacecraft in 1986, when flying close to the comet Halley, showed a black core containing carbon, hydrogen, nitrogen and sulphur, with dust grains a third of which were organic material. On this basis comets could well have supplied enough carbon to form the Earth's whole biosphere. Moreover, the Oort Cloud beyond the planetary edge of the solar system contains a vast reservoir of these comets, and calculations suggest that disturbances to this cloud eject most of its comets every few hundred million years. Other rocks are now known to have come from Mars, notably the SNC meteorites (an acronym for where they fell – Shergotty in India in 1865, Nakhla in Egypt in 1911, and Chassigny in France in 1815). A recent computer simulation predicted that, whilst most rocks discharged from Mars would be caught up in the sun, some 7% would end up on Earth[30]. Moreover, Mars could be more likely than Earth as the cradle of life because its smaller size would have made it less vulnerable to asteroid bombardment, its lower gravity would have produced less impact when an asteroid did strike (as opposed to the sterilization of the entire biosphere inflicted several times on Earth), and its formation heat was lower than Earth's so that its quicker cooling would have made it habitable earlier, even as early as 4.5 billion years ago. It is reasonable to conclude that if there ever was microbial life on Mars (as is likely), it is almost certain that viable Martian microbes would have reached Earth in the last four billion years – as equally the series of huge asteroid strikes on Earth about 3.8 billion years ago would have propelled quantities of life-bearing material to Mars, where conditions for their survival and development were much more favourable 3.8-3.5 billion years ago than on Earth, whilst Mercury and Venus were both much too hot.

Yet another variant on this theme is the idea of panspermia ('seeds everywhere'). Terrestrial organisms blasted into space by the cosmic pounding could have survived millions of years and then returned to re-colonize the Earth. This possibility could push back the start of life on Earth to well within the time of the intense bombardment, perhaps even to some 4.2 billion years ago. It is known that bacteria have extraordinary survival capabilities and amazing resilience to space conditions, including the radioactive effects of ultra-violet exposure from the sun. Moreover, this radiation exposure would have been much reduced if microbial spores hitched a ride on inter-stellar clouds which are common in the galactic spiral arms, and over a million years or so might be transported from star to star, including our solar system, or from another planet such as Jupiter's moon Europa, Venus, or another planetary nebula outside the solar system. It has been estimated that these clouds, together with the protective shield of ice and other space debris against cosmic radiation, could extend the life of spores even to several million years[31]. Moreover, the intensity and scale of the initial cosmic bombardments of both Earth and Mars would have blasted billions of tonnes of material into space, including millions of rocks capable of transporting life. But even if microbes arrived dead (which is likely in a high proportion of cases), the addition of a suitable RNA template might still offer the vital software ingredient from outer space to trigger a group of chemicals into replicating and creating life afresh. Nor are inter-stellar clouds the only plausible means for transporting microbial life through outer space. Comets may contain living organisms, and there are scenarios for a cometary panspermia[32]. The case for this has been made in explaining the correlation between the known passage of comets and the historical records of disease outbreaks, including the worldwide virulent Justinian plague of 540AD[33]. But whichever version of panspermia may turn out to be valid, it is not a theory of the origin of life, only an account of what may have happened in the very earliest stages of the development of life. Pushing the problem off into outer space does not solve the central issue of biogenesis: how did it actually start?

Life as an information-processing system

Molecular biology may one day offer a more complete account of the riddle of life, but it will never provide a comprehensive explanation because life is not to be equated with molecules. The understanding of a holistic 'organism' requires more than the cataloguing of the components alone. The mere reductionist approach misses out the hierarchy of levels and large-scale organisation which requires co-operative processes integrating the behaviour of a host of molecules into a coherent unity. The key to this is the genetic code – the means by which genetic infor-mation in DNA controls the manufacture of specific proteins by the cell. The code takes the form of a series of triplets of bases in DNA (known as 'codons') from which is transcribed a comple-mentary sequence of codons in messenger RNA, and the sequence of these codons then determines the sequence of amino acids during protein synthesis. Four bases can be arranged in sixty-four different permutations of three, and a group of enzymes which crucially can recognise both RNA sequences and the different amino acids then joins them up with the right designation. This code is universal in all known life forms, indicating it derives from a single common ancestor. But it raises perplexing questions as yet unanswered. How did this particular complex system come to be selected out of the 10^{70} range of possible codes based on triplets? Is this code best for the purpose, and if so, why? It cannot have been reached via Darwinian evolution incrementally over long periods of time because to change even a single RNA-amino acid assignment would be fatal not just to one protein, but to a whole set. One suggested solution is that the code assignments and the translation mechanism evolved together[34]. Another is that the universal code conceals abstract sequences like the energy levels of atomic nuclei, conceivably reflecting a property of super-symmetry, or even that there could be a code within the genetic code – a sort of palimpsest. But the crucial point for the origin of life, as Paul Davies makes clear, is understanding how mere hardware, the DNA, gave rise spontaneously to the encoded software[35].

There is a paradox involved here. Nearly all possible sequences in a nucleic acid molecule are random sequences, and thus a functioning genome is a random sequence, as it must be to contain great quantities of information. But at the same time it belongs to a tiny subset that encodes biologically relevant information, and it must therefore be highly specific. How then can a life form be created that combines such almost contradictory properties as randomness and specificity? Before Darwinian selection took effect, how could such very particular information (i.e. that which is necessary for life) have been obtained from the non-living environment and deposited in a genome? The problem is that informational concepts derived from communication theory – such as meaning, context, semantics – do not sit easily with biology, especially since they introduce ideas of purpose which are seen as alien to biological processes (though the latter often certainly seem to be purposeful).

Implications

The origin of life remains a mystery. There are several plausible theories which seek to explain how the first living molecular structure may have been created, whether by astronomically improbable chemical accident or by inevitability arising from autocatalytic sets. Equally there are several alternative theories, not mutually exclusive, as to how the earliest forms of microbial life may have survived and developed deep under the sea or from space or on land, but none connect to the very origin of life itself. And even to identify the first DNA does not answer the puzzle because what matters is not the composition of DNA itself, but the message written into its base pairs. It is the combination of this message with the necessary molecular environment, and the right semantic context, which is crucial for life. And this latter conundrum raises acutely the central issue about the nature of life – whether the laws of the universe have been engineered to serve a biological determinism and pave the way for life and thence in time its higher properties of mind, knowledge and understanding, or whether the orthodox view prevails that biological evolution is an endless series of meaningless accidents with no final causes. Significantly the latter view cannot answer the mystery, which Davies repeatedly presses, of where biological information comes from and how a living genome came into existence which generates random complexity and specificity together in a law-like manner. Maybe the emergent laws of complexity may explain how information was created, whilst the laws of physics are confined to explaining how it is disseminated. If that were so, then complexity would have real causal efficacy, which might explain how software control arose in the genetic code. If Davies is right – that molecular Darwinism needs to be supplemented by organisational complexity principles that confer specificity and information – it would significantly lead to sudden advances in complexity rather than the slow, incremental changes of Darwinian selection acting alone, which is very relevant to the next chapter.

Chapter 6

The Evolution of Life Forms

Pre-Cambrian: the first four billion years on Earth

After the formation of the Earth, when collisions of rock, ice, dust and gas generated huge amounts of energy heating the Earth to 5,000°C, a meltdown followed lasting 100 million years, during which the Earth's interior took on its present form. Heavy minerals sank to form a molten dense core some 2,200 miles across, while lighter minerals moved to the surface and formed a rocky outer crust. Between the core and the crust a layer formed of extremely hot rock, 1,800 miles thick, called the mantle. Large-scale volcanic eruptions of gas and steam produced the early atmosphere and the first surface water, and smaller land 'islands' gradually coalesced over the next billion years to form the first large landmasses. Over geological time vast changes in the distribution and shapes of continents and the extent and depths of the oceans were brought about by movements of tectonic plates (i.e. large pieces of the Earth's surface layer), which were themselves driven by huge flows of semi-molten magma within the Earth's interior. Geologists have good evidence that sequences of such movements over hundreds of millions of years caused continents to move thousands of miles over the Earth's surface and in some cases even to rotate, accompanied by massive shifts in climate and in atmospheric and ocean chemistry. But by about 3.5 billion years ago the Earth had cooled sufficiently for oceans and an early oxygenless atmosphere to form, though without protection from the Sun's ultraviolet rays.

The extremophile bacteria, the most primitive group of organisms known, called Archaebacteria, were able to survive the excess temperatures of boiling water, ice, acids, alkalines, and darkness. Like all life forms in the early Precambrian era, they were also anaerobic (i.e. they could survive without oxygen), because at this stage the Earth's atmosphere consisted almost entirely of nitrogen and carbon dioxide. By 3.5 billion years ago, primitive algae and bacteria had extensively colonized the edges of shallow, warm seas, growing as mats over the surface of the seabed sediment. When these mats were regularly covered by sediment, the primitive organisms migrated upwards towards the light, creating a new mat at a higher level. This succession of layers built up by photosynthesising blue-green algae into laminated mounds, called stromatolites, up to three feet high and easily preserved as fossils, as in Montana. Even before this, the 3.7 billion year old rocks at Isua in west Greenland contain traces of carbon which are probably the remains of microscopic photosynthetic bacteria, called photoautotrophs.

All these earliest primitive organisms had small cells and no cell nucleus, and are classified as prokaryotes. Amazingly, it took almost 3,000 million years for multi-cellular life and more complex life forms with large nucleated cells, such as animals and plants, to emerge. Such creatures are eukaryotic – they have a pattern of cell organisation in which genetic material arises within a membrane-bounded structure, the nucleus. This development probably occurred within the Vendian period which lasted from some 620 million years ago till the Cambrian era which began 543 million years ago, though the majority of these more complex multi-celled organisms have left no trace in the fossil record. However, the big exception is the Ediacaran fossils, the first larger organisms of which traces have been found, fossilised as impressions in seafloor sediments, despite their having no shells or other hard parts. They are named after the Ediacara Hills in the Flinders Range in South Australia, though some of the best preserved Ediacaran fossils have been found in the Vendian sandstone in Namibia in South-West Africa. They had a wide range of different forms, and though many looked superficially like jellyfish or worms, their body tissue may have been denser.

Rather little is known about the evolution of life between 3.5 billion and 0.6 billion years ago because there is only a fragmentary surviving fossil record. However, some of the chemical components of life can survive high temperatures and ultra-violet radiation, and chemical traces of life can be found, even if bodily remains cannot be recovered. Thus traces of oil and gas around two billion years old have recently been discovered in Australia and South Africa, and since oil and gas are created by the decay of minute marine life forms, their presence shows that primitive micro-organisms must have been abundant in the oceans during the Precambrian era. This micro-biota formed a vast potential food resource (similar to the krill today), and this raises two obvious questions. Why did take so long (nearly three million millennia) for bigger multi-cellular life, capable of consuming this food, to evolve?

There is perhaps just sufficient data to answer this question, by combining the insights of molecular biology and geochemistry, and Andrew Knoll has insightfully and painstakingly set out the evidence in his book 'Life on a Young Planet'[35A]. A tree of life can be built from comparisons of nucleotide sequence in genes from different organisms, and in such a construct plants and animals (including of course humans) form only small twigs of branches near the top of one bough in a tree of at least thirty other mostly more densely packed branches. Life's far greater diversity is microbial, and is concentrated on Bacteria and Archaea, the tiny architects of terrestrial ecosystems, leaving Eucarya as the classification for much larger multi-cellular creatures. Whilst size, shape and biological importance favour eukaryotic organisms (from slime moulds to human beings), prokaryotic metabolisms still provide the fundamental ecological circuitry of life, so that bacteria rather than mammals account for the efficient functioning of the biosphere.

What then is the evidence for the simpler precursors present on the early Earth and how did later biological molecules evolve from them? Sedimentary rocks of the Warrawoona Group in Western Australia, which formed 3.46 billion years ago, contain stromatolites and microscopic structures interpreted as fossil bacteria, though this is disputed. Equally, at Barberton in South Africa, also about 3.5 billion years old, the only other place in the world to contain well-preserved sedimentary rocks, cherts (extraordinarily hard flints) have been found which contain what could be fossil cyanobacteria or a primordial microbe long extinct. But if Archaean geology is uncertain, even more so is the question of how nucleic acids, proteins and membranes came to interact so intricately, thus ensuring the survival of each other, and ultimately leading to metabolism. The physicist Freeman Dyson has even suggested that life started twice, once by the RNA route and again via proteins, which then came together by protobiological merger, an early example of innovation by alliance. But once genes, proteins and membranes were in place, life probably developed quickly up the Tree of Life, driven by natural selection, gene duplication and gene lateral transfer. What is needed for biological expansion is that genes take control over many functions, though genetic takeover may well not be confined to one cell line. What is known is that 3.5 billion years ago, the metabolic diversification that paved the way for the perpetuation of life had almost certainly begun. Complex microbial communities cycled carbon and other elements through the biosphere, and even the elegant molecular assembly of photosynthesis may have been present.

In the Proterozoic aeon, however, around 2.4–2.2 billion years ago, the biogeochemical evidence points to a crucial change in the atmosphere. From at least 3.8 billion years ago primitive forms of bacteria had lived in the oceans, obtaining light energy from the Sun and producing oxygen from photosynthesis. But this oxygen was taken up by dissolved iron and deposited as insoluble iron minerals, forming layers of iron-rich sediments aptly named 'banded iron formations'. These rocks do not form in the oceans now and have not accumulated (with one exception) over the past 1.85 billion years, because iron entering the oceans today immediately encounters oxygen and precipitates as iron oxide. That must mean that in the Archaean aeon (4–2.5 billion years ago) the atmosphere and the sea surface had hardly any oxygen, probably less than 1% of present day levels. Confirmatory evidence comes from the presence of oxygen-sensitive minerals – pyrite, siderite and uraninite – in deposits older than 2.2 billion years ago, after which they fade from the scene. But what tipped the planet from a two billion year-long oxygenless state to a new stasis where oxygen was relatively abundant? This is disputed. It could have been increasing photosynthesis by early Proterozoic cyanobacteria removing dissolved iron from the oceans and thus releasing the brake on oxygen growth[36]. Or it could be that some of the methane produced by the dominant methanogenic Archaeans in the earliest Proterozoic Earth reached the upper atmosphere where it was destroyed by ultraviolet radiation, thus generating hydrogen gas which would have escaped into space and the hydrogen loss could have enabled oxygen to gain a foothold at the Earth's surface[37]. Or geological changes, shown by the highest carbon isotopic values ever recorded globally in the early Proterozoic limestones and dolomites, may have contributed to the rise of oxygen by increasing the burial of organic matter in sediments[38]. But whatever the causes, the early Proterozoic marked the point of transition which enabled the Earth to support a huge proliferating diversity of life. Whilst anaerobic micro-organisms retained their key roles in the functioning of the ecosystem, aerobic respiration became a dominant metabolism among bacteria. From about 2.2 billion years ago onwards, only oxygen and carbon dioxide were abundant enough to meet the needs of larger cells, and by

Vendian times oxygen had risen from 0.2% to 17% of the atmosphere, close to today's 21%, sufficient to support large multicellular organisms. The trajectory of subsequent evolution had been set.

By 1.5 billion years ago the cyanobacterial revolution was complete. Well-preserved fossils of that date from the Great Wall along the Kotuikan river in northern Siberia show that 'blue-greens' diversified early and continue today in almost unaltered form, illustrating their characteristic capacity to change rapidly but persist indefinitely. But soon after this time a further revolution occurred as eukaryotes broke the two billion year ecological hegemony of the bacteria. Full understanding of eukaryotic cell evolution remains elusive, but electron microscopy and molecular biology indicate that chloroplasts and mitochondria, the bases of energy metabolism in eukaryotic cells, arose by the lateral transfer of entire cells. The Russian botanist Merezhkovsky proposed in 1905 that chloroplast, the eukaryotic seat of photosynthesis, originated as a cyanobacterium which was swallowed by a protozoan. His hypothesis of endosymbiosis (two cells joined in mutually beneficial partnership, with one cell nested within the other) was rejected at the time, but revived by Lynn Margulis in 1967 and expanded to embrace the theory that mitochondria also, the compartmentalised site of respiration in eukaryotic cells, were descended from independent respiring bacteria. This altered the Darwinian view that evolution proceeds by branching and divergence, by proposing that new forms and physiologies could emerge from the fusing of branches. Molecular biology clinched the Merezhkovsky-Margulis endosymbiotic hypothesis for eukaryotic cell origins by showing that gene sequences from chloroplast DNA are more similar to those of cyanobacteria than to genes in the nuclei of plant and algal cells. Thus cyanobacteria take on a new significance as the source of photosynthesis in plants and algae, and ultimately by being yoked to a protozoan achieved the ecological feat of underpinning the greenery of the rain forest.

Many questions however still remain about this crucial biological development. Since algae scatter across several branches of the eukaryotic bough, did photosynthesis arise once and was later lost in some lineages such as ours, or did it come to eukaryotes several times by repeated symbiotic events? Comparison of a molecular phylogeny of chloroplast genes with parts of the tree of eukaryotic organisms shows that endosymbiosis must have brought photosynthesis to eukaryotes several times, including via secondary endosymbioses that incorporated eukaryotic symbionts. There is even one known case of tertiary endosymbiosis through a protozoan swallowing a unicellular alga, then being engulfed by a dinoflagellate member of marine planckton, and finally evolving by incorporation of a cyanobacterium into a eukaryotic host. Equally, just as photosynthesis is localised within chloroplasts, so aerobic respiration – the metabolism that fuels human bodies – is confined to mitochondria. Molecular phylogeny shows that they originated as bacterial cells which gradually evolved from casual symbionts to necessary organelles, returning energy to the host which supplied the sugar. Indeed, so far from demonstrating the higher order superiority of eukaryotes compared with 'primitive' prokaryotic organisms, this evidence shows clearly the limited capabilities of the former compared with the remarkable metabolic diversity of the latter and even the two metabolisms that power most eukaryotic cells derive from wholesale lateral transfer from bacteria.

Eukaryotes do, however, possess differences that are key for subsequent evolution. They are biochemically unique, with distinct transcription, translation and ribosome structures. Their cell contents are stabilised, not by a rigid wall as in the case of Archaeans and Bacteria, but by an internal dynamic cytoskeleton and a flexible membrane system. This co-ordination enabled eukaryote cells, crucially for evolutionary success, to engulf particles and thus incorporate chloroplasts and mitochondria. How this arose is still uncertain, but Martin and Muller[39] hypothesized that eukaryotic cell organisation developed from a primordial symbiosis between two prokaryotes – one a methanogenic Archaean needing fuel and the other a protobacterium able to respire aerobically with oxygen but also able to live anaerobically through fermentation. Having thus complementary metabolisms, they united to form a microcosmic carbon cycle. What however does still require explanation is why eukaryotic diversity accumulated so late – perhaps 1.2 billion years ago – having remained subservient to prokaryotes for 1.5 billion years previously. Once again evolutionary logic needs to be sought in the interaction between genetic possibility and environmental opportunity. The most likely reason is that there was a relative lack in the mid-Proterozoic oceans of the essential nutrient nitrogen, and algae cannot fix nitrogen; but as the nitrogen limitation reduced, seaweeds and planktons diversified and spread across continental shelves. Oxygen-rich oceans at the end of the Proterozoic aeon then paved the way for the last biological revolution – the rise of animals.

What caused the Cambrian explosion?

Contrary to the Darwinian view that Cambrian complexity emerged gradually over long periods of time in the Proterozoic era, it now seems likely that it developed only as the Cambrian period (Cambria being the Latin word for Wales where the English geologist Adam Sedgwick mapped a series of marine strata in 1835 above older, Precambrian, rocks and below younger Silurian strata) began about 543m years ago. Most end-Proterozoic fossils display unusual forms that distinguish them from, rather than link them to, Cambrian and younger fauna. The sandstone Nama rocks in Namibia, dating from 550 million years ago, reveal rounded disk-like fossils which are the commonest components of Ediacaran fauna and are clearly now an extinct taxa. These Ediacaran discs and vendobionts indicate that cnidarian-like animals filled the end-Proterozoic ecosystems, but there is no sign of the fossils deposited only 10-20 million years later in Cambrian rocks. How is this explained?

In Spitsbergen, the cherts containing hundreds of fossils in the Akademikerbreen rocks are separated from younger Cambrian rocks by thick beds of tillite, the sediment deposited by glaciers. Tillites are also found just below the Doushantuo fossils of southern China. In Australia, glacial rocks lie just below the sediment containing Ediacaran fossils above. The same stratigraphic pattern is found in northern India, Russia, Norway, Namibia, Newfoundland, and the Rocky Mountains from Death Valley to northern Canada. What this points to unmistakeably is an ice age that immediately preceded the Cambrian surge that heralded the age of animals. Brian Harland had already proposed in 1964 that Earth experienced a global ice age near the end of the Proterozoic aeon, and research since has confirmed that continental glaciers spread across the planet at least twice and possibly four times. Knoll contends that in the late Proterozoic the Earth froze about 765 million years ago (perhaps confined to Africa), again in two wholly global ice ages at 710±20 million years ago and about 605 million years ago, and then at least once more (relatively smaller) before the Cambrian got under way[40]. Other findings are also relevant here. Late Proterozoic glacial rocks generally have unusually high C-isotopic ratios, and these coincided with the break-up of one or more Proterozoic super-continents, which may bring about the burial of vast amounts of organic matter and explain the very high carbon ratios. In 1992 Kirschvink surmised that once glaciers expanded to within 30º of the equator, runaway refrigeration resulted, so that within a few thousand years ice sheets extended across all the land masses and covered oceans, producing a 'Snowball Earth'[41]. Hoffman and Schrag took this theory further by hypothesizing that volcanism would still have added CO_2 to the air above the ice and that concentrations of atmospheric CO_2 300-400 times higher than today's would have been needed to melt the kilometres-thick ice sheets. It would have taken millions of years to assemble such enormous stores of CO_2, but once a critical threshold was passed, de-glaciation would have occurred quickly. Others however adopt a less drastic view than the all-out Snowball hypothesis – that extensive areas of Equatorial Ocean remained ice-free and the ice began to retreat when atmospheric CO_2 reached perhaps only 4–5 times pre-glaciation levels.

If the Hoffman–Schrag scenario is correct, the advance of the ice would have eliminated almost all habitats, confining most organisms to escape havens like hydrothermal vents. Then in the rebound, they surmised, the survivors would have been roasted as the oceans heated to levels that most eukaryotes could not endure for long[42]. Through the extinction wrought by Snowball Earth first by ice and then by scorching, the unoccupied habitats then laid bare would have opened up the crucible that forged new forms of animal life. Populations that survive mass extinctions have the opportunity to radiate in the ecological emptiness that follows. But it still requires explanation as to why these new life forms were such radical departures from those that immediately preceded. Such weird creatures from the Middle Cambrian Burgess Shale in Canada so carefully analysed by Stephen Jay Gould as Opabinia, Wiwaxia, Anomalocaris and many others[43] are perhaps best seen as the products of environmental stress so extreme that it can induce mutations profound enough to spark major biological innovation. We know that Cambrian diversification proceeded, in geological time, quickly. Body plans identifiable as arthropods, brachiopods, molluscs, and even chordates took shape within 10-30 million years in the early Cambrian, and the Burgess Shale weird and wonderful organisms within forty million years. Again, the most likely reason is that mutations in regulatory genes facilitated rapid diversification.

Even then the analysis is still not complete. Super-continental break-up, planet-smothering ice, and violent disturbance at the Proterozoic–Cambrian boundary laid the foundations for the early evolution of animals, generating successive ecological waves that prompted metazoan diversification. But there has to be still another factor. If global or near-global glaciation leading to emptying of ecosystems ripe for re-colonization, why did the Cambrian explosion not occur earlier when there were at least four ice ages in the previous 220 million years in the late Proterozoic? A Canadian zoologist, JJ Nursall, has answered this by proposing that only in the latest Proterozoic period did Earth's atmosphere accumulate enough oxygen to sustain metazoan physiology[44], because until animals evolved sophisticated circulatory systems, oxygen levels must have determined their effective size. Evidence on this issue in the geochemical record comes from at least two sources. One is that high C–isotopic values imply that in late Proterozoic oceans organic matter was buried at unusually high rates, which breaks the metabolic balance between photosynthesis and respiration, enabling oxygen to accumulate in the atmosphere and oceans. A second piece of evidence is that it has been observed[45] that only at the end of the Proterozoic aeon did sulphur-bearing minerals begin to record the fractionation which would be expected in oceans full of oxygen. The geochemistry therefore strongly supports the view that animal evolution was fuelled by oxygen.

An answer can now be constructed to the complex question posed above. The reason it took an exceedingly long time, namely three million millennia, for multi-cellular creatures (and thus eventually humans) to develop from the original microscopic single-cell bacteria reflects the intricate interplay between environmental conditioning and genetic opportunity. During the Hadean era from the formation of the Earth 4.5 billion years ago till about 4 billion years ago, the boiling planet was repeatedly pummelled by major asteroid strikes scorching the rocks, drying out the oceans and producing a toxic atmosphere extremely inhospitable to life. With life forms originating around 3.8 billion years ago (or maybe up to 200 million or more years earlier), the long Archaean era 4.0–2.5 billion years ago saw the development of photosynthesis by cyanobacteria and the early stages of metabolic diversification, though the very low levels of oxygen in the oceans, less than 1% of today's levels, precluded the emergence of aerobic organisms. As the Proterozoic era (2.5 billion–543 million years ago) began, two developments opened the way to the development of larger creatures. First, the geological record indicates that the level of oxygen sharply increased, though whether from a biological or geological cause (or combination of causes) remains disputed. And secondly, soon after, a further revolution occurred with the emergence of the eukaryotic cell, almost certainly through endosymbiosis between prokaryotic bacteria. However, eukaryotic diversification was still delayed for as much as 1.5 billion years by the lack of the essential nutrient nitrogen in the oceans. But by end-Proterozoic, oxygen-rich oceans enabled large-celled eukaryotic algae to become dominant across continental shelves. By 555 million years ago, just before the start of the Cambrian era, large size had evolved in protozoans, sponges, cnidarians, and stem bilaterians (i.e. animals, including humans, with a single plane of symmetry dividing the body into left and right sides from head to tail).

Finally, also within the end Proterozoic period, several ice ages, including two of global or near-global reach, removed biology from most of the world leaving as the ice eventually ebbed huge areas of habitat with rare or weak competition. Such conditions uniquely enabled novel variants, many perhaps poorly functioning, to survive, at least until the forces of natural selection gradually winnowed them out. The key point is that genetic variation may be necessary for evolutionary radiation, but the extraordinary proliferation known as the Cambrian explosion would still not have occurred (and with it the path to homo sapiens, among others) if global glaciation had not cleared the way for novelties to survive and reproduce. Even then, it would still not have happened if oxygen levels had not, by this point, reached levels sufficient to allow larger creatures to develop. It had taken the combination of the break-up of the vast Gondwana continent, the methane-driven global glaciation (on the Hoffman–Schrag thesis), and the rise in oxygen levels above a critical threshold. In addition, at the Proterozoic–Cambrian boundary C-isotopic values plummeted, indicating a large disturbance in the Earth's carbon cycle, though radiometric dating shows that the isotopic anomaly lasted less than a million years. Mass extinction seems to mark the stratigraphic split and morphological divergence between Ediacaran and Cambrian animals on either side of the 543 million year ago divide. And just as the dinosaurs vanished at the Cretaceous–Tertiary boundary sixty-five million years ago, leaving the field to the mammals, and ultimately to us, so the disappearance of the Ediacarans at the Proterozoic–Cambrian boundary opened the way for bilaterian survivors to radiate across a relatively empty world.

The role of the mass extinctions

The Cambrian explosion, starting 543 million years ago, lasted only some fifty million years, fundamentally changing the course of evolution from its previous path of 3,000 million years of biological history. The early Cambrian strata reveal miniscule fossilised creatures, initially much smaller than the Vendian fauna which had grown up to three feet in length. Visible life, existing only within three inches above the seabed, included the shells of archaeocyathans, which were porous cones, and small shelly fossils with solid-walled cone shapes only 0.2 inches in size. In addition, a variety of fossilised spines, studs and small-scale plates appear, suggesting that life had become much more dangerous and effectively, on a miniature scale, a global arms race had begun. Although the archaeocyathans quickly spread worldwide, a major extinction event in mid-Cambrian times, about 530 million years ago, wiped out up to 70% of species. Though cone-shaped creatures became extinct, more successful and aggressive predatory creatures had evolved, like Anomalocaris and Laggania, with actively biting mouths, as well as arthropods (invertebrates with jointed limbs and segmented bodies), like the trilobites, many with increasingly armoured bodies. Perhaps the most important development of this time, however, was a small swimming animal called Pikaia, the first to possess the early characteristics of a backbone, composed of a long stiffening rod and spinal nerve chord – the ancestor of all vertebrate animals, including humans. The mudstone of the 530 million year old Burgess Shale from British Columbia in Canada, as well as other contemporary findings from Chengjiang in Yunnan Province in China and from Sirius Passet in Greenland reveal that arthropods were dominant, accounting for about half of all the preserved animals, with another third composed of echinoderms (including starfish), sponges and priapulid worms. But what is most significant about the sea animals of this era, 520 million years ago, is the first sign of head development seen in chordates such as Branchiostoma and Pikaia, processing by a swelling of the nerve chord (the brain) information about food from anatomical structures for seeing, feeling and smelling developed around the mouth.

The following Ordovician period (495 – 443million years ago) saw the beginnings of the evolution of fish, but most marine life – clam-like brachiopods, trilobites, and graptolites – was still very small, usually less than two inches. Jawless organisms (conodonts) were common, closely related to the first vertebrates. The appearance of the first fish-like jawless vertebrates (agnathans), found in the Harding sandstone strata 450 million years old in Colorado, was followed by the evolution of the first shark-like vertebrates which had jaws and teeth. Also, significantly, animals gained a foothold on land at this time, not directly from the sea, but through freshwater deposits, as revealed by parallel trackways 1/3inch wide found in 450 million year old late Ordovician freshwater deposits in northern England – probably made by a millipede-like arthropod. The global climate however became steadily wetter and cooler, and descended into an ice age at the end of the period that drove many of the 600 families of marine organisms into extinction. As ocean water was locked up in the polar icecaps, sea levels fell by 1,000ft, drying up the shallow seas of the continental shelves into bare plains. Whilst the trilobites, conodonts and graprolites never fully recovered, the Silurian period (443 – 417million years ago) saw a major revival as the oceans became warmer and sea levels rose. The closure of the Iapetus Ocean as the landmasses of Laurentia (North America), Baltica (northern Britain and Scandinavia) and Avalonia (southern Britain, Nova Scotia and Newfoundland) slowly came together created new shallow seas and basins, providing new ecological niches where marine life again flourished and diversified. But the most important development at this time for the long-term evolution of life on Earth was the spread of plants more complex than the Ordovician mosses, and in this period plants and invertebrate animals first became firmly established on land. Through photosynthesis the plants eventually created an oxygen-rich atmosphere which could later sustain a complex range of animal life on land. Their photosynthesised tissues provided vegetation for herbivores (plant-eating animals) to eat, and then later the herbivores themselves provided food for carnivores (meat-eating animals) to prey upon.

Vertebrate diversification intensified in the Devonian period (417 – 354 million years ago), as revealed particularly by the marine seabed deposits of Gogo in Western Australia. 'The Age of Fishes' in rivers, inland seas and freshwater lakes also evolved in the direction of terrestrial vertebrates. Fish groups of this period like panderichthyids (found at Lode in Latvia) became almost identical to the future tetrapods that eventually left the water for the land. But this transition is difficult. Fish propulsion, by sideways flexing of the body in a series of S-shaped waves, can work on land as shown by snakes, but cannot lift the body off the ground. Evolving short legs, as lizards did, puts more pressure on the backbone, so vertebrate skeletons had to become stronger and more flexible, which took a long time to evolve. The following Carboniferous (coal-bearing) Age (354 – 290 million years ago), sometimes divided into the earlier Mississippian and later Pennsylvanian periods, saw the steady drifting together of Gondwana, Laurentia and Baltica towards amalgamation into the single super-continent of Pangaea (the whole earth). The first extensive forests grew on earth, and four-legged animals emerged from the water and evolved into amphibians and reptiles. The hot 'global greenhouse' eighty million year state of the Siluro-Devonian periods gave way to a cooler and seasonal Earth. The first extensive forests grew in the lowlands which increased oxygen levels through photosynthesis from a mid-Devonian low of 15% to a peak of 35% in the late Carboniferous, the highest in the Earth's history. Tetrapods (four-legged animals) – extensively fossilized in East Kirkton limestone in Scotland – emerged from the water, and once a group of tetrapods had evolved which could lay shelled eggs, the age of (amniote) reptiles had arrived. In mid to late Carboniferous times, however, glaciers and polar icecaps formed, and an extensive glaciation persisted into the following Permian age. In this age (290 – 248 million years ago) the formation of the super-continent of Pangaea provided the environment for the global expansion of terrestrial life. The amniote tetrapods evolved into two branches – the reptiles and a group called synapsids. One of the later synapsid groups, called cynodont therapsids – from fossils of over a hundred species of therapsids found in the red sandstone of the late Permian Karroo basin in South Africa in the 1840s –

eventually became warm-blooded, and their lineage includes the first mammals in Triassic times.

At the end of the Permian the biggest mass extinction event occurred in the history of the Earth. Altogether some 95% of marine invertebrates perished, including brachiopods and trilobites which had lasted 300 million years to that point. Land vertebrates were severely hit. About twenty-one families of therapsids – nearly two-thirds of the total number of tetrapod families – and a third of amphibian families disappeared from the record. But marine creatures were hit even harder: marine diversity was reduced from a quarter of a million species to less than 10,000 – a kind of biotic Armageddon. What caused such huge decimation of life? No explanation is certain, but there are several theories. There was a major fall in sea levels at the Permo-Triassic boundary which eliminated much of the shallow marine life, but there were also huge volcanic eruptions in Siberia leading to global climate change. The catastrophe has also been blamed on great bursts of methane from ice stored on continental slopes, or again on an apocalyptic overturning of the Panthalassic (total sea) Ocean bringing to the surface waters low in oxygen but rich in CO_2.

Although this was the most devastating extinction known (so far), it was only one of many mass extinctions that have punctuated life on Earth. Reference is conventionally made to five – at the Ordovician-Silurian boundary at 443 million years ago when 52% of world species were wiped out, towards the end of the Devonian at about 365 million years ago when 40% died, at the Permian-Triassic boundary 248 million years ago when 68% died, at the Triassic-Jurassic boundary 206 million years ago when 45% died, and, most famously, at the Cretaceous-Tertiary boundary sixty-five million years ago when 42% died, including the dinosaurs. But even this catalogue is far from exhaustive. Reference has already been made to an extensive ice age about 765 million years ago and to two later ice ages which covered the whole Earth ('Snowball Earth') first about 710 million years ago and then again at 605 million years ago, as well as to yet another (though smaller) one which ushered in the Cambrian era at 543 million years ago. All of these must have severely reduced marine life, and predating these there would almost certainly have been other unknown but equally devastating extinction events. In addition, there is evidence of at least one, and perhaps three, extinction episodes during the 50 million year Cambrian era when at least 40% of species were killed. Mass extinctions are thus not exceedingly unusual and unexpected events, but written deeply into the weft of life on Earth throughout at least the last billion years.

There are two important issues here – their causes, and their role in influencing the evolution of life. Several different mechanisms have been put forward to explain why these extinction episodes occurred, not necessarily mutually exclusive and maybe sometimes in combination. The most dramatic postulated cause is a massive asteroid or comet impact which would kill both immediately through earthquakes and tidal waves, and over time through huge amounts of dust and debris thrown up which block out the sun's radiation and shrivel the food supply in the extreme cold. A colossal meteorite impact at Chicxulub in Mexico's Yucatan peninsula, leaving a crater more than sixty miles wide, was almost certainly implicated in the late Cretaceous extinctions sixty-five million years ago which destroyed the dinosaurs, though the dinosaurs were already gradually declining and large-scale volcanic eruptions also were occurring at this time discharging huge quantities of CO_2. In addition, there have been at least twenty-eight other asteroid strikes on Earth in the last 400 million years leaving craters between six - sixty miles wide. Massive volcanic eruptions are a second mechanism, and indeed massive volcanic eruptions, much bigger than any in modern times (far exceeding the largest, Tambora, in the East Indies in 1815 which discharged 15 km^3 of rock and debris and produced 'the year without a summer'), are known to have occurred because of the flood basalts, huge layers of volcanic rock, deposited. At least eleven flood basalt eruptions have been recorded in the last quarter billion years. Another mechanism is sharp changes in sea-levels, caused by climate change and tectonic plate movements. In the early Triassic around 240 million years ago sea-levels dropped to an all-time low in the last half billion years. A fourth mechanism is global climate change, especially the onset of global glaciation. What emerges clearly is that extinction events are usually associated, not just with one precipitating factor, but a combination of several.

The great significance of mass extinctions however is the profound role they play in altering the trajectory of life's evolution. It has long been noted by biostratigraphers that species appear in the fossil record fully formed, persist virtually unchanged for millions of years, and then disappear. This strongly suggests that changes in life forms occur episodically rather than continuously as posited by Darwinian natural selection, and that mass extinctions brought about by huge environmental change are the central mechanism driving these changes. Indeed, Niles Eldredge and Stephen Jay Gould enunciated a theory of 'punctuated equilibrium'[46] to describe this process as distinct from Darwin's view of imperceptibly gradual change over long periods of time. They posited that transformations take place rapidly and locally, after which their descendants are constrained by natural selection to stay much the same unless or until competitors or shifting environments overwhelm them. It has already been remarked that mass extinction performed precisely this role most notably prior to the onset of the Cambrian era but it applies at several other boundaries too, not least the Cretaceous – Tertiary boundary sixty-five million years ago which paved the way for the mammals and ultimately for homo sapiens. The significance of that evolutionary course of events is explored in the next chapter.

Implications

The story of the evolution of life over four billion years on Earth throws up several crucial conclusions. One is that it cannot be said to be a directed and straightforward process of ascent from micro-organisms to large creatures and ultimately to humans. The process was rather a haphazard mixture of almost frozen immobility over aeons of time combined with abrupt and violent upheaval at irregular intervals. Second, the achievement of more complex life forms depended on a succession of unpredictable environmental conditions being met – the development of photo-synthesis, a huge increase in oxygen levels, a rise in nitrogen as an ocean nutrient, the evolution of the eukaryotic cell from prokaryotic origins, to specify only some of the more important ones; and even over the elapsing of three million millennia life would not have proceeded beyond its most primitive forms unless all these conditions were met in the required order. Third, the trigger for genetic change and diversification was driven, not by any apparent preconceived plan, but by the blind force of overwhelming extraneous intervention, whether asteroid impact, vulcanism, global glaciation, or super-continent break-up. Fourth, because so many unpredictable variables were involved, the outcome of the evolution of life forms must at each stage have remained uncertain, indicating that a different combination of external pressures played out over time could have produced a different set of life forms from those we now recognise. Life could well have diverged repeatedly to follow a wholly separate trajectory or set of trajectories. Fifth, it follows from that as a corollary that the species at the outer limits of the Tree of Life owe their existence in many cases to a wildly improbable concatenation of circumstances – a conclusion that applies partic-ularly to the arrival of humans.

Chapter 7

The Advent of the Human Species

The rise and fall of the dinosaurs

The earliest amphibians, direct ancestors of the human race, crawled ashore about 360 million years ago. In the next 300 million years animal life evolved in four main developments which Robert Bakker has categorised as Megadynasties[47]. In the first the amphibians, which were cold-blooded, could live and feed out of water, but had to return to the water to reproduce, though some species freed themselves of this need by developing – a major evolutionary advance – the hard-shelled egg. These egg-layers, called reptiles, were however cold-blooded lumberers with low metabolic rates, spreading out over land recently colonised by plants. Then around 270 million years ago this rather somnolent world was swept away by Megadynasty II in the 'Kazanian Revolution'. Some species became warm-blooded and proto-mammals appeared with a higher metabolic rate, able to run fast in pursuit of prey – a huge advantage over cold-blooded creatures totally dependent on external warmth. These semi-reptilian early mammals evolved in two main groups – diapsids which retained typical reptilian characteristics (ancestors of lizards, crocodiles, and birds), and therapsids (ancestors of cats, dogs, whales, and humans). This latter group included Probainognathus, furry creatures with a skull, jaw and teeth very similar to mammals and which may have even suckled their young. Their descendants evolved into three kinds of early mammal, one of which –Kuehneotherid – became the ancestor of every other mammal alive on Earth today.

These proto-mammals looked set for twenty million years to continue to dominate the world, until they were struck down by the greatest disaster in the geological record, 251 million years ago at the end of the Permian. After these terminal extinctions over a 10 million year period which wiped out 75-90% of all existing marine species, the surviving smaller therapsids and the more reptilian diapsids were thrown together in competition, an equal battle which the former (our ancestors) lost – a sobering fact indicating that mammals possess no intrinsic superiority on any supposed evolutionary ladder. In this Megadynasty III era, their reptilian rivals, thecodonts, competed increasingly successfully, and some species grew to half a tonne weight. As they diversified and developed further, the thecodonts were soon replaced by archosaurs, forerunners of the dinosaurs, crocodiles and flying reptiles. By the end of the Triassic period 213 million years ago, the therapsid cynodonts had been all but eliminated by the early dinosaurs. The survivors, the line from Probainognathus to Kuehneotherid to humans, managed to eke out a living by evolving into small, mouse-like creatures too insignificant to attract attention from the dinosaurs, probably developing a nocturnal lifestyle and living off insects and perhaps plants.

Throughout the 150 million years of the Jurassic and Cretaceous eras the dinosaurs dominated the Earth – a period 1,000 times longer than the time since homo sapiens migrated out of Africa to take over the world. They were as numerous as mammals today, and ranged from the lead predator Tyrannosaurus Rex and the tank-like herbivorous brontosaurus down to dinosaurs no larger than today's goats or chickens. Their demise, normally dated to sixty-five million years ago, was not necessarily sudden. Their numbers dwindled over a period of at least ten million years from thirty genera to thirteen found in the fossil remains of Montana and southern Alberta. The predisposing factors may have been the fall in sea level as a result of tectonic activity, leading to the drying out of the shallow inland seas and to continental interiors, bereft of the equable effects of large masses of water, becoming liable to harsh winters and baking summers. With animal populations already weakened by the consequential substantial loss of food supply, it is likely that the coup de grace was administered by a meteorite impact or by eruptions of volcanism, or even both.

One interesting question remains: why did the dinosaurs not evolve intelligence? One answer might be that the environmental pressures that prompted the rise of human intelligence simply did not exist in the Cretaceous in a way that threatened Megadynasty III. However, one tempting hypothesis developed by Canadian researchers, Dale Russell and Ron Seguin, suggests that maybe such evolution of dinosaur intelligence was indeed under way sixty-five million years ago[48]. Their 1970s study of the fossil remains of a dinosaur specimen, Stenonychosaurus, showed that it had a relatively large brain, walked on two legs, and had four-fingered hands with opposable digits which is the key to the sensitive grip required for precise digital manipulation. The ratio of brain to body weight of this dinosaur placed it in the same range as large modern birds or less intelligent modern mammals. The researchers then built a model of the kind of creature which Stenonychosaurus might have developed into by extrapolating forward the evolution of the relatively large brain, upright posture and dexterous hand. Russell calculated that at the rate of evolutionary change prevailing in the late Cretaceous, a creature with the same body weight as a modern human, and a brain to match, could have emerged within twenty-five million years (i.e. by forty million years ago). The dinosaur model built to these specifications looked more like a human being than a dinosaur[49]. Russell argued that this form "may have a non-negligible probability of appearing as a consequence of natural selection within the biospheres of Earth-like planets". He even concludes that "the humanoid form may be a special (non-random) solution to the biophysical problems posed by intelligence". We return to this point later in this chapter.

Megadynasty IV after the cataclysm of sixty-five million years ago once again saw the balance reversed between mammals and reptiles. In Megadynasty II the proto-mammals had dominated, with the more reptilian creatures relegated to small-animal niches. In Megadynasty III the reptilians out-competed their mammalian rivals and established an overriding physical dominance never equalled before or since, with mammals confined through the Mesozoic era to a small scurrying existence in the interstices of the ecology. In Megadynasty IV mammals turned out better able, after the removal of the large dinosaurs from about the size of Stenonychosaurus upwards, to diversify and fill the ecological space in the niches left vacant. However, it is reasonable to surmise that if the intelligent dinosaur had been only slightly smaller, the evolution of life on Earth may have rolled out quite differently – one of many cusps of contingent variability that abound along the pathways pursued by life forms over aeons of time. But in the absence of that intelligent competition, probably the mammals were able to succeed because of the skills honed under pressure of natural selection in order to survive at all in a world dominated by dinosaurs over a very long stretch of time (213-65 million years ago).

The primate ascendancy

Primates – that is, a mammal with a large brain, good stereoscopic vision, strong clasping hands, and all-purpose teeth – appear in the fossil record before the cataclysm sixty-five million years ago, in what is now Montana, though at that time it was closer to the equator. After evolution throughout such a long period, primates remain today, given these characteristics, highly adapted to tree life, though significantly one line – humans – departed from this primate lifestyle. As life gradually recovered from the catastrophes, the first mammal boom was in place within a few million years, and many mammals grew in size and developed bigger brains to fill the niches left vacant by the dinosaurs. During this period too the super-continents were breaking up, so that some species evolved in some parts of the world but could not spread elsewhere (e.g. the marsupials in the southern continent).

From the human point of view, a central development of the Cenozoic era (from the global disaster sixty-five million years ago till today) was the emergence of the first monkeys about fifty million years ago, though the fossil record is sparse on how or why this happened. Interestingly, monkeys evolved almost identically in two different land masses cut off from each other, South America and Africa. It suggests that when the ancestral primate was confronted with the evolutionary challenge of adapting to the tropical jungle and living off fruit and leaves, it produced virtually the same result twice – an example of parallel evolution. The gene pool of primates inherited from ancestors does allow for a degree of variation and adaptation of the basic mammal form, and gene changes occurring by chance that are selected by evolution operate within those limits to tailor the outward physical form to the niches available. Parallel evolution, whereby different species are tailored by natural selection to fit a given ecological niche in a similar (optimal) way, also underlies the observation cited earlier of an intelligent dinosauroid developing like a human being.

From 40-32 million years ago a series of marine extinctions indicate a drastic change in the weather of the planet. The disappearance of species that liked warmth from the microfossil record and the major drop in both surface and deep water temperatures, maybe exacerbated further by an asteroid strike around this time, suggest a substantial global cooling across the planet. Accompanying this was the development for the first time of seasonal variations, but also more importantly as the world cooled, sea levels fell leaving continental interiors farther from the sea and with lower exposure to rain, so that thick forests in many parts of the world were transformed into open grassland. It was probably these fundamental ecological changes that prompted the emergence of the ape-like variation within the monkey line, and hence the later development of the human species. For whilst the ape first became prominent in northern Africa where these environmental changes were marked, the ape did not develop in South America, which remained an isolated continent straddling the equator and covered in lush jungle. Further evidence that massive climate change lay behind that the emergence of the ape line comes from the fossil skull found in the Fayum Depression in Egypt, hence known as Aegyptopithecus (from the Greek word for ape or monkey). Found in strata twenty-eight million years old, just after the huge upheavals of the previous eight million years, it is the earliest ancestral ape known, with a supple back, long grasping hands and a larger brain relative to body size (it was only the size of a cat) than any other known mammal from that time. By twenty-five million years ago there were several other proto-ape lines in northern Africa, recognisably of the same family (Hominidae) as humans. Thus about twenty million years elapsed before apes split off from the monkey line, and a further twenty-five million years before homo sapiens split off from its sibling apes – spacing that again indicates the crucial importance of environment and particularly climate change in driving evolution.

The period after twenty-five million years ago, the mammals' heyday, also saw an explosive radiation in ape varieties round Africa, taking advantage of the cool, dry conditions (related to the large ice cap that formed over Antarctica from thirty-five million years ago) and the widespread open forest and extensive grasslands. Following the collision between the African and Eurasian continents around eighteen million years ago, apes spread out further into Eurasia and diversified more till apes outnumbered monkeys by twenty to one by fifteen million years ago. Of the various ape groups, Ramapithecus, found in deposits between 14-7 million years ago, is now thought to be the ancestor of today's Asian apes like the orang-utan, evolutionary cousins to humans, though the latter are even more closely related to the African apes. However, it is not until 3.6 million years ago that a definitely hominid ape appears in the fossil record, the earliest known ancestor of the human line, separate even from the other African apes.

The point at which the hominid line split from that of other African apes can now be measured by the difference between the genetic material, the DNA, of humans and other apes. The difference between the genetic material of human beings and the other two African apes, the chimp and the gorilla, is about 1%, while the molecular 'distance' between humans and the orang-utan is about twice as much, suggesting that the line leading to both humans and the African apes split from the orang-utan line about twice as long ago as the three-way split in the African ape line. If then Aegyptopithecus just after thirty million years ago marks the point at which the apes split from the African monkeys, and we know that the genetic 'distance' between the living apes and the African monkeys is about three times (or a little more) than the distance between all the African apes and the orang-utan, the difference between African apes must correspond to some nine million years of evolution, and the difference between humans and the other two African apes must correspond to about half this, i.e. some 4-5 million years of independent evolution. This date coincides with the time when the East African forests were retreating amid a general regional drying out, offering new habitats of open woodland and grassy plains. Further DNA tests suggest that among the African apes, the gorilla line split off first, around eight million years ago, significantly at about the same time as Ramapithecus disappeared from the record while the humans-chimps split occurred around five million years ago. The genetic evidence for this dating neatly matches the climate-driven turbulence of the period. By 3-4 million years ago the fossil record from the East

African rift containing several varieties of ape-men shows clearly where the hominid line began.

The environmental driver behind these processes is quite clear. As the forests shrank, the apes faced a choice: either stay in the trees and become even more competitive in the face of diminishing resources (they are the ancestors of the gorillas), or emerge from the forests and learn to adapt to life in the more open woodlands on the edge, still using trees but having to get food from the ground as well (they are the ancestors of the chimps). A third branch of this family, perhaps least adept at tree life and forced out on to the plains after losing competition with their more successful cousins, had to find a new way of life to survive. Over long periods of time they evolved into upright walkers, ate whatever they could catch, formed the habit of sharing food among family members or a wider group, and needing greater skills to survive, gradually developed larger brains. Ultimately they became human. Interestingly, however, baboons also split from the ancestral monkey family around 4-5 million years ago and began living in the open plains – the monkeys' response to the dwindling forests. But they could not walk upright, unlike their related hominid line – the apes' answer to the same ecological challenge. As Mary and John Gribbin have noted[50], maybe the world is dominated today by descendants from the apes rather than the monkeys because, coincidentally, the lifestyle of a tree-dwelling ape, hanging from branches and swinging between them (known as brachiation, from the Greek word for arms), gives it a body structure fitted to walking upright whereas the monkey body, used to running along the tops of branches, is not well-suited for this purpose.

The arrival of homo sapiens

The bipedal brachiator lifestyle of the early human line conferred several important advantages. It enabled an all-round view of surroundings, both to obtain food and to get advance warning of predators. It is a more efficient form of locomotion on the ground than going on all-fours, and consumes less energy. It also frees the hands to carry, whether weapons, implements or food. The development of intelligence came later, prompted by a succession of climatic pressures after two million years ago. From three million years ago ice sheets began to spread down from the north, but did not initially impact on East Africa. But around the start of the Pleistocene era from 1.8 million years ago, rainfall in the region fell markedly, linked with the spread of ice at higher latitudes. It was this dramatic cooling in the northern hemisphere and the concomitant drying out in Africa which pushed the early hominids out of the trees and into the wholly different lifestyle on the plains. But it was the ice epoch of the last two million years – the ebb and flow of massive ice-sheets across continents – which set the premium on intelligence for survival and forced the hominid development into homo sapiens – an extraordinarily rapid spurt in evolutionary change.

The earliest hominid in East Africa, named homo habilis ('handy-man'), dates from 2.5 million years ago. This was an ape that walked upright, about 1.2 metres tall, with a slender build and a large head averaging some 675 cm^3, only half that of today's homo sapiens. He was a tool-user, more sophisticated than other close members of his genus with whom he shared the African rift valley, Australopithecus africanus, which had a smaller brain only some 440 cm^3 in volume, and Australopithecus robustus, heavier built, taller at 1.6 metres and with a brain some 520 cm^3 in size. It seems clear that all three were descended from a recent common ancestor, and claims have been made that this 'missing link' has been found in Ethiopia in the form of a skeleton, 40% complete, dating from about 3.3 million years ago[51]. Familiarly entitled Lucy, this female ape-person was formally designated in 1978 as Australopithecus afarensis, just over 1 metre in height (though males of the species may have been up to 1.7 metres tall).

Looking very much like a modern pygmy chimp, it may perhaps best be seen as a proto-human body with an ape's head on top.

The Pleistocene glaciation reached a peak when the area covered by ice amounted to 45 million km^2, three times the area covered by Greenland and the polar regions today. The volume of ice actually reached 56 million km^3. In the face of these extremely harsh conditions and challenged by the climatic convulsions arising from these enormous ice-sheets, homo habilis had evolved by 1.5 million years ago into homo erectus, a more human-like ape which was taller at 1.6 metres and equipped with a much larger brain about 925 cm^3. Later specimens had had larger brains up to 1100 cm^3 in size, not far short of the modern human average today of 1360 cm^3. Homo erectus was much more human, with more modern teeth and a less prominent jaw, and walked fully upright (hence the title). It was this species which led the homo line out of Africa and into Asia and Europe.

It is now realised, through the use of the isotope thermometer technique that fifteen or more full ice ages occurred during the Pleistocene in the last two million years, as well as six ice ages in the past few hundred thousand years. Each full ice age, with 30% of the entire land surface of the Earth covered by a blanket of ice, lasted for 80,000-100,000 years, while the periods between the ice ages – the inter-glacials – lasted only 10,000-15,000 years (which suggests, since the last ice age ended about 10,000 years ago, that another ice age is due within the next 5,000 years). These ice-age rhythms are best explained by the Milankovich model, named after the Serbian astronomer who calculated the rhythmic variations in the amount of heat reaching the northern hemisphere according to the Earth's tilt and wobble as it orbits the sun and the constant changes between circle and ellipse in the orbit itself.

The significance of this new pattern, unique in the history of the Earth, for life forms across the globe was very considerable. It was not, as previously, gradual steady climate change over long aeons of time to which species could slowly adapt, nor was it abrupt and violent ecological change causing widespread extinctions and leaving niches vacant to be filled by the few survivors. For a previously tree-living ape totally unsuited to these new conditions, it put a premium on agility, cunning and adaptability finding new ways to survive in terms of habitat and food. It forced the rapid development of intelligence and hastened the evolution of the human line. Unsurprisingly, an environmental rhythm that drastically cut back both shelter and food for up to 100,000 years before easing up briefly and then plunging back again into a bitterly harsh ecology, repeated over a dozen times, winnowed out the less adaptable through widespread death and starvation and left only the sharper and cleverer as survivors. This is confirmed by the steady increase in cranial capacity in the homo erectus line throughout the Pleistocene.

However, between 400,000-200,000 years ago a much bigger increase in brain size occurred, accompanied by thinner skull bones. Homo sapiens had arrived, but soon after the line split. By 100,000 years ago two sub-species had developed. One, homo sapiens neanderthalensis (from its discovery in Germany), was bigger in size, had a larger brain, and lived from across western Europe to central Asia, dying out for reasons that are disputed (eliminated by conquest or absorbed by inter-breeding within the other sub-species) around 40,000 years ago, in the middle of the last ice age. The second, homo sapiens sapiens, probably emerged out of Africa, as homo erectus had done previously, judging by part of a 115,000 year old human skull discovered in a South African cave, and then moved across the world in one or two waves through Asia to Australia about 33,000 years ago and through Europe over the land bridge to America some 25,000 years ago. So when the current inter-glacial finally arrived about 10,000 years ago, homo sapiens sapiens had already adapted to every continent on Earth and had endured and survived the harshest and most inhospitable excesses of a very long-lasting ice age, and had thus honed his skills and intelligence to the point

99

where he could now in a more equable climate dominate the world and create for the first time on Earth a series of civilizations. But already, during the ice age itself, homo sapiens was already fully human, no less intelligent than we are today, able to talk and to form complex societies, and from the evidence of burials having religious ideas and concepts.

Inevitable convergence or wild improbability?

What this whole story seems to reveal is an endless series of contingencies where a large and varying concatenation of forces and events have produced outcomes which could so easily have been quite different, leading to an unpredictably alternative world. Such alien outcomes might never have included humans, or even the development of intelligence. If all the turns and twists in this enormous zig-zagging saga were assembled together, with even the smallest opening up bigger and bigger divergences from the geological and biological route actually recorded, the advent of humans might indeed be seen as an absurdly negligible unlikelihood. Thus Stephen Jay Gould argues "the awesome improbability of human evolution"[52].

A contrasting assessment stresses the facts of evolutionary convergence: the recurrent tendency of biological structures to come up with the same or similar 'answer' to a given challenge. In the field of biochemistry there are often multiple solutions to a specific problem, but nevertheless particular motifs recur. Indeed it has been said that "convergence offers a metaphor as to how evolution navigates the combinatorial immensities of biological hyperspace"[53]. The evidence is ubiquitous among insects, birds and mammals. The emergence of the sensory modalities in different taxa – eyes in particular, but also such features as balance, hearing, olfaction, echolocation, and electrogeneration – are all remarkably convergent. Such complex systems may arise from wholly different starting points, but still repeatedly converge on the same evolutionary end-point.

There are several lessons to be drawn from this. The number of evolutionary solutions to a given problem is limited, and the emergence of biological complexity may be much more constrained than is often supposed. It is also highly significant that what is possible has often been arrived at multiple times and in wholly independent contexts. Thus, to take just a few examples out of hundreds, the convergence of mimicry of insects and spiders to an ant morphology has evolved at least seventy times[54], while the evolution of flight, the fusiform body shapes in aquatic vertebrates and above all the development of viviparity (live births rather than hatching eggs) and matrotrophy among vertebrates (which have originated independently over 130 times) are all rampantly convergent. What this means is that the emergence of these various biological properties is virtually inevitable. What may have been impossible billions of years ago becomes increasingly likely in the trajectories of evolution. It also suggests that 'mammal-ness' is not the exclusive preserve of one single evolutionary group, and that implies that if humans had not emerged, then some alternative warm-blooded, viviparous, vocalizing and intelligent species would have developed.

But even if many of the evolutionary features that contribute to defining human beings are clearly convergent, and even if mammal-ness is a biological property rather than a historical contingency, that still may not explain such distinctive characteristics of humans as intelligence, culture, tool-making, and bipedality. The question then is whether the basic architecture regarded as essential for human existence – in effect the biochemical scaffolding – was in place at much earlier times in the history of life. Recent research has indeed uncovered levels of complexity in lower organisms that correspond interestingly to the social behaviour of animals and higher organisms, including in respect of foraging and cooperative hunting, specialised dispersal forms, genetic altruism, and communication using various chemical signals[55]. These reveal convergences in behaviour, clearly indicative of adaptation, between micro-organisms and larger creatures (birds and animals). But that still does not explain how human complexity arises from the molecular substrate. However, it is well understood that evolution is highly skilled at co-option and redeploying existing structures (after all, humans have less than 30,000 genes, with multiple functions). But that still leaves open the question whether humans as a biological property are inevitable because as well as possessing with other creatures a complex social system, culture, placentas and live birth, warm-bloodedness, and vocalization, we also display bipedalism, manual dexterity, and a very large brain.

In fact there is clear evidence that all three evolved indepen-dently and long before the hominid line. Fossils of the Miocene ape, Oreopithecus, from what is now Tuscany (but were then isolated islands in the Mediterranean), strongly indicate that some three million years ago it developed bipedality, based on analysis of the hip and foot bones. It probably did so because its insular location meant it was not threatened by large predators and could readily collect food from low-hanging trees. When the islands reconnected to the continent, the carnivores returned, the ape disappeared, and it took another two million years before other bipeds with a precision grip evolved. Nor in the history of life was the use of fore-limbs for skilled manipulation limited to the higher primates: it was also found among frogs and rodents as well as some marsupials and lemurs.

Even in the case of the very large brains that humans possess (seven times bigger than might be expected in relation to body size), there is good evidence that other species had developed large brains long before the hominids. From at least four million years ago dolphins had the largest brains of any creature and only about 1.5 million years ago, in the era of homo erectus, were they overtaken by the hominid brain size. In both cases the trigger for enlarging brain size was probably environmental – the pressures imposed by the extensive glaciation of the planet in the case of homo erectus and the dramatic cooling of the Southern Ocean in the case of the dolphins. And not only dolphins, but also some other species (e.g. bonobo chimps and African grey parrots) may have developed sufficient cognitive complexity to allow them to understand a simple but symbolic system of communication rules[56]. Whether however animal communications foreshadow the origins of human language is much disputed, but it may well suggest that language has long evolutionary roots. This issue of human uniqueness or otherwise will be discussed further in the next chapter, but all this evidence clearly indicates that evolutionary convergence plays a much bigger role than has been generally recognised.

Implications

The issue as to whether the advent of the human species was entirely fortuitous or virtually inevitable is readily answered by the available evidence. Both facets played a role in a complex interactive process. As Rob Foley has noted[57], 'while contingency plays a part in the timing and location of evolutionary events, the way these events are played out, the final biological outcomes, are strongly influenced by selection, adaptation and function', and he concludes: 'should the tape of life be replayed, undoubtedly there would be many differences, but there would also be a very significant number of similarities'.

The derivation of the human lineage over the last quarter billion years from the semi-reptilian proto-mammals, via their near-elimination first in the biggest mass extinction in the Earth's history and then being out-competed in the rise of the dinosaurs, can only be viewed as an exceptionally chancy and haphazard contingency. It could clearly very readily have turned out otherwise, and the advent of the hominids could very easily not have happened at all. Yet there is ample evidence that the principle of evolutionary convergence applies across all species, and even in the case of the dinosaurs the discovery and analysis of a recognisably humanoid-type specimen suggests evolution towards something resembling a hominid form was already well under way sixty-five million years ago and might well have been completed by forty million years ago. How closely the ultimate form would have reflected homo sapiens with similar character-istics and potential can only be conjectured. But the repeatedly observed principle of over-determination in nature – parallel evolution in different species and different locations leading to the same or similar results – suggests that the emergence of a human-type species, in one form or another, could well still have developed.

For the evolutionary sequencing to the hominid line that did occur, however, massive and continuing environmental upheaval throughout the last sixty-five million years played a decisive role. Successively, the breaking apart of the super-continents like Gondwana, drastic global cooling across the planet, possible asteroid strikes, continental interiors transformed from forests to open grassland, and finally the spread of massive ice-sheets across the continents put a premium on adaptability, intelligence and cunning, and honed the development of creatures that most excelled in them. But these powerful climactic pressures of course formed only the final chapter (so far) of a much longer and more profound process of environmental conditioning which suggests it is difficult to view the emergence of humans as a 'planned' development, rather the highly contingent variable in an extremely slow process of evolutionary convergence towards an intelligent being – a process that may well still be in its early stages.

Chapter 8

Are Human Beings Unique?

What distinguishes us from other creatures?

The last chapter indicated that many of the typically distinctive characteristics of humans are not confined to the human species (though often developed to an unprecedented high degree in humans), but have been found to a greater or lesser degree in other creatures long before the hominid emergence. But does that apply to all human attributes, including some of the most profound such as consciousness, self-awareness, moral sense, aesthetic appreciation, and religious/spiritual understanding? It might be argued that humans are unique in their capacity to construct vast technological systems that can even override the natural dynamics of the planet, in their ability to use culture rather than genetic selection to ensure survival and comfortable living, in their skill at manipulating abstract information in pursuit of scientific investigation, in their development of complex moral systems, in their achievement of aesthetic buildings, landscapes and art, and in their spirituality reaching out to religious experience and (as some would claim) in their possession of a soul. If indeed these are distinct capabilities of humans, from whence do they derive?

All life is based on chemistry, and evolutionary science has shown that every single living thing today is ultimately descended from a single cell that originated on Earth nearly four billion years ago. More striking still, molecular biology has found that all living creatures contain evidence of this descent within every cell of their bodies. It is therefore relevant to ask whether these traces reveal any significant differences between humans and all other living things. In human beings there are some three billion DNA base pairs, whilst in a single human cell the amount of information in the DNA is similar to that contained in the words of three sets of Encyclopaedia Britannica. The DNA of two human beings differs in about 0.5% of these base pairs, and between human and chimpanzees the difference is just 2%. As an indication of how DNA compares with other species, the overlap for example of the cytochrome-C molecule (a common workhouse molecule enabling chemical reactions for cells to generate their energy) is 100% between humans and chimpanzees, 90% in the case of dogs, 86% for rattlesnakes, and 71% for pumpkins. This suggests that we share most of our cellular chemistry not only with other primates, but with all living things. Whether investigation is via the fields of anatomy, evolution or biochemistry, the same conclusion is reached, that our similarities to other organisms in molecular structure overwhelmingly exceed our differences from them, and that where distinguishing features clearly exist, they tend to be subtle.

A more common assumption is that what separates humans from other creatures is our capacity for complex and intelligent behaviour. Yet caution is needed even here. Examination of the phyla across the animal kingdom shows that a complex nervous system is not necessary to produce complex behaviour, and whatever intelligence is exactly, it is not the exclusive preserve of primates or even of mammals. Nor are humans alone in their capacity to make tools, or eve in the possession of language – though the vocal chords of chimpanzees are constructed such that large repertoires of articulated sounds cannot be produced. Animals can certainly communicate with each other, and can also communicate between species, as sheepdog trials indicate. In terms of naming objects, recognising words, and even answering simple questions, some animals, most notably parrots, can certainly function verbally. There is however equally clearly a point in the scale of mental tasks, for example conceptualising another's mental state as well as more obviously certain levels of abstract reasoning, which only the human brain is able to perform.

If then the overall genetic differences between chimpanzees and humans are strikingly small, how does one explain these key divergences in capacity? There may well be more than a single explanation. One theory[58] notes that the atomistic notion that each organic trait is controlled by a single gene is incompatible with our observed anatomical dissimilarities, so certain kinds of genes must have far wider and more far-reaching effects than merely single traits – a view confirmed thirty years later by the discovery that humans do indeed have only some 30,000 genes, hugely less than previously imagined. King and Wilson therefore postulated that part of the genetic system had the function, not of determining specific traits, but of controlling the timing of developmental events within the organism – turning other genes on and off at the appropriate time – and that mutations in this regulatory system might then explain the big divergence between the two species. What gives this theory increased plausibility is the separate evidence of differences between apes and humans in the timing of gene expression during development. As Stephen Jay Gould has strongly argued[59], homo sapiens is basically a neotenic species, evolving from apelike ancestors by a general retardation in the developmental rate. Uniquely in man, nearly 30% of his entire life-span is spent on growing, thus greatly extending the time available for learning by experience and developing the brain, the source of human beings' greatest advantage.

The human brain
Another and more usual explanation of human uniqueness lies in the almost unbelievable complexity of the human brain. It contains some 100 billion neurons, highly interconnected and grouped together in spherical conglomerates (nuclei) and in flat sheets (cortices), each of which performs a very specialised task.

Signals travel along a single neuron by a complex chemical process (not like an ordinary electrical current running through a wire or microchip), and are conveyed to other neurons by the emission and reception of specialised molecules. In addition to these neurons the brain is laced with blood vessels which bring oxygen and nutrients into its cells and carry away wastes, as well as bringing other molecules into it. Furthermore some nine-tenths of the cells in the brain are not neurons at all, but glial cells whose role may be to set the threshold at which the neuron fires.

Just above the brain stem sits the diencephalon, a region which acts as the major co-ordinating centre of the brain. The thalamus is located here, which provides the main relay station for nerve signals between the brain stem and the upper reaches of the brain. Beneath it is the hypothalamus whose functions not only relate to the sex drive, hunger, thirst, pleasure and pain, but also send molecules to the pituitary gland, the master gland of the endocrine system, which influence the production of hormones in the pituitary itself. The outer part of the brain is formed of two lobes (cerebral hemispheres) connected by a thick cable of nerve fibres and divided into regions (lobes). Neurons in the frontal lobes control conscious movement, while the back of the head (the occipital lobes) is the location for the initial processing of vision. Between them are the parietal lobes where data on the state of the body is processed, while the temporal lobes deal with hearing, memory, learning and emotion. The outermost layer of the brain (the cerebral cortex) is associated with the higher mental faculties. However, it is wrong to stress the functional separation of different components of the brain since its key characteristic is that it operates as a coherent, complex system where large numbers of interacting neurons constantly communicate with each other.

What are the implications of this process? One is that the brain is not designed ab initio, but rather grows and develops synapses in accordance with well-defined chemical signals – and not even

very efficiently since half the neurons that begin making connections end up 'committing suicide' and disappearing. Another
factor concerns its operation: it is still not fully understood how
the brain assembles the preliminary building blocks of vision
into a coherent visual picture, though it seems that groups of
neurons fire in concert at a rate of forty times a second and it
may be that this co-operative phenomenon (parallel processing)
answers the 'binding problem' of how the various threads of
reconstruction of the visual image move forward in the brain.
But research has still only uncovered glimpses of a full understanding of the brain. It involves spectacular complexity, with
perhaps 100,000 neurons beneath each square millimetre of the
brain's surface. It probably combines the greatest range of
complex functions with the most densely and tightly packed
structure existing anywhere in the universe.

The evolution of intelligence
This raises the obvious question as to how an organ of such
staggering complexity as the human brain could have developed
from an initial primitive form. Evolution requires that every
single change in this development over millions of years must
have conferred an advantage on the individual who first
possessed it. This may not have been directly planned at each
stage as a heuristic process, but gradual changes from given
mutations may have offered an evolutionary advantage for other
reasons which then coincidentally opened up other opportunities leading ultimately to an enhanced brain and greater intelligence. Several instances of this have been postulated in other
species. Cooling fins for example might have been developed in
cold-blooded creatures like insects in order to mediate heat more
efficiently, the larger the fin the greater the survival advantage,
but at a certain size the fins could have been large enough to
enable the insect to glide. Once that threshold is crossed, a new
ecological niche opens up and the development of full wings

happens naturally. But it cannot be said to have been the original purpose. The process is not even necessarily logical, but may be surprisingly anomalous. In the design of the human eye, for example, the ganglion cells that initially process the visual signal are actually located in front of the cells that receive the incoming light, thus casting shadows on the light receptors (*59A). What this indicates is not only that the evolutionary process has no requirement to be moral, it doesn't even have to be perfectly efficient either. All that is necessary is that it generates organisms that are efficient enough to bring about survival.

This process in which a particular organ is useful first for one purpose and is then found to be useful for some entirely different purpose is common in the history of evolution, and may best be described as 'tangential evolution'. A good example is the panda's thumb, first gradually discarded as superfluous, but then developed again as environmental imperatives changed[60]. How this process may have developed in the case of the human cerebral cortex is inevitably speculative since a fossil skull cannot indicate how the neurons in that brain may have been connected or whether particular groups of connected neurons may have existed performing specialised functions deep within the brain. One reasonable hypothesis is that the move to upright posture may have played an important role in the evolution of the human brain inasmuch as freeing the hands opens up adaptations like grasping, throwing and tool-making which would be favoured by natural selection. And walking upright may well have been prompted by tectonic processes some thirty million years ago which not only pulled the continents apart (e.g. the Red Sea and the Great Rift Valley in East Africa), but changed the ecology from rain forest to open plains and savanna, giving survival value to those great apes that could move quickly from one forest sanctuary to another.

The neuro-physiologist William Calvin has taken the theory of tangential evolution still further[61]. He hypothesizes that there is a region of the brain, perhaps in the left hemisphere near the language centres, which deals with planning and analysing sequences, like those involved in arranging words into sentences. Once hands were freed for throwing, survival advantage would lie with those great apes which could throw stones or weapons accurately to obtain food. Now it has been found that if a very rapid movement of the arm and hand takes less than a fifth of a second to complete, the brain doesn't have time to correct the motion while it's proceeding; a pre-programmed set of movements needs to be in place for instant action. Natural selection would thus facilitate the rapid development of this skill. But once this planning ability had been honed for this purpose, this same skill, Calvin suggests, could have been co-opted laterally for the entirely different purpose of helping human to develop language, since both involve the application of similar higher mental functions. Such a theory is certainly tentative, but it does have the incidental merit of perhaps explaining also the development of human musical ability, which otherwise is not readily warranted on purely natural selection grounds.

The conundrum of consciousness

The next question is: whatever is the way that human intelligence has evolved, has it developed a capability which might be called 'consciousness' which is unique to humans, indeed at the very heart of human uniqueness? That of course immediately raises further questions about the meaning and exact physical and metaphysical nature of consciousness itself. What is special about human consciousness that is different from the operations of a computer, however advanced? What precisely is the connection between the purely physical-chemical firing of neurons in the brain and the non-physical mental experience of perceiving a colour? Whatever set of criteria is deemed to describe human consciousness, can it be applied equally to a chimpanzee or to, say, a frog, and if not, where is the dividing line? Or to put it in another way, how does a system like the human mind and body produce the perception of self in a way that may not be true, if that is the case, of other animals? It is fair to say that this is one of the most discussed and least agreed, areas of dispute about the whole human condition.

Some have thought it useful to elucidate the problem by depicting the human brain as some kind of computer. But this is to ignore very distinctive differences, both in quality and quantity, between their respective methods of operation. A computer performs at colossal speed in completing numerical calculations and keeping track of data while the brain operates in a massively parallel way, putting together different parts of the picture simultaneously, though each operation is relatively slow. Whilst it takes a neuron a few milliseconds to fire and for the nerve signal to travel along its axon and then for the system to clear ready to fire again, a transistor in a PC can turn on and off in a billionth of a second, that is it operates a million times faster than neurons, and the latest models can operate a thousand times faster even than that. Consequently computers and brains work best at different problems – computers can memorise huge lists of random numbers or inconsequential pieces of data which human beings never could, while brains can understand grammatical speech and the use of idioms which computers can't. In other words, computers and brains are not so much rivals at the same tasks as complementary in proficiency at different tasks.

There are other important differences too. The human cerebral cortex developed over a long evolutionary process that was not designed to produce higher level cognition, so that the wiring of the brain (so far only partially understood) is likely to have many functional differences from the electronic logic of a machine specially designed for the purpose. Computers work through the movement of an electrical charge in a semiconductor; the brain operates on the basis of chemical reactions. A neurotransmitter in the brain can either stimulate or inhibit according to the type of receptor to which it attaches; there is no analogue for this in a computer. Above all, whilst a computer has discrete electrical functions, the brain operates wholly inter-dependently in the most complex manner with the central nervous system, the hypothalamus, pituitary gland, and hormone levels at every stage. This biochemical truth shatters any idea that the mind is somehow located in the skull separately directing the body; rather, mind and body are intimately and fundamentally connected at every point. However, the fact that the human brain is not analysable as a digital computer does not mean that it cannot be theoretically understood by some other model, merely that the science to achieve that has not yet been developed. Roger Penrose postulates that this new science may lie at the nexus of quantum mechanics and unified field theories[62].

Other approaches however have been adopted towards the consciousness dilemma. One is to deny there is a problem at all – once the activities of the neuron s are understood, all else is illusion, and there is nothing special about human consciousness[63]. But such reductionism simply sidesteps the holistic nature of the conscious 'I' that observes and seeks to make sense of the reality out there. Another approach is the opposite – acknowledging that consciousness exists, but arguing that it is so fundamental that it should be seen as one of the basic properties of the universe and therefore unable to be defined further[64]. However, the history of the physical sciences repeatedly shows that what may be seen as elemental at one time and at one level of explanation becomes explicable at another time and derivable at another level of explanation. Yet another approach is the scientific materialists' view that the sense of personal identity and free will are nothing more than the behaviour of a vast assembly of nerve cells and their associated molecules[65]. This is not necessarily a re-statement of the argument from denial (above) or simply a re-formulation of the concept of the brain as a computer and the mind as an algorithm or systematic procedure. It is essentially an argument that theoretically at least a machine could be built with billions or even trillions of neuron connections, far in excess of the human brain, which could not be denied to be intelligent or even conscious, and therefore there is nothing unique about human consciousness. Is this view tenable?

Complexity and emergent properties

Given that the brain is indeed in one sense a physical system, does the thoroughgoing materialist approach adequately explain human experience whilst excluding consciousness? There are good reasons for doubting this, based largely on the nature of highly complex systems. Thus it was previously believed in the history of science that if we knew the position and velocity of every particle in the universe, we could then via Newton's Laws predict the entire future, thereby incidentally eliminating human free will. We now know that that is not possible because inter alia the advent of quantum mechanics, in particular the establishment of the Heisenberg Uncertainty Principle, showed that it was impossible to obtain both these pieces of information (position and velocity) at the same time. On this basis it is likely that the new science of complexity may well contain features that prevent us in practice understanding a system as complex as the brain.

There are other similar arguments too. Beyond a certain threshold of complexity, it may be that, whatever our theoretical understanding, the laws governing this feature of reality mean that it is impossible to construct a working material model that reproduces the brain. The precedent here is that the special theory of relativity showed that under extreme conditions (e.g. a super-cyclotron attempting to break down particles into the ultimate constituents of matter by accelerating them near to the speed of light and then smashing them together), the fundamental terms of the equation change (i.e. in this case the particles become heavier), making it impossible or at least extremely difficult to achieve the objective. On this basis it may be that the new science of complexity might involve laws that preclude any material reconstruction of the brain, indicating that there are features of the brain that go beyond material explanation. And yet another argument might be that when a sufficiently complex system is put together, at a very high level of complexity indeed, a Gödel-type theorem might apply in that its properties cannot in practice be predicted because the connection between the individual parts and the final behaviour is just too complicated to detect[66].

But the reason the purely materialist explanation of the brain is inadequate is that it neglects the development of emergent properties in such a hugely complex system. At certain thresholds as the level of complexity increases, the system becomes capable of performing new functions, and these new emergent phenomena gradually change the very nature of the system itself. Indeed, given the complexity of a single neuron and the degree of connectedness of the brain, it is reasonable to assume that a cascade of different emergent properties could appear at successive stages in the growth of complexity. The logic of this is that as a system gathers complexity, it proceeds through a series of discontinuous jumps, with each avalanche characteristic of a new higher level of complexity corresponding to a new type of emergent property. At a macro level, the Cambrian explosion around 540 million years ago might be regarded as an example of this process over millennia. But at a micro level, the phenomena described as consciousness, intelligence, artistic and cultural awareness, and spirituality can be seen as emergent properties at the higher levels of the cascade. Arguably, when there appears to be a large gap between the mental capacities of one species and another, particularly in the case of a near relative, the difference is probably to be explained by an emergent phenomenon in the former.

The implications of the concept of new emergent properties are crucial in explaining many aspects of human evolutionary history. When the addition of neurons reaches a certain mass, perhaps 500 million, certain capabilities such as learning, memory, and quite detailed and comprehensive analysis of visual fields can be achieved, as shown by the octopus which has these abilities and has a brain composed of about 500 million neurons. The same principle probably explains the development of hominids, some 2 million years ago, into something recognisably human. It equally explains how human beings, who have the largest (relative to size) and most complex cerebral cortex amongst all animal species, are qualitatively different from other animals in their mental functioning, even though almost identical at the chemical level.

Having said that, the precise nature of consciousness remains unclear, even mysterious. The neurobiologist Antonio Damasio believes consciousness develops from a constantly updated picture of the state of the body conveyed both electrically and chemically, interacting with memory and other higher cognitive functions[67]. Gerald Edelman, focusing on the development of the brain and the formation of synapses, proposes that consciousness arises from a complex reciprocal flow of information between groups of neurons, or 'maps', and that groups of neurons not selected for this purpose as the development of the brain matures die off or are eliminated, typical of a broader evolutionary process. Francis Crick identifies the origin of consciousness in the high-frequency oscillations of signals which occur in the brain, with interactions between specific neurons developing an ongoing complexity[68]. Whichever, if any, of these is correct, or whatever any combination may contribute in part to a final theory, it is clearly possible and indeed likely that a full and complete understanding of consciousness will embody the principle of emergent properties.

Whatever the ultimate explanation of the nature of human

intelligence, self-awareness and consciousness, the question obviously arises as to whether, even if human beings can at present be seen as in some sense unique, that uniqueness is merely a transitory stage between the animal kingdom and the development of a new higher intelligence, maybe silicon-based and machine-engineered. Will such super-machines, whether or not they can be described as 'life forms', supersede the human race just as mammals replaced the dinosaurs sixty-five million years ago? It is true that the latter process only happened because of catastrophic external intervention (global glaciation or an asteroid strike, or both in succession), but that does not rule out a gradual but decisive change – an emergent phenomenon again – in less violent circumstances. However, the real lesson of the nature of change over geological time is that it is non-linear and unpredictable, but rather divergent, tangential, and qualitatively novel.

This has been repeatedly demonstrated in the unfolding of Western thought throughout the last 300 years, even though that is such a minutely short period of time in evolutionary terms. Newton (1642-1727) postulated through his inverse square law a universe of perfect order and regularity, leading to a view of the universe as a kind of clock which God wound up at Creation and which is now ticking along on its own according to the predicted laws of motion. Newtonian mechanics appeared to banish chance from the universe, until Heisenberg found that the laws of quantum mechanics re-opened the whole question of unpredictability. Equally then it must be an open question whether the conflict between the materialist concept of the brain on the one hand and the principle of human uniqueness on the other will play out in a similar way. Given that the complexity of even the most advanced microchips is still negligible compared with the almost incomprehensible interconnectedness of the 100,000,000,000 neurons in the human brain, there can be no guarantee that the straightforward exponential development of artificial (or any other) intelligence will somehow equal or surpass the capabilities of the brain. Just as the theory of relativity showed that Newtonian mechanics couldn't be applied to bodies moving at speeds comparable to the speed of light, in the same way there may be a certain level of richness in the logical system of the brain which defies reproduction beyond a certain point. Maybe therefore the human brain can indeed be seen as a material system governed by the same laws as other physical entities, but one whose complexity is of such an order as to be non-reproducible and unique.

Implications

Any uniqueness of human beings is clearly not focussed on DNA when human DNA overlaps almost entirely with that of chimpanzees, humankinds' nearest relative, and to a very large degree even with reptiles and plants. Equally clearly it is focussed rather on the human brain, the staggering complexity of which opens up potential capabilities in the fields of intelligence, consciousness, morality, aesthetics, and spirituality which are precluded from other lesser endowed animals. What is most significant however is that the human cortex was not designed ab initio for its current purpose, as is evidenced by its faulty or less than perfect construction in certain respects and also by its much smaller size and potential at earlier stages of evolution. There are different explanations, not necessarily mutually exclusive, of how and why it developed as it did – whether genetically through mutations in control genes which retarded development in humans (neoteny) and thus favoured a much longer learning period before maturity, or environmentally because of survival imperatives as the landscape changed radically from rainforest to open plains, or tangentially as natural selection favoured one dimension of evolutionary development for one purpose which at a certain threshold then opened up further, altogether different dimensions for competitive advantage. Whatever part these contingent factors played in the interaction of causes directing human, and in particular cranial, development, they were only the latest in a long line of previous contingent formative forces evolving the hominid line. And however remarkable the complexity of the human brain as the highest point of this development so far, there can be no anthropocentric suggestion that this point represents in any sense a culmination or pinnacle.

Another important facet that has arisen from much recent biochemical evidence is that there is such close and complex inter-operability between the brain and each of the main controlling systems of the body that it cannot be conceptualised as Cartesian dualism. Nor however can the brain be viewed as purely a materialistic phenomenon, but rather that at a certain threshold of complexity – perhaps an intimately inter-connected network of around 500 million neurons – it develops novel emergent properties and maybe a growing series of novel faculties over time as complexity continues to extend further. However, cranial size is not by itself necessarily the overriding determinant of evolutionary success. The Neanderthals, a sub-species of homo sapiens, had a larger brain, but died out some 40,000 years ago. Elephants also have a larger brain than humans, though a much smaller one relative to body size, so that brain-body ratio in terms of manoeuvrability and rapidity of response is clearly also crucial. Nevertheless the rapid growth in the size of the human cortex over the last two million years has unquestionably played the major role in the achievement of human dominance, even if there are still widely different analyses of precisely what are the key factors in the operation of the brain as a system of almost mind-numbing complexity.

Chapter 9

The Evolution of Spirituality

The origins of religion

The stirrings of a religious sense, in at least its crudest form of a perception of forces over and beyond the natural world with which (or with whom) human beings sought some kind of relationship, are traceable almost to the earliest records of human settlements in all the main continents. These records date back to the fourth millennium BC (i.e. some 5,500 years ago), and it is likely – though only conjecture – that similar perceptions existed in the millennia following the end of the last Ice Age before recorded evidence was written down, i.e. for perhaps the last 10,000 years or so. In that last Ice Age which prevailed for almost 100,000 years, the developing homo sapiens species (Cro-Magnon man among other Ice Age peoples) clearly, on the basis of surviving cave paintings from 40,000 years ago, developed complex societies and a significant degree of culture, and judging by the evidence from burials, they had religious feelings and ideas. Thus it is arguable that at least a sense of the numinous, which might be described as an experience of a dynamic external presence, may well accompany the development of human civilisation even from its earliest stages.

After the last Ice Age (that is, the last so far in a cycle of well over a dozen full Ice Ages during the Plesistocene Era of the last two million years) ended some 11,000 years ago, the origins of human civilisation can be traced to the 'Neolithic Revolution', the beginning of permanent settlements, and the domestication of animals and crops (wheat and barley) around 9-8,000BCE. The first walled town in the world, Jericho, covering 10 acres, was founded between 8,000-7,500BCE. Rice cultivation appears in

Thailand about 6,000BCE. The first evidence of farming in Europe dates from about 6,500BCE in Greece and the Aegean, and it then spreads up the Danube to Hungary about 5,500BCE, to Germany and the Low Countries about 4,500BCE, along the Mediterranean coast to France about 5,000BCE, and about 4,000BCE to Britain (which had become an island as a result of two mega-floods, first around 435,000 years ago and a second some 200,000 years ago, to form the Channel). Around 6,250-5400BCE Çatal Hüyük, the largest city of its day, flourished in Anatolia with the first know pottery and woollen textiles, and about 5,000BCE the Mesopotamian alluvial plains were colonised by groups practising irrigation. Agricultural settlements appeared in Egypt about 5,000BCE, and bronze casting begins in the Near East about 4,000BCE, with the first use of the plough and wheel in Mesopotamia and of the sail in Egypt about 3,500BCE.

In the fourth millennium BCE the first signs of a more systematic civilisation are apparent. The earliest Chinese city is founded at Liang-ch'eng chen about 3,500BCE, and the Lung-shan culture is established. Early Cycladic civilisation established itself in the Aegean 3,200-2,000BCE, King Menes unites Egypt about 3,100BCE and the dynastic period begins, major cities develop in Sumer about 3,000BCE, and the megalithic stones and circles in Brittany and the Iberian peninsula date from about 3,500BC and in the British Isles (Stonehenge) about 1,700BCE. Significantly, pictographic writing is invented in Sumer about 3,100BCE, and at about the same time the use of bronze develops in Thailand, copper-working (after early experiments with copper ore in Anatolia about 7,000BCE) spreads to Europe, arable farming techniques spread to central Africa, and the first potter appears in the Americas (Ecuador and Colombia). Then about 2,750BCE the growth of civilisations is seen in the Indus Valley, the 'Old Kingdom' pyramid age extends in Egypt 2,685-2,180BCE, and Sargon I of Agade founds the first empire in world history 2,370-2,230BCE. Further empires begin to be established with the invasion and settlement of the Peloponnese about 2,000BCE by Indo-European speakers (early Greeks) and the beginnings of the Minoan civilisation in Crete which lasted 2,000-1,450BCE, and similarly in Asia Minor with the Hittite invasion of Anatolia (2,000-1,650BCE), the establishment of the Assyrian state by Shamsi-Adad about 1,850BCE, and the founding of the Babylonian empire by Hammurabi (1728-1686BCE) and the promulgation by him of the first known code of laws. In Asia, the Aryan invasion about 1,550BCE destroys the Indus Valley civilisation and leads to the Aryan settlement in North India. At the same time the first urban civilisation in China dates from about 1,600BCE, with the development of the Shang Bronze Age culture.

In the mid second millennium BCE the development of writing opened the way to the recording of literature and the beginning of religious texts. By 1,500BCE ideographic script was in use in China, 'linear B' script in Crete and Greece during the Mycenaean civilisation 1,600-1,200BCE, and Hittite cuneiform in Anatolia. In India there is evidence of Brahma worship about 1,450BCE, and the composition of the Vedas (the earliest Indian literature) begins. In Egypt the Pharaoh Akhenaten enforces monotheistic Sun worship about 1,370BCE. About 1,200BCE, following the Israelite exodus from Egypt and the settlement of Palestine, the Jewish religion centring on the worship of Yahweh begins to be established. About 1,100BCE the Phoenicians develop the alphabetic script, the basis of all modern European scripts, and their spread throughout the Mediterranean regions till about 700BCE, including their colony at Carthage founded about 814BCE begins to extend this facility. The Upanishads, the Sanskrit religious treatises, are composed 800-400BCE. Amos, the first great prophet in Israel, calls on his people to turn again to Yahweh about 750BCE, at about the same time as Homer's Iliad (the story of the gods in the Graeco-Trojan war) and Hesiod's poetry were first written down.

This outline history of some of the turning points in the early part of the present inter-glacial period provides the context in which to assess the emergence of religious thought and practice from the earliest recorded times. It is clear that religious ideas are woven into the evolution of societies even from that earliest period. The first evidence of what humans thought and believed comes from the stories and fragments from Sumeria and Egypt following the invention of writing in the former about 3,250BCE. After the three main developments of agriculture – not only in the Fertile Crescent between Egypt and Mesopotamia, but also in the Indus Valley in India and the Yellow River Valley in China – the first writings present contrasting images of wilderness and the natural order, of conflict and sustenance, and of sacrifice and care.

One of the earliest fragments is the Enuma Elish[69] from the early Babylonian civilisation. It reveals a picture where early agricultural settlements had given way to stone cities with strong defences and power hierarchies, including also the building of temples to the gods. In a story which predates Genesis by 2,500 years, it unfolds a story where everything has originated from primal chaos signified by water, an element without diversity or form, which gives life, but which threatens storms and floods. From the formless abyss of primal being derive the pairs that symbolise all creation, and from these pairs arise two great gods. The sky-god maintains all things under the rule of cosmic law, ensuring the regular succession of the seasons, while the god of wisdom is the god of creativity and originality, bringing about new and surprising events. A similar creation story comes from ancient Egypt where the gods are portrayed as arising in pairs from primeval chaos. Despite the much greater concern of the Egyptians with death and the after-life, there are still the same themes of involvement in cosmic conflict, in divine sacrifice and thus the generation of new life. There is a sense of a wider spiritual reality which can sustain the empires of the earth and control the forces of chaos and wilderness, and can be harnessed to the service of kings by priests, poets, prophets, and deliverers of oracles. However, there is still no general agreement on the nature and development of archaic religion, and the mass of ancient myths that have survived in many cultures have been subject to a wide range of interpretations[70], notably from a Jungian viewpoint of the collective unconscious.

The Axial Age of transformation

Between 800-200BCE a profound saltation occurred in the evolution of religious thought which Karl Jaspers has described as the Axial Age[71]. This spiritual revolution occurred against a background of turmoil, displacement and war. In China it started after the collapse of the Zhou dynasty and ended when Qin brought back unity to the warring states. In India it followed the break-up of the Harappan civilisation and ended when the Mauryan empire was created. In Greece it followed, though some time after, the collapse of the Mycenaean kingdom and ended with the rise of the Macedonian domination. In the Middle East it was prompted by the destruction of the Jewish lands through conquest and the deportation of their tribes, and despite resettlement through counter-conquest its flowerings persisted into the first century CE.

In four quite separate regions the great religions of the world that have gripped the human consciousness ever since came into being – Confucianism and Daoism in China, Hinduism and Buddhism in India, monotheism in Israel, and philosophic rationalism in Greece. During these six centuries of intense creativity, spiritual and philosophical geniuses with their unique insights – Buddha, Confucius, Jeremiah, Socrates, the Upanishad mystics, Mencius (or Meng Ke), Euripides, among many others – developed a wholly new form of human experience. The Axial Age was perhaps the most creative period of intellectual, philosophical, religious, and psychological advance in recorded human history, unequalled until the Reformation, Enlightenment, and Western transformation of the last 400 years. Indeed the insights of the Axial Age have never been surpassed inasmuch as all the great religions of Rabbinic Judaism, Christianity and Islam can be regarded as later flowerings of the prime Axial vision, though translated into an idiom that spoke directly to the different cultures and problems of their own times[72]. In fact the insights were so radical that later followers toned down the freshness of the vision with a cloying religiosity which often obscured the profoundness of the original truths – a tendency to dilution which is still marked today.

Key to the Axial viewpoint was not a set of beliefs or propositions of a creed, but living a moral and compassionate life. Theology was not discussed; it was even rejected as inappropriate or unrealistic to seek for the certainty about ultimates which some improperly expected from religion. Rather, all the Axial traditions, in advancing the fields of human consciousness, opened up a transcendent dimension within their own being, but they did not view this as supernatural. Sages like the Buddha would not discuss it precisely because the experience was ineffable and unable to be contained within any metaphysical analysis. Indeed, so far from trying to impress on others their understanding of the ultimate reality, they insisted that nobody should accept religious teaching on faith, but rather they should test everything against their own experience. Religion was about behaviour that fundamentally changed your life at a profound level. For these reasons the Axial prophets played down the rituals and animal sacrifice which had previously been central to religious activity. Religion was not about being a spectator or participant in some kind of external sacred drama of worship or appeasement of supernatural forces. It was about putting morality at the heart of personal life, about disciplining behaviour to a habit of benevolence and concern for others; not starting from a conviction of the Absolute before embarking on the spiritual life, but committing to an ethical lifestyle which might, unsought, yield intimations of the transcendent.

The aim of the Axial prophets was not to provide a bit of spiritual uplift, but to create a fundamentally different kind of human society. They enunciated a spirituality of compassion and responsiveness to others' needs, and a repudiation of selfishness, greed and violence. Going further still, they insisted not only that murder and aggression were wrong and unacceptable, but so were even unkind behaviour and hostile language. Indeed the golden rule of Judaeo-Christianity and Islam – do not to others what you would not have them do to you – was already embedded in the Axial philosophy centuries beforehand. For the protagonists of Axial enlightenment, religion was not a matter of submitting to orthodox belief, but of living a life respecting the sacred rights of all beings. They broke too with tribal or local boundaries by declaring that kindness and benevolence towards one's own people were not enough; these qualities had to be applied to all, friend and enemy alike, irrespective of nation or race. This was all the more remarkable when such claims were made, not in a world of peace and quiet piety, but amid societies torn apart by violence, warfare and instability. And when they sought the sources of such conflict within the human psyche, they began to open up a previously unexplored dimension of human experience.

The development of the Axial ideals did not occur uniformly either in the same manner or in the same period of history. In Israel it proceeded disjointedly until the exile in Babylon (586-538BCE) produced a spurt of intense spiritual creativity. In China, by contrast, development was slow and incremental. Lao-tse (c.570-500BCE), despite a political nihilism coupled with a wholly negative attitude to contemporary worship, held that true religion was to obey the law of nature and preached the ineffable joy of the sense of being in communion with the Absolute

(Taoism). But it was left to K'ung Fu-tsu (Confucius, 551-478BCE) to inaugurate the first full Axial philosophy – a formal humanitarianism expressing itself in a love of mankind rooted in filial piety, since only through the proper regulation of family life can national life be appropriately organised. Mozi (480-390BCE) however, succeeding him in the turmoil of fifth century China, argued that Confucius had distorted the compassionate ethic by limiting it to the family and wanted to replace the egotism of kinship with a more generalised altruism – "others must be regarded like the self". Similarly, Zoroaster (or Zarathustra), living in an earlier age (perhaps around 800BCE), founded the religion of ancient Persia and of the Parsees on the basis of the much older polytheistic Aryan folk-religion, but profoundly modified it, purging it of its licentiousness and cruelty, and instead inculcating hospitality, philanthropy and benevolence. On a different plane Siddhartha Gautama (the Buddha, c.565-483BCE), in northern India, through his unremitting gentleness, serenity and fairness, exemplified what a human being could or should be. Like all the great sages of the Axial age, he claimed that by reaching beyond themselves to a reality that transcends their rational understanding, by practising total self-abandonment, by curbing the voracious and frightened ego that wreaks such damage, men and women can become fully human. Parallel to this essentially psychological religion but coming from a more rationalistic provenance, the fifth century Greek philosophers developed the art of argumentation as a way of liberation to a better understanding of the self. Socrates (470-399BCE), a paradigmatic model of the Axial age and martyr to nonconformity, relentlessly chastised the rulers of Athens for their lamentable ignorance of the only kind of knowledge of supreme importance, the knowledge of how to make one's own souls and those of others as good as possible.

The essential saltation of the Axial Age lay in the transformation away from perceiving religion as a means of relating to supernatural powers in order to achieve human goals and escape human disaster to regarding religion as pursuing the good life by participation in one supreme objective value. There was indeed a transcendental breakthrough within this Age, but like the ancient religion of Israel, it was often deeply agonistic, often preceded by massacres and followed by hostilities. Even Isaiah's insistence (around 740BCE) on humility and surrender might seem to fit within the Axial spirituality of kenosis ('emptying' or self-surrender), but it also inflated the defiant patriotism of Judah against its gathering enemies. Significantly, the religious traditions in all four regions were rooted in fear and pain. They did not seek to suppress that, but rather to insist that this suffering should be fully acknowledged as an essential prerequisite for enlightenment. This was most dramatically portrayed in the Greek myths, from the Homeric epics to the trilogy of the fifth century BCE tragedians – Aeschylus, Sophocles, and Euripides – where a consequential succession of terrible and unnatural deeds had to be ended by purification (katharsis) as the only way to appease the gods and disperse the contagious power of evil (miasma).

The rise of world's great religions

Arising out of these Axial transformations of understanding, the theistic model of religion was developed in the Near East from the 8th century BCE onwards by a nomadic tribal people, the Jews, who believed that God had called them to found a homeland in territory beside the eastern Mediterranean. It began with partial and ambiguous insights into a God that had delivered them from slavery in Egypt and then passed down to them a fundamental law of justice and mercy, but it steadily evolved into a faith in the general providential ordering and moral purpose of history. Hebrew Scripture is an account of the gradual awakening, led by the Prophets, that Yahweh was not a tribal/nationalistic deity warring and vengeful on behalf of the children of Israel as displayed in the Pentateuch, but a unique God loving and caring for all the human race, the creator of the whole universe, calling on all human peoples to fulfil his divine purpose.

Ethical monotheism can therefore be said to have originated with the ancient Hebrews and with their belief that God had chosen them – the children of Abraham, Isaac and Jacob – to enter into a special relationship or covenant with him. It was a conviction resolutely maintained throughout Jewish history in defiance of wholesale disasters (and likely a main cause of them) – from the Assyrian destruction of Israel in 722BCE, the Babylonian deporting of the Jewish population in 586BCE, the 2nd century BC Maccabaean revolts, the Roman destruction of the temple in Jerusalem in 70CE, and the Jewish Diaspora at the hands of the Romans in 132CE – until the foundation of Israel as a secular state in 1948 was seen as the final restoration of a homeland lost over two millennia before. Yet the stories underpinning this belief are probably not historical[73]. Israeli archaeological excavations after 1967 have found no traces of the mass destruction of Canaanite cities bloodily portrayed in the book of Joshua, no signs of foreign invasion or Egyptian artefacts, and no indications of tribal replacements. The general scholarly view is that the settlers who created the new colonies in the southern highlands (of what is now Palestine) in the 13th century BCE were probably migrants from the failing city-states of the coastal seaboard, not foreigners but Canaanites, not liberated from Egypt but freed of Egyptian rule in their own land. What the early parts of the Bible, written in the 7th or 6th centuries BCE were portraying was not history, but epic stories that offered a distinct identity and a meaning to existence. The covenant agreement that bound together the different ethnic groups into the new entity of 'Israel' was born of upheaval and constantly living under threat, but held together by their unique relationship with their god, Yahweh.

Rabbinic Judaism, centred round the Torah revealed by Moses and the Noahide Covenant, makes claims to universal truth – that there is one God, one judgement and one basic moral law – but continues to exist as a highly specific socio-cultural model which resists incorporation into any universal global faith. However, Jewishness is generally an attribute of birth, custom, sensibility and practice rather than encapsulated by a certain set of beliefs, even though the mediaeval Jewish philosopher Maimonides established thirteen principles which have been widely accepted in the Jewish prayer book since the 16th century CE, but without authoritative status.

Christianity developed the theistic model in a rather different way, beginning as a Jewish messianic movement, but corrupted by absorption in 312CE by the emperor Constantine as the official religion of the militaristic Roman Empire. The Christian Church which began as a persecuted pacifist millennial Jewish sect was transformed into an authoritarian imperial cult, manipulated to impose an orthodox uniformity and to suppress dissent. Yet Christianity never lost its primary focus as an inward and spiritual faith based around the life, crucifixion and resurrection of Jesus Christ (who was born, according to conflicting evidence, between 6BCE and 4CE and was executed between 29-37CE). The Jews amongst whom he was born were looking for a Messiah as a figure of deliverance, but rejected him and had him executed partly because he scandalised the dominant priestly caste and partly because of the risk to the Jewish nation from the Roman power in the event of an uprising. For his followers however, Jesus represented the fulfilment of the Jewish Prophets, the one who would bring forgiveness of sins and reconciliation between enemies, but in a radical Christian reinterpretation of the concept of Messiah (the 'chosen one' of God) he does so through suffering and dying on the cross, thus demonstrating the unlimited love of God and not only for the chosen people, but for all.

The question of the divine-human status of Jesus has been a

matter of contention from the time of the early Christian Church onwards. The Council of Chalcedon in 451CE decided that Jesus was fully human, but his humanity was so united to the divinity of the eternal wisdom (or Logos, the 'Word') of God that he is the Son of God in full human form. After his death, the Gospels relate that Jesus was raised to the presence of God, thus permanently uniting humanity to the divine nature. To Christians, by taking on a proper human nature without ceasing to be God and without at the same time overwhelming that human nature, Jesus made the fullest possible revelation of the nature of God[74].

The subsequent history of Christianity has been marred by its hijacking by successive imperial powers. The eastern half of the Roman Empire, centred on Byzantium, rent by interminable quarrels about seemingly unintelligible theological quibbles as well as weakened by war with Persia, collapsed under the Islamic onslaught at Yarmuk in 636CE. The western half equally collapsed under repeated waves of attacks by Visigoths and other barbarian hordes in the 5th and 6th centuries CE. Europe, plunged into the Dark Ages, and did not emerge again as a Christian civilisation for another 1,000 years, only when the European powers conquered the Americas, Africa and Australasia did Christianity attain the dominant global role it holds today, with some 1.97 billion adherents worldwide, compared with 1.18 billion Muslims, 0.78 billion Hindus and 0.36 billion Buddhists. But the price paid by transforming into the spiritual arm of European world-dominating colonial powers is that Christianity can lose the integral individual simplicity of its fundamental message of forgiveness through the endless self-giving love of God.

Islam by contrast has presented a theistic model which avoids the Christian doctrinal contortions over the incarnation, Trinity and atonement – that a man was God and that God is both three and one at the same time. The prophet Muhammad (570-632CE) never claimed to be more than a man, but said that the Qur'an was dictated to him by the angel Gabriel. It offers a simple but powerful message of the transcendent simplicity of God, the reality of divine judgement and the hope of Paradise. Divine forgiveness is dependent on penitence, not on any sacrifice, still less on the suffering or death of an innocent man identified as God. Islam is an individual faith – no church teaches authoritative scriptures, no priests intermediate between God and humans, no philosophers dispute the inner nature of deity. Its rapid expansion in the century after Muhammad, which overran North Africa, Spain and threatened Europe till repelled at Poitiers in 732CE, was seen as a liberating mission against oppression by other empires, and it established a great civilisation and culture in the 8th-10th centuries CE while Christian Europe was benighted in the Dark Ages. It founded universities and hospitals, was largely tolerant towards Christians and Jews, and achieved an academic Enlightenment half a millennium before Europe.

Yet Islam, like Christianity, has at times in its history been appropriated by an intolerant and violent imperialism. The caliphate after Muhammad was beset by assassinations, feuds and treachery. The goal of spreading God's law by force and imposing the law in all its crude purity on infidels, dissidents and unbelievers has often disfigured the faith as both Christians and Muslims regard each other as infidels and betrayers of God. After the collapse of the Ottoman Empire (1453-1918CE) and the end of European colonial rule in the Muslim countries, the call to jihad (translated by some Muslims as 'holy war') has echoed forcefully across the Islamic world, summoning fighters to kill in the name of God. This is no more a reflection of the Qur'an than the Crusades were of the Bible. It reveals rather, as so often in Christian history, the utilisation of a distinctive faith to pursue political ends – in this case anger and frustration at domination and manipulation by the Western powers. In the same way as Christian 'just war', jihad is aimed at defence against unjust attack and protection of the innocent, whether in Palestine, Bosnia, Chechnya, or Iraq. It is both Christians and Muslims who need greater awareness of the frightening human capacity to extend what they proclaim as justified violence beyond the limits set by divine law, and then justify it by appeal to God. All three Semitic religions – Judaism, Christianity and Islam – can co-exist, but only if they forego compulsion over matters of faith and learn to respect and empathise with the spiritual traditions of others.

By contrast with the West, the dominant model in the Indian and Chinese spiritual traditions has been the liberated consciousness. No prophets proclaimed the law of God, the need for repentance or the hope of Paradise. A personal God was seen as unduly anthropomorphic and hard to reconcile with a world of suffering. Rather the material world was seen as existing for ever, in which human beings were trapped by attachment and desire in a cycle of suffering and rebirth. The goal of both the Jains and Sankhya Yoga was therefore to gain freedom from this cloying attachment and live as a pure spiritual being (nirvana). Freeing oneself of greed, hatred and ignorance and uniting with the supreme state of wisdom, compassion and bliss was the highest value, attained above all by Siddhartha Gautama. Buddhism, which he founded in northern India, was absorbed there by the spread of Hinduism, but developed strongly in Sri Lanka, Japan, Korea and South-East Asia, was dominant in Tibet and Thailand, and in 379AD became the State religion of China. It has however in modern times been particularly vulnerable to attacks by a virulently anti-religious communism, though it continues to retain extensive influence even in the face of persecution through monasteries of monks, not least in Burma, who teach meditation and tolerance without insisting on commitment to any specific set of beliefs.

Buddhism is a practical faith where practice takes priority over theory. It does embrace authoritative sacred texts, but these contain the teachings of the supremely Enlightened One, not the revelation of God through prophets. It contrasts with the Semitic traditions in that Buddhists do not have any marked sense of a personal relationship with God or a longing for future redemption or a global just order. But they do display an overriding compassion for the sufferings of all beings and a reverence for all life which is more all-embracing than in the Semitic religions. Essentially Buddhism teaches that methods of mental training can produce a life not only liberated from hatred and selfishness, but achieving awareness of a transcendent state of compassion, detachment and wisdom – even if, as some Buddhist traditions would have it, it may take a few million lifetimes.

What might be seen as an ideal unification of the theistic emphasis on personal devotion, love for others and striving for a just world order with a Buddhist sense of serenity, mindfulness and compassion has been attempted by many Hindu traditions. They interpret the many gods they worship as personal expressions of one ultimate reality, Brahman (the Self of All), which embraces all things and is described as consciousness, intelligence and bliss. The Upanishads, the sacred texts encapsulating this doctrine, have been revealed to inspired individuals (seers) by the gods, and these 'heard' scriptures are accepted as inerrant authority. The Supreme Self is not counter-posed to the cosmos, but the underlying reality of the universe itself which is not material at all, but spiritual. In the Shiva interpretation of Sankara, the goal of religion is to experience oneness with the Supreme, through becoming aware of the illusion of individual identity and of the material world. In the Vishnu (or Krishna) interpretation, persons are seen not as specific bodies, but as purely spiritual souls and tiny but distinct parts of the Supreme Self. The essence of Hinduism is that at the deepest level the human soul is one with the Divine Soul, that human life is a spiritual journey towards realising and achieving that truth which comes from freeing the self from egoistic longings and devoting the self instead to the Supreme Lord. This has not however prevented Hinduism deploying a caste system of extreme inequality, as well as countenancing self-immolation of widows, animal sacrifice and many frenzied rituals.

In China Confucius and Lao-Tzu founded movements based on harmony with nature and identifying the Way of Heaven in social and political life. Both pursued the same theme, that human conflict results from an imbalance in natural forces and the religious goal is to restore that balance and maintain it so that the Way of Heaven can be achieved on Earth. In accordance with the radical reinterpretation of the Buddhist way when Buddhism reached China, spiritual reality is not seen as separate from the world or as a personal being or even a hidden Supreme Self of the entire world, but as a matter of balance, harmony, calm and dispassionateness. When Buddhism reached Japan about 538CE, similar themes gained dominance, with the indigenous Shinto based on reverence for spirits of the natural world and for ancestors combining with Chinese forms of Buddhism. East Asian spirituality therefore is a monist tradition, not centred on a realm after death or on attainment by ascetic denial, but on understanding the true nature of the actual social and material world. For these very reasons it has been under sustained attack from modern ideologies which are driven not by conformity with the inner laws of nature, but by exploitation of the material environment and revolutionary change in human society.

In the 20th century Chinese religion came under catastrophic assault from Maoist communism on the grounds that it was hierarchical, backward-looking, and possessed of an obsolete value-system. Japanese religion was similarly undermined by the forces of Western capitalism which were wholly antagonistic to the quietist Buddhist values of anti-acquisitiveness, non-competitiveness, reverence for the natural world and indif-ference to material wealth. Korea suffered a double onslaught, from communism in the north and capitalism in the south. Whereas communism has now largely been subverted by the attractions of materialistic consumerism, the gross excesses of the latter in hugely widening global inequalities combined with the devastations of climate change, over-exploitation of global natural resources and over-rapid increase in populations with yet further pressure on resources may set off a powerful reaction. The challenge for East Asian spiritual traditions is whether they can harness this to an adaptive religion compatible with a more dynamic and egalitarian culture and a more democratic social organisation.

Enlightenment and the scientific counter-revolution

The first outpouring of the belief in the power of reason and of respect for the inherent dignity of humanity, as opposed to compliance with an organised Church, appeared in Europe in the 11th-13th centuries in the writings of Anselm (1033-1109) and Peter Abelard (1079-1147) and in the theological summation of Thomas Aquinas (1225-1274). Whereas in Islam the focus shifted from scientific investigation to submission to the divine law, in Christianity God's will was seen as justifiable by reason, so scientific inquiry to discover the underlying cause of things was merited. The Protestant Reformation then claimed the right for individuals to interpret the scriptures for themselves in the light of personal conscience, even against the express authority of the Catholic Church. This not only led sometimes to questioning the authority of the Bible itself, but it also set free rational thought from over-dependence on Aristotelian and Platonic doctrine and unleashed empirical investigation in preference to a priori speculation. The discoveries of Copernicus (1543) and Galileo (1633) challenged not so much the Church as such, but pure Aristotelian reason as supported by the Church. This critical rationalism of the new humanism (symbolised by Descartes' Discours, 1637), when combined with the development of the experimental method paved the way for the European Enlightenment and ultimately the rise of modern science. But the new evidence-based rationalism, when combined with the world-view of Newtonian science, also raised significant doubts about the historical Bible and the inerrant authority of the Church came to be widely disbelieved.

The empiricists' restriction of religious experience to evidence observed by the senses was however challenged by the Prussian theologian Schleiermacher (1768-1834). He held that non-sensory perceptions or intuitions (Anschauungen) can also provide knowledge of objective reality, though he recognised that such revelatory experiences were not always readily describable, even if vivid and life-changing. This approach saw the Bible as a record of personal experiences derived from the original inspirational experiences of Jesus, and it gave authority to public experiences (e.g. the resurrection of Jesus) as well as private experiences (e.g. the transformational power of a spiritual perception) without assuming the recollections were necessarily accurate in every detail. This fits well with Christianity where the Gospels were written 30-40 years after the death of Christ, but less so with Islam where it is claimed that the scriptures were dictated by God, though even there the suras of the Qur'an may be said to reflect the inspired Muhammad's overwhelming experience of God as commanding and merciful. A further extension of this approach was made in the 20th century by the German theological realist Rudolf Bultmann, professor of New Testament Studies at the University of Marburg (1921-51), in his programme of de-mythologizing the supernatural language to uncover the authentic historical message of Jesus.

Another response to critical rationalism, which took root in the 18th century and flowered in the 19th-20th centuries, was a wholesale rejection of religion and attempts to explain it away as a social or psychological illusion. Hume's Natural History of Religion, published in 1757, argues that "the primary religion of mankind arises chiefly from an anxious fear of future events"[75], and its cause is ignorance of the ultimate causes of things, while the belief in invisible, intelligent powers is "at least a general attendant of human nature", though these are fantasies of the stupidity, weakness and timidity of the great majority of mankind. Similarly, Frazer[76] from his comparative study of ancient religions concluded that they were based on fear and propitiation of angry gods. Durkheim[77] argued that religions are social and moral phenomena which provide rituals that subordinate the individual to the group by making the group's moral ideals the dominant code for its members. Weber by contrast saw religion, not as a conservative consolidation of the status quo, but as associated with social change through 'elective affinities' between some religious ideas and some social goals (e.g. the Protestant ethic and early capitalism, or currently radical Islam and martyrdom/terrorism). Marx however in his polemic against latter 19th century capitalism saw religion as functioning to justify an oppressive social order and compliance towards the established authorities. The 20th century saw yet another raison d'etre proposed. Freud, arguing a reductionist materialism in the psychology of religion, traced the origins of religious belief to infantile neuroses which create forces such as repression and compulsion. Jung, however, adopting a more positive attitude, saw religious symbols as contributing to personal integration and mental health, and postulated the collective unconscious as the origin of archetypes or primordial psychic forces found in many religious symbols. In summary, what is perhaps most striking about this list of explanations for religion, far from complete though it is, is its wide diversity of mutually incompatible ideas, despite a finality of truth having been claimed by each.

Secularisation and re-awakening

The evolution of spirituality has thus progressed from local myths and rituals, through the insights of the Axial sages to the canonical codification of the scriptural texts of the great religions, thence via the sceptical inquiry of critical faith in the Reformation and Enlightenment to the wholesale rejection of religion in some strands of sociology, psychology, evolutionary biology and State ideology, and then currently in the light of the increasing penetration of scientific understanding to a growing de-mystification of religion and an avowedly secular society. However, the present global religious landscape presents a complex picture. One dimension of this is that whilst in the US and Europe an artificially demand-driven all-encompassing consumerism has suffocated much of the religious influence, in many parts of the Southern world in East Asia, Africa and Latin America the reach of the churches has been growing. Within the West, while the traditional churches have been in decline, particularly the more liberal traditions since the 1960s exemplified by Bishop Robinson's Honest to God (1963), there has been a revival of the evangelical and eschatological sects, especially in the US and among minority black and Hispanic groups.

There have been several very different responses to growing secularisation. One has been the proselytising effort of a virulent atheism as symbolised by Dawkins' The God Delusion (2007). Another has been the emergence of what Epstein has called the concept of 'minimal religion'[78], a reaction to a militantly atheist regime where spirituality is lived out in one's own immediate circle with family and friends rather than in churches. Because this 'religion' has developed outside any confessional structures, it expresses a spontaneous and unreflective ecumenicism where the coexistence of plural forms of worship and spirituality are readily accepted. Another aspect is the series of nagging dissatisfactions with the modern moral order, the rapid disenchantment with its easy-going impulses, and a continuing sense that there is something more. This increasing challenge to the hegemony of the mainstream narrative of secularisation is now opening up fresh possibilities at the start of a new age of religious searching, though this is likely to reflect a wariness of confessional leadership and an unwillingness to return to traditional religious authority. It is more likely to maintain the importance of following one's own spiritual itinerary and keeping in mind Berdyaev's stricture that "knowledge, morality, art, government and the economy should become religious, but freely and from inside, not by compulsion from outside"[79].

This flowering of pluralism has also impacted on perceptions within the world religions in the sense that, in John Hick's words, "the great post-Axial faiths constitute different ways of experiencing, conceiving and living in relation to an ultimate divine Reality which transcends all our varied visions of it"[80]. This rejects the exclusivist approach that only one faith expresses the essential basic truth, but again it opens up alternative views. Some would argue that this Reality is completely unknowable, whilst others would insist that it can be genuinely, if also very imperfectly, known in various partial ways in different religious traditions. The latter can be seen as the trajectory from 16th century Europe currently reached away from infallible propositional statements towards the mosaic of experiential views of revelation. On this understanding religious truth can most likely be found in a dialectical interaction between many traditions where 'truth' is always provisional and not confined to any one leading faith. It is important however that this is not seen as merely a form of individual eclecticism or as an arbitrary mishmash of conflicting doctrines, but rather as a convergent spirituality. The compassion for all things in Buddhism and Jainism, the reverence for humanity in Christianity, the complete dependence on the divine will in Islam, the love of life in Judaism, the inner harmony in East Asian spirituality, and the deep sense of the unity and inter-connectedness of all things in the cosmic self in Hinduism are all seen as facets of a single underlying reality. Just as the explosive growth of scientific knowledge, the technologies of communication, the ambitions of an international economy, and the rising tide of emigration and tourism are driving a global perspective, so the pressures on religion are driving a faith that is critical, experiential, personal, yet also global.

Implications

Religious belief and practice is a virtually universal phenomenon throughout all human records and in all parts of the world. This can, and has, been explained as caused, successively through history, by fear of unknown forces and the need to appease supernatural powers, by incorporation within the governing forces of society as a means of consolidating kingly rule, by the need to provide a foundation for morality and the rule of law and order, as a device to make socially oppressive regimes more amenable by a promise of justice in another world, as a wish fulfilment for life hereafter to overcome fear of death, and even as an externalisation of infantile neurotic drives within the unconscious. Even if religion has in certain circumstances served some of these purposes at particular times in history, it is hard to believe, given the incompatible proliferation of competing claims, that any can explain the universality of religious experience. It is certainly true that religion has been frequently manipulated for murderous purposes in the interests of militaristic or ideological dominance (e.g. the Crusades, the Inquisition, and European colonialism), but that does not prove it is inherently bad, only that political and military power can subvert any human structures, at least for a time, for malicious ends.

What the history of religion in this chapter has shown is that whatever the revelations of inspired prophets and sages about an overarching spiritual Reality and whatever their call to justice, compassion and concern for others, it is the self-centred needs of humankind in each age that have all too often prevailed – originally for a warrior or fertility god, then for security against political suppression, and then in the contemporary age of (relative) peace and materialism there seems little or no use for God. Again, that does not reflect on the underlying reality, whatever that may be, only that the harnessed manipulation of God has lost its immediate purpose. Feuerbach, Marx, Darwin, Nietzsche and Freud all, like Laplace a century before, found no place for God. And indeed when religious ideas have lost their validity, they have often faded away painlessly. Yet however much the philosophers proclaim there is no use for God and those like the mystic poet William Blake declare that God is dead, the fact remains that people who have no conventional beliefs keep returning to religious ideas. A central message of this chapter is that human beings cannot endure emptiness and desolation; they always create new symbols to act as a focus for spirituality[82]. They fill the vacuum by creating a new focus of meaning, though once again that does not necessarily guarantee its ontological reality. Moreover, even when such restorations of faith do arise, as they have in the latter 20th century, they still display the close connection with ulterior human, usually political, purposes – the US Christian fundamentalist association with the Neo-conservative Right, the Muslim fundamentalist link with al-Qaeda and mass terror against Islam's perceived enemies, and the Jewish fundamentalists of the Occupied Territories and the Gaza Strip. God, if he exists in the revealed conception of the prophets, dies when he is so hideously misrepresented and will continue to die with every such misappropriation until, if ever, his true nature is comprehended.

੭∽ৎ

Part II

Assessment of the Evidence

੭∽ৎ

Chapter 10

The Status of Religious Claims

Approaches to the existence of God

Thomas Aquinas (1225-74), the most rationalistic of mediaeval theologians, produced five 'proofs' for God's existence. The first was Aristotle's argument for a Prime Mover. The second, rather similar, maintained that there cannot be an infinite series of causes, so there must have been a beginning. The third argued from contingency, as propounded by Ibn Sina (980-1037), the Arab polymath known in the West as Avicenna, which requires the existence of a 'Necessary Being', as enunciated also by Aristotle. The fourth was derived from Aristotle's Philosophy and argued that the hierarchy of excellence in this world implies a Perfection that is the best of all. And the fifth was the argument from design, asserting that the order and purpose observable in the universe was of such supreme intricacy and beauty that it could not be the result of chance. These arguments are no longer widely regarded as valid today although some proponents remain. All imply, with perhaps the argument from design excepted, that God is simply another Being, albeit the Supreme Being, the Necessary Being, the Most Perfect Being. He is another link in the chain of existence, albeit the final, causative, teleo-logical link (although that in itself, of course, whilst suggesting God is powerful does not necessarily make him all-powerful). Although Aquinas certainly intended to differentiate God from all the other links as being First Mover or Necessary Cause, the arguments seemed to support the reductionist view that God was simply at the end of the line the Highest Being or the Most Complete Being – a view perhaps held by many in the West today, but one where pure logical deduction does not, and cannot, prove the existence of an entirely separate entity.

Once it had been realised by the Muslim philosophers in the 11th century that reason alone could not reach a religious understanding of what was called 'God', debate began to focus on blending philosophy with mysticism, though religious experience had to be subjected to the critical intelligence and discipline of philosophy if it was not to descend into self-indulgent emotionalism. The proponents of mysticism however, whilst proclaiming that it was capable of reaching an incomparable transport of joy in some kind of union with God, have always also insisted that its nature is incommunicable, which makes it very difficult to understand or convey. A leading mystic, St. Teresa of Avila, described it thus:

> God, when he raises a soul to union with himself, suspends the natural action of all her faculties. She neither sees, hears, nor understands, so long as she is united with God. But this time is always short, and it seems even shorter than it is. God establishes himself in the interior of this soul in such a way that when she returns to herself, it is wholly impossible for her to doubt that she has been in God, and God in her. This truth remains so strongly impressed on her that even though many years should pass without the condition returning, she can neither forget the favour received, nor doubt of its reality.....But how, you will repeat, can one have such certainty in respect to what one does not see? There are secrets of God's omnipotence which it is not given to me to penetrate. All I know is that I tell the truth, and I shall never believe that any soul who does not possess this certainty has ever been really united to God[83].

The indescribability of the mystic experience is made even plainer by another of the great mystics, St. John of the Cross. He wrote that the soul:

... finds no terms, no means, no comparison whereby to render the sublimity of the wisdom and the delicacy of the spiritual feeling with which she is filled....We receive this mystical knowledge of God clothed in none of the kinds of images, none of the representations through the senses, which our mind makes use of in other circumstances. Accordingly in this knowledge, since the senses and the imagination are not employed, we get neither form nor impression, nor can we give any account or furnish any likeness, although the mysterious and sweet-tasting wisdom comes home so clearly to the inmost parts of the soul.....The soul feels as if placed in a vast and profound solitude, to which no created thing has access, in an immense and boundless desert, desert the more delicious the more solitary it is. There, in this abyss of wisdom, the soul grows by what it drinks in from the wellsprings of the comprehension of love,...and recognises, however sublime and learned may be the terms we employ, how utterly vile, insignificant and improper they are, when we seek to discourse of divine things by their means[84].

This language and imagery may have an archaic ring to a modern age, and is easily dismissed as ecstatic trances couched in pre-scientific terms. In fact however there are very good reasons why such statements should be treated as serious evidence of a non-sense-datum reality. First, the mystical tradition has been a powerful strand, even a central one, in all the world's major religions over the last 3,000 years. The prophets of Israel attributed their own passions and emotions to God. The Hindus and Buddhists had to offer personal devotion to avatars (embodiments of the divine). The three great monotheistic religions developed a mystical tradition which elevated God to transcend the personal category and to assume a nature more similar, perhaps, to nirvana (ultimate reality) and Brahman-Atman (breath, sacred power). In both Judaism and Islam mystics developed very similar concepts of the divine, with kenosis (the self-emptying ecstasy of God) crucial to both the Jewish Kabbalah (inherited tradition) and to Islamic Sufism. In all three faiths the God experienced by the mystics became normative among the faithful until quite recently, and mysticism became the chief vehicle of religious experience. Only in Western Christianity was this development slower, until an explosion of mystical religion in northern Europe in the 14th century, notably Meister Eckhart in Germany and the unknown author of 'The Cloud of Unknowing' in England.

A second reason for regarding mystical experience as serious evidence of an opening to an overarching reality is the ubiquitousness of the phenomenon throughout history, including in modern times. The prophet Muhammad, when he made his Night Journey from Arabia to the Temple Mount in Jerusalem – a central tenet in Islam – then ascended till he reached the divine sphere, though he did not see God himself, only symbols that pointed to the divine reality. Using the same imagery of ascent implying that worldly perceptions had been left behind, St. Augustine described his ascent as a rapturous mental flight: "Our minds were lifted up by an ardent affection towards eternal being itself....We ascended even further by internal reflection and dialogue and wonder at your works"[85], though he was silent about the climax of the flight, stressing instead its transcendence of space, time and ordinary knowledge. Few persons are capable of true mysticism, but of those that have been, monotheists describe this climactic insight as a 'vision of God', Plotinus interpreted it as experience of the One, Buddhists have seen it as an intimation of nirvana. Even for those few the joy and peace of contemplation could sometimes only be achieved for a few moments after enormous struggle: the 6th century Pope Gregory the Great, a master of the spiritual life, wrote that the soul "pants and struggles and endeavours to go above itself but sinks back, overpowered with weariness, into its own familiar darkness"[86].

For others the experience has not been laborious, but of suddenly being overpowered by inexpressible joy. To give a modern example, Leslie Weatherhead, Minister of the City Temple in London till 1960 and dissentient from conventional religion, described an episode fifty years previously in a dingy railway compartment:

> For a few seconds only, I suppose, the whole compartment was filled with light. This is the only way I know in which to describe the moment, for there was nothing to see at all. I felt caught up into some tremendous sense of being within a loving, triumphant and shining purpose. I never felt more humble. I never felt more exalted. A most curious, but overwhelming sense possessed me and filled me with ecstasy. I felt that all was well for all mankind – all men were shining and glorious beings who in the end would enter incredible joy. Of this they were heirs....An indescribable joy possessed me[87'].

It may of course be objected that such manifestations are the extravagant dreams, hallucinations or even the projected wish-fulfilments of the over-excited, the over-emotional, or the over-zealous. But the third consideration is that such a description fits hardly any, or even none, of those who have reported such overpowering visions. Muhammad was a trader with, it is reported, a quick and economical manner, who was never idle and always determined, with great human feeling for the sufferings of others. The great Spanish mystics were highly efficient organisers and had indomitable spirit and energy[88]. Ignatius de Loyola, a former soldier, has been described as one of the most powerfully practical human engines that ever lived. Teresa of Avila was an energetic reformer who enhanced the monastic life of women in the order of discalced Carmelites. Pope Gregory was a powerful Roman pontiff with a distinctly pragmatic view of spirituality. Meister Eckhart was a brilliant intellectual who lectured on Aristotelian philosophy at the University of Paris. Maimonides, the great Jewish mystic philosopher, held high government office in Egypt and was the physician of the sultan. Leslie Weatherhead was Hon. Chaplain to her Majesty's forces as well as President of the Methodist Conference. And so the list goes on. These were not persons who in their ordinary life were given to hypnoid states of ecstasy.

A fourth point is that visionary experience, which developed first and most intensively in the Eastern and Middle East traditions, is anyway far from alien to the more rationalist Western approach. Jung's concept of the collective unconscious can be seen as a more scientific attempt to explore this common imaginative experience of humanity. Yoga, embodying the idea of personal transcendence, is widely practised in the West and is based on persevering exercise involving diet, posture, breathing, intellectual concentration, and moral discipline. It could be argued too that the popularity of psychoanalysis in the West represents an interest, however inadvertent, in the ideas of mysticism since there are such striking similarities between the two disciplines. Despite obvious differences, mediaeval mysticism and modern psychotherapy both evolved comparable techniques to bring about healing and personal integration. The 13th century Spanish mystic Abulafia regularly spoke of 'unsealing the soul, untying the knots that bind it' a phrase also found in Tibetan Buddhism, but resonant also of the psychoanalytic attempts to unlock the complexes that cause mental ill-health. And given the same Greek root for both 'myth' and 'mysticism', it is noteworthy that both Freud and Jung turned to the ancient Greek myths of Oedipus to illustrate their new science in explaining the inner workings of the psyche. Maybe all these trends show, particularly since the 1960s, that people in the West are looking for new sources of inspiration in religious experience uncluttered by an inadequate theism.

Having said all that, however, mystical experience cannot of course be accepted automatically as an inerrant revelation of divine reality. Quite apart from the fact that 'mysticism' is frequently, and ignorantly, associated in the West with cranks or New Age hippies, so-called mystical states can also be character- istic symptoms of delusional insanity or paranoia. A critical, rational judgement needs always to be applied to mystical utter- ances to assess their validity and profoundness, though where such utterances have threatened the prevailing order or ideology, rationalism is readily overridden by murderous retaliation as many of the great mystical figures such as Jesus, al-Hallaj and Suhrawardi have found to their cost.

Subject to these strictures, mysticism therefore deserves to be taken very seriously indeed as an approach to God. Indeed it can be said that there is no authority for God's existence except the inward conviction that is born of mystical experience. Yet that experience remains puzzling and bewildering. Eckhart declared that God was Nothing[88]. By this he did not mean that God was an illusion, but that he was like no-thing known to us – he had an existence utterly different. Humans had to abandon simplistic preconceptions and anthropomorphic imagery. The mystic, Eckhart argued, must not succumb to any finite ideas about the divine because only thus could he achieve identity with God whereby "God's existence must be my existence and God's Is- ness is my is-ness"[89]. Thus again the intellect might perceive God as Three Persons, but once the mystic had achieved union with God, he or she saw him as One. It was indeed better to speak of God in negative terms, as Maimonides had proposed, to appre- ciate God's transcendence. In language replete with paradox and metaphor, Eckhart thus distinguished between the Godhead as 'desert', 'wilderness', 'darkness' and 'nothing', in contrast to the God revealed as Father, Son and Spirit.

The portrait of God that emerges from the mystical literature is always incommunicable and ineffable, and referred to only in highly symbolic and allusive terminology. The experience of pushing language to its limits and metamorphosizing it into a non-linguistic meaning created a sense of the utter separateness of God whom mystics encountered as an overwhelming, even terrifying, holiness. The visions utilised reflect the culture of the mystic: a Jewish visionary will visualise the seven heavens, Buddhists the Buddha and bodhisattvas (followers of the Buddhist way), Christians the Virgin Mary, and Muslims the Night Vision of Muhammad and his divine ascent. These appearances are neither hallucinations nor objective, but a means to reach a deeper and inexpressible religious experience. Indeed the God of the mystics is not an objective reality at all, but profoundly subjective. The interior journey of access often involves systematic contemplation through the image-creating rather than the cerebral logical faculty of the mind, with demanding physical and mental exercises that may yield the final vision. Only sometimes does the dramatic vision appear abruptly and without warning. This facet of mysticism was developed further in the Eastern tradition, particularly by the 6th century Greek Christian known as Denys the Areopagite, with its emphasis on apophatic or silent experience. The mind needed techniques of concentration to cultivate an interior tranquillity and waiting silence. In order to achieve an intuitive apprehension of God, it was necessary to strip the soul naked, to annihilate ego, almost in the manner of a Christian yoga using techniques that had been practised for centuries in the oriental religions.

Mysticism, perhaps the only means by which God (if, as would be said today, God exists) is directly experienced, remains a difficult and uncomfortable concept in contemporary culture, with its overwhelming emphasis on materialism and instant gratification. It also leaves behind several unanswerable questions. How is it possible to know an incomprehensible God? In what sense can a human soul achieve union with a transcendent God? What are the means by which an immaterial God can impact on a material world? Why do certain, rather few, persons have mystical experiences so that if such experiences are the only means of assured knowledge of God's existence, why is this confined to such a small minority of people? All that can be said – and it is admittedly an inadequate response – is that those who have experienced such mystical communion, even for a few moments, from all walks of life, in historical times and at the present day, invariably confess a conviction, more certain than of anything else they have ever known, of God's presence and their absorption within the divine. St. Teresa again:

> If you nevertheless ask how it is possible that the soul can see and understand that she has been in God, since during the union she has neither sight nor understanding, I reply that she does not see it then, but that she clearly sees it later, after she has returned to herself, not by any vision, but by a certitude which abides with her and which God alone can give her"[90].

In more modern guise a similar claim can be selected from any number of such attestations:

> I regard belief in God as something everyone should and must question furiously until a moment comes in their life when they can question no longer; when in fact they find themselves saying, like Jung, 'I don't believe, I know'. This moment came for me some years ago when I had an experience of God so vivid and shattering that I knew that either God existed or I must be stark, staring mad. And I didn't feel mad, only much happier than I have ever felt in my life before or since....The brief moment I refer to seemed, and still seems to me, the most real thing in my life; the pearl of great price compared to which everything and everyone else I value, however dearly, is a copy which makes me homesick for the original"[91].

Revelation

As a variant of mystical understanding, the German historian of religion, Rudolf Otto, used the term 'numinous', from the Latin 'numen' meaning a divinity to be worshipped, to refer to "an ultimate category of religious experience which is defined by this sense of mystery and awe"[92]. He posited that this sense of the numinous was the basis to religion, and its force could induce a great range of powerful emotions from wild ecstasy to deep calm, and at other times a dread sense of awe and humility in the presence of the strong mysterious energy encompassing all things in life. He described this transcendent reality as a mysterium tremendum et fascinans, terrifying because it broke down any normative sense of reality and fascinating because, paradoxically, it generated an irresistible attraction. Otto also saw this overpowering experience as a non-rational paradigm, similar to the power in extreme cases of music or the erotic, inexpressible in language, and classically reflected in the Old Testament in the apparition of Yahweh to Moses on Mount Sinai. So far from being a source of enlightenment, as achieved by the Buddha, it could induce a sense of mortal terror which brutally overthrew all arrogant sense of human beings as the lords of existence, a perception all too widespread today.

But apart from this overawing numinous power, the only other direct source of knowledge about God comes from revelation. Both Christianity and Islam derive from this source, the former in the manifestation of Jesus Christ as recorded in the New Testament Gospels (written between 62-100CE) and the Acts of the Apostles (written about 100AD), and the latter through the words dictated to the prophet Muhammad by the angel Gabriel over a period of two decades between 610-630CE brought together as the Qur'an. Judaism looked to revelation, first from the Old Testament prophets of Israel, then from the long-awaited Messiah, though all of those proclaimed as such – Jesus, Abraham Abulafias, Jacob Frank' and (embarrassingly)

Shabbetai Zevi were all over the centuries rejected.

Claims of divine revelation immediately raise questions about the status of the claims. In the case of Christianity, the historicity of Jesus Christ is certain. The pagan historians, the younger Pliny (61-114CE), Tacitus (55-120CE), Suetonius (75-150CE) and Josephus (37-100CE) all refer to Jesus, and none had any vested interest in partisanship. Josephus actually states:

> About that time lived Jesus, a wise man, if man he may be called, for he did wonderful works – a teacher of those who joyfully received the truth. He won to himself many Jews and many Greeks. He was the Christ, and though Pilatus condemned him to death, he was our Messiah and appeared on the third day"[93] –

Some scholars have taken this as an interpolation by a Christian apologist after the death of Josephus. Jesus himself never claimed to be God, rather he used to call himself 'the Son of Man'. Although this phrase is much disputed, the original phrase in Aramaic, Jesus' own language – bar nasha – appears simply to stress the weakness and mortality of the human condition, so that Jesus seems to have been deliberately emphasising his frailty as a human being who would suffer the vicissitudes of human life. However, the Gospels record that Jesus had certain divine powers (dunameis in the Greek) which enabled him, despite his mortality, to heal the sick and to forgive sins. But he did not claim these powers alone, insisting rather that his disciples, if they had faith (meaning not a particular set of beliefs, but an inner surrender and openness to God), would enjoy the same powers too. Significantly, St. Paul never referred to Jesus as God, and clearly did not believe that Jesus had been the incarnation of God himself. Rather he called him 'Son of God', as one who possessed God's powers and 'spirit' which made manifest God's activity on Earth, but did not mean that Jesus was identifiable with the inaccessible divine reality. This is the terminology reported in all three Synoptic Gospels at the transfiguration of Jesus when a voice from the mountain top cloud (a bat qol, 'daughter of the voice', in Rabbinic tradition) declared: "This is my Son, the Beloved; he enjoys my favour. Listen to him".

The nature of the historical Jesus however is clouded by centuries of philosophical and ecclesiastical accretions. The Virgin Birth, to which the Church attaches central importance as evidence of the divinity of Christ, is never mentioned by Mark, Peter, Paul or John. Since the Jews had a saying that for every child born there were three partners, the father, the mother and the Spirit of God, perhaps the New Testament story is only a poetical way of conveying that whilst Jesus had a human father, the Spirit of God was operative in his birth in a unique and special way [94]. Or it may suggest the 'sacred marriage' rite widespread in the Near East in ancient times whereby the high priest or king played the role of divine messenger and was 'married' to a virgin with whom be cohabited, since Luke records that Mary entered the house of Zacharias, the priest on duty in the temple, stayed there three months, and then returned to her own house [95]. Another sign claimed of Jesus' supernatural powers are the 'miracles' ascribed to him, like those later attributed to St. Francis Xavier, St. Thomas a Becket of Canterbury, and Muhammad – though never claimed by themselves. Perhaps such stories are best understood either as events within the natural laws where Jesus released energies belonging to a plane of being higher than humanity at its present stage of development has reached, or where long after the event details were inflated or heightened or simply invented out of reverence for a personage who was the subject of worship. Consistent with all else that is known of Jesus' central message of love, he would never have used such events to impress his audience or to win converts, only to express compassion and help for those in need.

Even the central meaning of Jesus' life and ministry is shrouded by later encrustations. The doctrine of atonement, that Christ died to atone for the sins of mankind, which became central to Western Christendom, does not derive from any claim of Jesus recorded in the Gospels, but can only be traced back to St. Paul. There is no recorded saying of Jesus in which he explicitly connects his death with the forgiveness or remission of sins. Perhaps the cross of Christ should be better understood as an acted parable of his symbolic marriage to all those thereafter who followed him. The Passover was regarded by the Jews as God's marriage to his people; at the last supper Jesus expressed his great eagerness "to eat this Passover with you"[96]. In a Jewish wedding the bridegroom first brought the bride to his own home; Jesus invited the twelve disciples to supper in the upper room lent to him since he had no home. Then the bridegroom knelt and washed the feet of his bride; Jesus washed the disciples' feet. Then the wedding feast followed; Jesus ate the last supper with his followers. Then the bridegroom and bride were joined in the words of the wedding covenant; Jesus made 'a new covenant' with the symbols of the broken bread and the poured out wine. In a Jewish wedding four cups of wine were used. The first was drunk by all as a cup of blessing. The second represented a curse and was 'poured out'; at the last supper it seems Jesus drank it alone[97]. The third was an overflowing cup, the cup of salvation, which all drank. The fourth was 'the cup of the Kingdom'; at the last supper it seems all drank except Jesus[98]. When then at the crucifixion his body was broken and his blood poured out, the message must have been clear to them that he was 'married' to them, committed to them for ever[99]. On this reading, Jesus is not a lamb sacrificed to appease or propitiate an angry God, let alone the expiation by an innocent man for the sins wrought by humankind throughout history; the message is rather a revelation of the nature of God, and a pledge, as in an enduring marriage covenant, that however much God is hurt and hindered by sin, he will not cease an endless outpouring of love.

The other central issue for assessing the meaning of Christ lies in the claim of resurrection. There are good reasons for regarding this as a historical event. First, the disciples who were traumatised and utterly disillusioned by the crucifixion as well as physically terrified of the consequences of acknowledging any connection with Jesus, suddenly only six or seven weeks later became missionaries preaching his resurrection within a mile or so of where he had been put to death. It is difficult to believe that these terrified men could have been so totally transformed, at very real risk to their lives, unless they were utterly convinced that Jesus was not dead but, in some sense, alive again. If they were lying or simply disingenuous, they could so easily have been exposed by anybody pointing to the corpse in the tomb behind the stone. As to whether the resurrection was a physical one, the evidence suggests it was not. The disappearance of the body while the grave-clothes were left exactly as they were[100] suggests not a bodily departure, rather some kind of de-materialisation, almost evaporation, in a way that in our state of knowledge we do not understand – referred to by Huxley as trans-natural events rather than super-natural[101]. It is also significant that St. John's Gospel records Jesus as saying beforehand: "In a little while you will not behold me (using the Greek verb 'theoreo' for physical sight through the optic nerves), and again in a little while you shall see me (the Greek word here 'horao' means mental insight or spiritual vision) because I go to the Father"[102]. It is therefore most likely that what the disciples saw after Easter Day was some special kind of apparition, though certainly not an hallucination – Paul's recording of Jesus' appearing to five hundred people at once[103], in hiding and in despair, not in any animated state of expectation whatever, rules that out. But whatever exactly happened to his body, the key spiritual meaning of the resurrection is that his personality survived and was recognisably active thereafter in the world.

The New Testament never equates Jesus with God, but the resurrection reveals he was more than just a man – truly man, but in a
unique category of avatar (embodiment of the divine).

Revelation in Islam was very different. Muhammad, repelled
by life in 6th-7th century Mecca as a trader amid the ruthless drive
for wealth among the merchant class, began solitary contemplation in a cave a few miles from the city, and there around
610CE when he was forty he began to receive visions which he
described as of a 'Glorious Being' whom he later identified as the
angel Gabriel rather than God himself. The angel told
Muhammad to recite the words revealed to him, and later his
Companions, using the pre-existing oral poetic tradition,
memorised the recitations. While visitations from the angel were
the prime source of transmission of the words later assembled in
the Qur'an, in other cases the words were transmitted without
the agency of an apparition, sometimes with Muhammad strug-
gling to find the right phrases for the inspiration within his own
mind (where the Qur'an refers to God speaking from 'behind a
veil') and sometimes from an exterior mystic 'suggestion'. The
voice of the Qur'an is usually unidentified and addresses
Muhammad in the third person, which is consistent with his
believing that the revelations came from outside himself. The
Muslim interpretation is that this was the voice of God, through
the agency of the angel Gabriel, speaking via Muhammad to the
world. The power of the Qur'an is not obvious to a non-Arabic
speaker since it appears difficult to read and lacking any order or
logical thread or conclusion. The rich and dense text, however,
when proclaimed in classical Arabic by an accomplished chanter,
had a mesmerising effect –as is illustrated in contemporary terms
by the incendiary power exerted by Osama bin Laden's post-9/11
televised tapes drawing on the Qur'an and delivered in the same
classical idiom. And for Muslims the dense phraseology of the
Qur'an hides an inner meaning which can only be discerned,
through God's grace, by those with true faith.

The components of the Qur'an were first collected and put together by Zayd ibn-Thabit, Muhammad's main scribe, partly from men's memories and partly from writing on parchment, stones, boards, even bones. But no copy of this original collection has survived. No definitive text was in circulation till 'Uthman began the third caliphate in 655CE and ordered an official version to be compiled, and the earliest complete copy of the Qur'an dates only from 688CE, fifty-six years after Muhammad's death. Thereafter it has survived more than thirteen centuries in largely its original form, despite constant textual refinement by scholars over 200-300 years (which some argue produced the magnificent language so characteristic of the Qur'an) and despite some later interpolations like the infamous Satanic Verses.

The central message of the Qur'an[104] is of one omnipotent God, demonstrated by his power to create, in relation to whom man is utterly subordinate, unable to do anything unless God allows so that total surrender to his will is the only real response. Other spiritual beings exist, including jinns good and bad, angels who are wholly pure acting as servants of God, as well as Shaytan, the fallen jinn. The role of Muhammad as prophet is set out, bringing God's message to mankind who will be punished if they ignore it. The Qur'an also warns of the Last Day when man will be judged either to endless bliss or to endless torment, and there are many graphic descriptions of Paradise and Hell. Laws are also prescribed for the faithful, including the Five Pillars, the commandments of Surah 17, prohibitions against certain foods and alcohol, and precise social provisions (the Shariah). There is also lengthy description of the history of salvation involving messengers before Muhammad who is giving the final warning of God, as well as of the brotherhood of man uniting all over and above ethnic or tribal differences and demanding tolerance of Christians and Jews whose prophets are accepted as men of God. Altogether, there is little new teaching in the Qur'an that went beyond the pre-existing monotheistic traditions of Christianity and Judaism, though to Muhammad's audience it was mostly new and in particular it was a distinctly Arab message, and thus a unifying force among the warring tribes, and recited with entrancing force as powerful desert lore.

Though there is a considerable degree of broadly overlapping beliefs between Islam and the Judaeo-Christian tradition, there are still significant differences. A key one is the idea of predestination where the Qur'an speaks of certain people created 'for Hell' and others 'for Paradise', and does not resolve the dilemma between the omnipotence of God controlling all destiny and man's accountability for his own actions, whilst Christianity asserts that humans do have free will for which they will be held responsible in the Last Judgement. Muslims see access to salvation coming from adherence to a holy book claimed to be the Word of God, while Christians look to salvation through a redeeming Saviour. Muslim dogma embraces angels and jinns with parallel but unseen physical lives, a three-dimensional Heaven and an ever-burning Hell, a living Shaytan, and a crowded Last Day, while Christian interpretations of these concepts have treated them not as physical replicas but as metaphor for experiencing the endless love of God or suffering through being excluded from it. Muslims regard Jesus not in any sense as the embodiment of God, but rather as having a mission to foretell the ministry of Muhammad, for which they call in evidence the New Testament itself[105]. The Qur'an also seems to support a version of creationism (as do apparently a majority of Americans), whilst in Europe and among the great majority of Christians the theory of evolution is accepted. And central to the Muslim faith is the belief in the Qur'an as the (dictated) Word of God, though many Christians might perhaps accept that God could intervene in history at different times and in different ways.

Implications

Since God (even if he exists) is unknowable, ineffable, inexpressible, any knowledge about his nature can only come either from direct, personal, mystical experience or from revelation in some perceptible, spiritual form. Since spiritual experiences have to be interpreted and since even the God of the mystics is not an objective reality but profoundly subjective, that immediately raises questions about the genuineness of the claims propounded. Spiritual insights are not susceptible to scientific proof or to the application of the methodology of verification or falsification, but on the other hand statements clearly cannot be trusted simply because someone alleges that it was revealed to them. As Keith Ward has said; "the specific information provided – whether in the form of visions or of 'heard' messages – depends very much upon cultural expectations, general background beliefs and the imaginative ability of the human mind to construct vast edifices of ontology from the merest hints of mystery"[106]. Separate criteria for the assessment of the validity of spiritual claims are therefore obviously needed. At least four present themselves. Such claims based on personal or mystical experience should have to meet the bar that they are:

(i) consistent with material reality, not obviously contrary to it, and consistent with known and tested life experience, not any charlatan misrepresentation of it.

(ii) reported by persons who on known evidence are judged to be balanced and integrated, and whose account can therefore be relied on to be sound and thoughtful, not wild or hysterical.

(iii) are life-transforming in ways clearly perceived by others and can be seen to increase the wisdom, insight, sensitivity and caring concern of those who experience it.

(iv) meeting the highest standards of moral goodness that

humans are aware of, and increasing love and compassion for others.

It can thus reasonably be concluded that there are three channels for gaining genuine access to spiritual insights or understanding of what is perceived as God. One is a personal vision so totally compelling and dynamic that the person is utterly convinced as to its transforming meaning and whose life thereafter bears witness to that meaning. But very few people indeed do have such a vision in the course of their lives, and for that large majority who don't, they can only rely on the evidence of such visions provided by others. However, such an invitation almost always provokes a healthy scepticism, if not outright disbelief. Such a response is entirely understandable, and many may never be prepared to move away from that. But on the balance of evidence, as stringently filtered by the four criteria set down above, it does not seem reasonable automatically to discard such visionary experiences attested by certain others where they ring true as a revelation, albeit incomplete, of some ultimate spiritual reality. That is the second channel of access, though because it depends on rational judgement rather than on the integrity of own personal experience, its force is inevitably weaker. The third is the transforming power evinced by the life and actions and teaching of those who are perceived, again only on the strongest evidence, as embodiments of the divine or imbued with some special or unique relationship with a transcendent spiritual reality. In the case of Christianity, Jesus' intense awareness of God as attested in the Gospels, the transformation of the apostles at Pentecost, and the revelations of the resurrected Jesus are primary attributes of religious commitment. Even in the case of Islam, where the fundamental claim is that the scriptures were dictated by God, the prophet's overwhelming experience of God as both commanding and merciful may be seen as underpinning the message he 'heard'. It is the perceived self-disclosure of God to Muhammad which inspires the Muslim belief that the poetic discourse of the Qur'an conveys the underlying spiritual truth of the rule of God, even if some of the ideas and images reflect the limiting culture within which they were located.

The essential point is that it is a category error to ask whether a religious belief is true as if it were a matter of fact to be independently ascertained by replication and experiment. Religious statements do not relate literal truths, but use imaginative stories or poetic exposition because there is no other way to convey spiritual truths about an inexpressible spiritual reality. A religious claim is paradigmatically different from a scientific statement in that the latter can be checked irrespective of the mood or disposition of the investigator, while the former (if genuine) reflects the impact of a dynamic power on inspired human minds. The 'truth' of a religious claim, insofar as such language is appropriate at all, lies in the psychological response to that all-pervading power which itself depends on the predispositions and receptivity of the human mind[107].

Chapter 11

The Issue of Purpose

The last chapter showed that science and religion operate in wholly different domains and impact on humans through very different paradigms. Yet there may well be cross-over between them that carry important messages for concepts relating to the meaning and purpose of the universe and the human role within it. At the point that the scientific-religious interface has reached at the present time, several important questions arise, though the evidence required to answer them seems markedly inconsistent. Such apparent contradictions between the scientific and religious world-views centre primarily round the validity of teleology and the notion of final cause. The evidence for and against will now be weighed, and then a proposal made as to how they might be reconciled.

Arguments against the claim of purpose

The modern religious concept regards the universe as dedicated to the development of human beings whose fulfilment lies in their capacity to respond to an ultimate divine reality. Such a view seems hard to reconcile with the analysis of chapters 2,4,5,6 and 7. If that really were the case, it might be thought strange that the context chosen for this was a stupendous universe of almost unfathomable proportions where humans occupy one miniscule planet within the solar system of one mainstream star among 100 billion such stars in one galaxy which is among 100-200 billion such galaxies, even leaving aside the even more unimaginable concept that this colossal universe is but one within a vast ensemble of universes (see chapters 3 and 4). It seems such a grossly inefficient use of space-time if that were all the universe was about or was designed for.

As an extension of this last point, it is also curious that, if human beings are the teleological end point of the universe, it has taken so long to reach them. Homo sapiens did not evolve till about 200,000 years ago on an Earth that is 4.45 billion years old in a universe that is some 13.7 billion years old. Humans in their currently recognisable modern form did not arrive till 99.9993% of the lifetime of the universe had already elapsed. Of course it can be argued that given how it is now believed the universe formed and developed and how the Earth a great time later came into existence and then later still life forms gradually appeared on Earth and slowly evolved, that simply reflects – no more, no less – how long the process took. Besides, theologians will point out that time is only a limiting factor for humans and other similar physical creatures whilst for God, who is beyond and outside time, the passing of aeons is no restraint or inhibition whatever (in the words of the hymn, 'a thousand ages in thy sight is but an evening gone'). Nevertheless, it seems odd to design a world for humans – if that is the view taken – in a way that leaves humans off the stage until the last 0.0006% of the time of the performance.

There is a further, third, important consideration which seems to militate against the God-designer view. That is that the emergence of the human race at all was quite extraordinarily fortuitous. The set of highly contingent conditions that led from the time of the dinosaurs ultimately to the human species are set out above, but even that excludes the wildly improbable and unpredictable evolution of life forms in the 3.5 billion years before the downfall of the dinosaurs. For almost 3 billion years within that colossal period of time only single-cell organisms existed; multi-cellular life and more complex life forms from which plants and animals (and ultimately humans after an exceedingly complicated lineage) later emerged did not evolve till almost the end of this huge traverse of time. The US palaeontologist Stephen Jay Gould has described this whole process of multiple layering of the unlikeliest contingencies and zig-zagging genealogical tangents with no apparent causal trajectory combined with glacial immobility for aeons as a "story of massive removal followed by differentiation within a few surviving stocks, not the conventional tale of steadily increasing excellence, complexity and diversity."[109]. It is true, in contrasting mode, that the history of evolution shows multiple examples among mammals, birds and insects of over-determination whereby biological structures repeatedly produce the same or similar functional solution to a given challenge so that even if one or several pathways are blocked by extinction of a species, 'Nature' returns to the same solution by another route [110]. To that extent, the extreme unlikelihood of a particular species reaching a distant evolutionary destination, given the extraordinary vicis-situdes of the intermediate pathways, is matched by the inevitability that that evolutionary solution, given its functional optimality, will sooner or later, over hundreds if not thousands of millions of years, ultimately emerge. One interesting example already noted in this text suggests that had the mass extinction of the dinosaurs not occurred around sixty-five million years ago, an intelligent large-brained, bipedal, four-finger-handed dinosaur – now named Stenonychosaurus (narrow-nailed lizard) – with clear indications of a prototype human might well have developed some forty million years before homo sapiens finally took the stage. Nevertheless, it seems bizarre that the planned human design, if planned it was, should be liable to the vagaries of alternative competing transmission mechanisms as a result of which human beings in their present form might never have developed at all.

Certainly there is no evidence in the fossil record of the comfortable anthropocentric scenario of steady progress towards the human apogee. Three instances out of very many may be plucked from our known evolutionary history to illustrate this point. Pikaia, not a two-inch annelid worm as Walcott in his analysis in 1911 of the Burgess shale assumed[112] but a chordate within the phylum to which all vertebrates including man belong, was the first recorded member of humans' immediate ancestry. If this tiny Middle Cambrian organism had not survived the Burgess decimation 530 million years ago, the eventual tiny human twig might well never have had a chance to emerge on the mammalian branch, like so many other species in a lineage with interesting possibilities that were never realised. At another hinge in man's ancestry it may be noted that during the 165 million years of dinosaur supremacy mammals registered no significant changes towards dominance, larger brains or greater size, but merely scampered as small creatures in the interstices of the world of much larger-bodied vertebrates to evade the attention of predators. Since the development of much larger brains may lie outside the potentials of reptilian design[111], consciousness may never have evolved on Earth if a mass dying of the dinosaurs had not been triggered by an asteroid collision. Then again at a third turning point in human evolution, it might be argued that if homo sapiens had succumbed to extinction like so many other species, another branch of the same stock – homo erectus or the Neanderthals – could well have developed the same pathways towards abstract intelligence, and numerical and aesthetic skills. But the Ice Age evidence indicates they did not. The most likely explanation based on allopatric theory is that homo sapiens arose as small populations that became isolated from their parental group at the periphery of the ancestral range[112] – a separation that promotes favourable genetic variation because natural selection is intense in geographically marginal areas where species are under great pressure to retain a foothold.

There is yet another facet of the evolutionary landscape which perhaps most of all casts doubt on the idea of a pre-ordained plan. In the post-Cambrian period of Earth's history from about

540 million years ago at least five mass extinctions occurred when respectively some 52%, 40%, 68%, 45% and 42% of world species currently alive were wiped out. Even this catalogue of devastating extinctions is far from complete since it is known that there were at least three extensive ice ages between 765 and 605 million years ago which must have drastically curtained marine populations, as well as at least one and perhaps three extinction events during the Cambrian era when at least 40% of species were destroyed. All these took place in the last billion years, but over the previous 2.5 billion years that life has existed on this planet it is reasonable to assume that some, perhaps many, extinction episodes also occurred in addition to the ten or more of which we have some evidence. Given then the all-encompassing global catastrophes that each of these episodes entailed, it is hard to credit that the goal of man and survival of all the intermediate species was part of a long-prepared and systematically organised strategy.

For all these four reasons it cannot be concluded that there was some kind of overall predetermined plan behind the universe of which the human race was the ultimate purpose. There is such fortuitousness piled on fortuitousness at every level – cosmological, geological, and genealogical – in the hugely elongated and fragile thread of evolution leading to humans, such a cascade of the most improbable and unpredictable events and processes at almost every stage throughout this near fourteen billion year story, that any concept of pre-ordained destination simply cannot be validated. An alternative model is needed. The most obvious hypothesis is that in the absence of any undergirding teleology the universe, the solar system, the planet Earth, and pattern of life forms have all developed on an entirely mechanistic and random basis. As the celebrated physicist Steven Weinberg once exclaimed, the more knowledge one has of the universe, the more pointless it seems to be. However, this too is not readily borne out.

Arguments against the assumption of pointlessness

Within the cosmic universe and the natural world on Earth there are many observable facets which do not suggest a pointless arbitrariness at all.

(a) Fine-Tuning: fortuitous or designed?

The most striking example is the spectacular degree of fine-tuning both of the fundamental forces and particle masses underpinning the structure of the universe, discussed at length in chapter 3. The balance between the centrifugal and centripetal forces at the singularity from which the universe sprang had to be fine-tuned to about one part in 10^{55}, a mind-blowing degree of accuracy, to prevent on the one hand over-rapid expansion precluding galaxy formation (and therefore the emergence of carbon life, including humans) and almost immediate re-collapse on the other. The hypothesis of 'inflation', posited to solve the so-called flatness and smoothness problems, itself requires phenomenally accurate fine-tuning, again to the tune of an accuracy of around one part in 10^{50}. If the strengths of the nuclear weak force and gravity differed from their current values by an amount even so absurdly tiny as one part in 10^{100}, it could destroy the balance between the two most fundamental forces holding the universe together. If the nuclear weak force had been stronger, all the hydrogen would have burned to helium at Big Bang, so there would have at later stages no water or long-lived stars (and hence no life). Only the nuclear weak force at exactly its current strength allows neutrinos to interact with stars weakly enough to escape the incredible gravitational force in a collapsing supernova whilst at the same time strongly enough to blast the outer layers of the star into space to yield the material to build planets like Earth (without which again there would be no life). If the nuclear strong force were only slightly stronger, protons would not be formed and hence no atoms, while if it were slightly weaker, the deuteron would not bind together, so stars could not burn and hence the key carbon component of life would not be created. If the third force, electromagnetism, were only very slightly stronger, stars would not explode, so necessary elements heavier than iron would not arise, while if it were only very slightly weaker, stars would burn out quickly and not over billions of years steadily produce life-creating material. If gravity, the fourth force, were not 10^{39} weaker than electromagnetism even by some utterly miniscule amount, stars would be a billion times smaller and would burn a million times faster, so life would be extremely unlikely to emerge. Equally, particle masses have to be exceptionally finely calibrated for living forms to arise. If the difference in mass between neutrons and protons (0.1%) had not been virtually precisely double the mass of the electron, the hundreds of stable atoms from which the biology of life derives would not have been created. If the electric charges of the electron and proton were not in precise balance, the instability of matter would yield a universe full of radiation and gases, so again life would never occur.

These are just a few of the main examples, but the list of what the astronomer Fred Hoyle called a 'monstrous series of accidents' is a very long one[113], as compiled in particular by astrophysicists such as Bernard Carr, Martin Rees, Brandon Carter, John Barrow and Frank Tipler. Life clearly depends very sensitively indeed on an extraordinarily finely calibrated set of physical laws and conditions honed to utterly breathtaking precision. Gribbin and Rees concluded that "the conditions in our universe really do seem to be uniquely suitable for life forms like ourselves"[114], while Hoyle commented that it looked as if "the laws of nuclear physics have been deliberately designed with regard to the consequences they produce inside the stars" and that the universe looked like a "put-up job"[115] – a remarkable example of an agnostic scientist feeling compelled to acknowledge the possibility of a teleological basis to the laws of physics.

What then can be the explanation for this degree of fine-tuning? It cannot be accidental. The chances against many of these force strengths, particle masses and relational variables being coincidentally set with such almost unbelievable precision at exactly the level (the Goldilocks principle – not too much, not too little, but just right) required to produce a universe favourable for life must be gigantic, and the chances against all of them being coincidental is simply unimaginable. Penrose's calculation, that without initial conditions guaranteeing a smooth beginning, there would need to be accuracy of around 10^{123} in selecting our exceptionally highly ordered universe from the range of all physically possible ones (i.e. a chance of one in a hundred trillion trillion trillion trillion trillion trillion trillion trillion trillion) is simply beyond the radar screen of human comprehension. And if some Grand Unified Theory were proposed to explain these necessary initial conditions, that would be merely re-introducing the fine-tuning in another form which the inflationary scenario was devised to evade.

If then fortuitousness is ruled out, is a universe structured with such almost unbelievable precision compatible with an assumption of random and arbitrary pointlessness? One response has been to advance the anthropic principle: it's not surprising we find a universe so suited to our needs because if it were not so, we would not be here to observe it. But this is a tautology, not an explanation. A second response is to hypothesize the existence of a huge ensemble of universes, possibly infinite in number, within which sooner or later will be found one or more like ours that display the special laws of physics enabling life to emerge. This hypothesis seems unlikely for several reasons. First, there is no evidence for the existence of alternative universes, let alone an almost infinite number of them, independent of the argument that they are needed for purely dialectical reasons to solve the problem of this highly fine-tuned universe we inhabit. Secondly, the list of extremely unlikely coincidences is so large and the odds against their happening by chance so monumentally colossal in many individual cases that, when all are taken in combination, the number of universes required to meet all such possible contingencies rises exponentially to ultra-astronomic levels – an example of obscurum per obscurius, as the lawyers say (solving a difficult and obscure problem via an explanation even more difficult and more obscure). It is not a credible conclusion when other, much simpler, alternative explanations are available.

Third, even if the multiverse postulate were taken seriously, it still has to be explained how such an enormous, perhaps semi-infinite, array of universes was generated in the first place. Six proposals were examined in chapter 3. But these again all involve imaginative hypotheses of extreme conditions for the existence of which there is no independent verifiable evidence – an open universe with infinitely many regions (Ellis and Brundrit), an inflationary cosmos growing at an incomprehensibly gigantic rate and then at phase transitions separating into an almost infinite number of regions with different force strengths, particle masses and gauge symmetries (Linde), almost infinitely many universes generated by an endless variety of quantum vacuum fluctuations (Tryon), an oscillatory cycle continuing indefinitely of Big Bangs followed by re-collapses at which space-time properties undergo complete reprocessing at each bounce (Wheeler), a near-infinite number of universes generated by the postulate that every change which quantum theory recognises as possible actually occurs in some branch of reality or mini-universe (de Witt), and a huge growth in 'child universes' in the form of regions of an expanding false vacuum which are pinched off once surrounded by true vacuum (Sato) or where child universes are generated by quantum-tunnelling from their mothers (another Linde hypothesis). Whilst some elements of some of these hypotheses may have some plausibility, none of them avoids the pitfalls of improbable explanation, i.e. either they require the generation of a virtual infinity of universes, or they introduce metaphysical appendages more extreme than the theory of design, or they push the logic back to ultimate premises which then imply the same staggering degree of fine-tuning which their whole argument was calculated to avoid. If then for these reasons the fantastic degree of fine-tuning manifest through the universe and on Earth cannot plausibly be explained by any of these hypotheses, the balance of evidence – unless some alternative, more credible theory were found in future – would point to the universe being in some way designed. The weight of evidence on fine-tuning is such that it might by itself alone refute the argument of a mechanistic or purposeless universe, but there are several other considerations, of differing weight, which also point in the same direction at the planetary level.

(b) Gaia as an adaptive control mechanism

First was the insight of James Lovelock and Lynn Margulis who defined the "notion of the biosphere as an active adaptive control system able to maintain the Earth in homeostasis"[116]. The Gaia theory proposed that we are not just a collection of accidentally cohabiting selfish species and agnostic geochemical cycles; it posited the existence of feedbacks at global level that have served to keep the Earth's surface habitable within a tolerable range, despite significant external changes, including changes in radiation from the Sun. It involved two radical departures from the conventional view. One was that life profoundly affects the non-living environment, such as the composition of the atmos-phere, which then feeds back to influence the entirety of the living world. The second was that this tight coupling between life and non-life produces the unexpected 'emergent property' that Gaia – the Earth system as a whole – is able to maintain key aspects of the global environment, such as global temperature, at levels favourable for life despite shocks and disturbances both within and outside itself. This ability for self-regulation is shared by all living things, including the human body, which can regulate its internal temperature at optimum level when confronted by wide variations in external temperature[117]. This led some to refer to the Earth, misleadingly, as in some sense 'alive'.

For this reason Darwinian biologists in the 1980s attacked the concept of Gaia as teleological, in that it implied action purposefully directed towards an end. However, as a 'system' rather than an 'organism', the theory does show that there are regulatory mechanisms which have kept the environment fit for life over 3.8 billion years. Such mechanisms can explain the relative constancy of the climate – surprisingly when the Earth's atmosphere is far from equilibrium –, the unexpectedly moderate levels of salt in the oceans (from the action of bacteria in tidal flats), the constant level of oxygen within 50% of present values in the atmosphere for the past 300 million years, the control of temperature in the air above by algae in the oceans through the seeding of clouds, the removal of CO^2 from the atmosphere through the weathering of rocks which is largely determined by living organisms, and many other remarkable findings. Even so, Gaian balance and self-regulation is clearly only part of the story. At the strong global cooling about 2.5 billion years ago, for example, when the photosynthetically produced oxygen had been fully absorbed by the iron and sulphur in the sea and oxidation was exhausted, the escape of oxygen into the atmosphere killed off vast quantities of organisms, creating not only a climate shift but also a holocaust which changed irreversibly the world ecology. Thus Gaian stasis, powerful as it is, can be overridden by cataclysms whether generated by comet bombardment, destruction of shallow seas when continents collide and merge, oxygen shortage in the oceans, or dramatic climate change leading to horrendous wipeouts of species in up to a dozen mass extinctions before and since the Cambrian period 540 million years ago. But then, it is claimed, once one control mechanism has been stretched to breaking point, another replaces it till the next catastrophe. Nevertheless, the role of Gaia in homeostatic regulation is clearly not total. Not only therefore, on Gaian theory, is Earth's inorganic world extraordinarily fine-tuned in a manner conducive to life, but living creatures themselves also manipulate their inorganic environment within narrow ranges of tolerance in order to enhance their own survival and welfare (the Goldilocks effect for life forms). Since living creatures do not act in this way consciously with that intended purpose, this may be regarded as another facet of the anthropic principle – if they had not behaved in this way, we would not be here to observe the results. But again a logically deductible consequence is not a substitute for causation. The Gaian framework of complex interconnectedness between living and non-living forms must be construed as pointing to a world designed to be favourable to life, though subject from time to time to irruptions of extreme and overwhelming violence, within a universe that seems to be designed for a similar purpose.

(c) Darwinian competition or symbiotic network?

A third consideration lies in the driving forces behind evolution. The Darwinian theory of natural selection proposes that mutations which occur blindly (i.e. not purposively directed towards any 'development' of 'improvement') have the effect that some mutated organisms will be more efficient at reproducing and will thus tend to survive in the constant struggle for life which eliminates most of the others. This is unquestionably a powerful theory in explaining why organisms are selected which are more efficient at obtaining food, overcoming competitors and reproducing themselves, but again it does not explain, certainly cannot guarantee, the emergence of complex conscious life-forms from hugely simpler unconscious microbial forms. Nor can it readily explain the development of distinctive human characteristics such as consciousness, morality, aesthetics, science and art on the grounds purely that they were conducive to more efficient domination or replication (despite attempts in human socio-biology to do so). Equally, it seems too simplistic and mono-thematic to explain all biological and metaphysical evolution of living creatures as the outcome of a universal struggle for survival in the absence of any independent corroborating evidence or any falsifiability criterion by which its predictive power could be ascertained. Indeed, Eldredge and Gould[118] have postulated an alternative, or complementary, hypothesis of 'punctuated equilibria' whereby very long periods of gradual mutation are suddenly interrupted by large and fast genetic saltations (changes by big rapid jumps) in conditions of relative genetic isolation. Under this 'allopatric' theory (meaning, in another place), new species arise in very small populations that become isolated from their parental group at the periphery of their ancestral range[119].

However, whilst natural selection and allotropic saltation may drive evolution blindly and seemingly purposelessly via competitive advantage and chance ecological opportunity, Margulis has argued that other forces operate equally powerfully, or even more pervasively, via continual co-operation, strong interaction and mutual dependence among life forms. This theory of symbiosis premises the growing complexity and multiplication of life forms, not on elimination of competitors, but on co-opting others and networking. For the first two billion years Earth was inhabited solely by bacteria. During this vast expanse of time, almost half of the entire history of the Earth, prokaryotes (organisms composed of cells without a nucleus, i.e. bacteria) continuously transformed the Earth's surface and atmosphere. They invented all of life's essential, miniaturised chemical systems (achievements that so far humanity has not approached), leading to the development of fermentation, photosynthesis, oxygen-breathing, and the removal of nitrogen from the air.

These staggering events at the earliest stages of life derived from at least three dynamics of evolution only discovered in the last fifty years. One is the remarkable orchestrating abilities of DNA by which the living cell can self-replicate whilst at the same time being susceptible to mutation, which randomly tinkers with identity, so that the cell has the potential to survive change. A second is the natural genetic engineering whereby prokaryotes routinely and rapidly transferred bits of genetic material to other individuals. Thus any bacterium at any time might have the use of accessory genes, visiting from sometimes very different strains, which performed functions beyond the repertoire of its own DNA. Some genetic bits might be recombined with the cell's own genes, or be passed on further. The significance of this is enormous: it means that all the world's bacteria potentially have access to a single gene pool and hence to the adaptive mechanisms of the entire bacterial domain[120]. That has two other crucial implications: the speed of recombination is vastly superior to mutation – a few years perhaps compared to a million – and the constant rapid adaptation to environmental conditions supports the entire biota since the global microbial exchange network ultimately affects every living plant and animal. The driving force therefore is a cross-communicating and co-operating worldwide super-network of bacteria which renders the planet fertile and habitable for larger life forms. The third dynamic was a symbiotic alliance that became permanent. The ancient bacteria combined with other micro-organisms which took up residence inside, offering waste disposal and oxygen-derived energy in return for food and shelter, and the merged organisms then later evolved into more complex oxygen-breathing life forms.

Symbiosis, the merging of organisms into new collectives, can thus be viewed as a major evolutionary driver – maybe the main driver – of change on Earth. Darwin himself, who died in 1882 almost a century before DNA, genetic transfer and symbiosis were uncovered, wrote presciently that: "We cannot fathom the marvellous complexity of an organic being. Each living creature must be looked at as a microcosm – a little universe, formed of a host of self-propagating organisms, inconceivably minute and as numerous as the stars in heaven". Long after Darwin's death the discovery of mitochondria strongly reinforced his observation. These tiny membrane-wrapped inclusions in the cells of animals, plants, fungi, and the intermediate organisms between plants and animals (protists) lie outside the nucleus in modern cells, but without mitochondria the nucleated cell – and hence the composite of cells forming the plant or animal – could not utilise oxygen and hence could not live. This suggests a dramatic scenario. It has been hypothesized that the descendants of the bacteria that swam in the primeval seas three billion years ago are now found in human and animal bodies as mitochondria. By creating organisms that were not just the sum of their combined parts, but more like the sum of all the possible combinations of their parts, symbiotic alliances pushed developing beings into uncharted areas of complexity. Nor is this just a facet of palaeon-tological history: the process continues unceasingly today. At least 10% of our own dry body weight consists of bacteria, some of which, though not a congenital part of our bodies, we cannot live without. Our DNA is derived in unbroken sequence from the same molecules in the earliest cells that formed at the edges of the first oceans. To that extent our bodies, like those of all life, preserve the environment of an earlier Earth, and still today we co-exist with microbes and harbour remnants of others which are symbiotically subsumed within our cells.

(d) Quantum entanglement
In addition to fine-tuning, Gaian inter-connectedness and symbiosis, there is a further dimension (though certainly not fully understood) which seems to point away from a concept of a purposeless world. Erwin Schrodinger discovered in the 1930s that in quantum mechanics, when two subatomic particles

interact locally and then move very far apart, they still must be treated as an indivisible whole because measurements performed on one of the particles will depend in part on the state of the other. Einstein referred to this non-locality as 'spukhafte Fernwirkungen' (spooky action at a distance), and refused to believe it, but repeated experiments have confirmed beyond doubt that such non-local effects are real. Once entangled, it makes no sense to talk about the properties of just one of them because all the information about the particles, such as their momentum and spin, lies only in their joint properties. Recent experiments have gone further and found that the quantum phenomenon of entanglement, which was thought to be confined to the infinitesimal world of subatomic particles, can produce effects that remain measurable on macroscopic scales[121]. Some believe that entanglement is everywhere, that almost all quantum interactions produce entanglement whatever the conditions, and that the constant interactions between electrons in the atoms in the human body are also a mass of entanglements. Even more weird, further experiments by Brukner and Vedral in 2003 found that moments of time can become entangled too – for example, the very act of measuring a photon polarisation a second time can affect how it was polarised earlier on. This bizarre result suggests that quantum mechanics seems to be bending the laws of cause and effect and perversely implies putting space and time on an equal footing in quantum theory. Maybe the laws of classical physics have to be reformulated when entanglement indicates not only instantaneous cause and effect across cosmological distances, but even extends this 'impossibility' to events separated in time as well. But despite our uncertain knowledge at this stage concerning quantum entanglement, certain conclusions still stand out. A collection of particles must be treated holistically. The Newtonian and thermodynamic paradigm, which portrays the universe as a sterile machine composed of individual units in decay, needs to be replaced by a new paradigm of a creative universe which emphasises the collective, cooperative, innovative and inter-mingled character of physical processes. The notion is subjective and holistic rather than analytic and reductionist. Certainly the picture of quantum geometry in terms of networks is still developing, and it still needs to find a way to combine with other approaches to quantum gravity, especially string theory. Indeed, just as Leibniz's relational philosophy of space and time enabled Einstein's general relativity to move beyond the concept of fixed background space, so string theory needs to be reformulated as a theory of pure relations. But again, even at this stage, our understanding of the quantum world gives a perspective, not of pointless arbitrariness, but rather of tightly interwoven organisational networks and of the fundamental nature of inter-relations between physical things even at miniscule level.

(e) Facts and values in the human condition

Whilst the macroscopic construction of the universe, the forces of biological evolution, and the nature of the physical world at the subatomic level all reveal strong evidence of purposive operation, human activity has been subjected to a contrary analysis over the last three centuries. Whilst it is difficult to describe human behaviour without recourse to the category of purpose, the breakthrough in the 16th and 17th centuries that gave birth to modern science was only achieved through the methodological elimination of the idea of purpose from the study of physics and astronomy. This technique was successful enough to convert much, perhaps even most, modern thinking to believe that purpose has no place as a category of scientific explanation, including analysis of animal and human behaviour. Even though purpose plainly remains an inescapable element in human life, science has created a mental world where explanation is offered uniquely as the effect of antecedent causes. This abandonment of teleology has produced two of the most striking features of modern Western culture – the dichotomy between the public and private worlds and between the conceptualisation of 'facts' and 'values'[122]. This fissure has led to the search for 'objective' explanation of the human condition in terms of 'value-free facts', as though it were not the case that human beings were not only essentially purpose-driven creatures but also almost universally imbued with a sense of the need for achieving purpose in their lives. Just as it is bizarre for sociology to regard value-free facts as the only really valuable things, so it is illogical to regard the universe as pointless when it contains conscious, creative, sentient beings on Earth (and very likely elsewhere throughout the cosmos) with an overriding sense of ulterior purpose in their lives. The relentless search for cause and effect has increasingly concentrated attention on endlessly smaller sub-systems and micro-systems, but it is at the expense of the loss of appreciation of an organism understood as a whole. It has led to ever-growing specialisation, individualism and fragmentation, to the neglect of necessary focus on the function of the whole. What is missing is the recognition that a complex living organism is so much more than the sum of its parts, and that its integral meaning can only be understood holistically.

Implications

This chapter has pointed up the apparent contradictions in the evidence regarding the crucial issue of teleology in the nature and role of human beings. On the one hand the superfluity of scale in both the extent and duration of the universe, the repeated catastrophic irruptions which several times ended most of existing life on Earth in mass extinctions, and the utterly fortuitous emergence of humanoids after millennia of the most improbable genealogical twists and turns all militate against any idea of the human race as the pre-ordained purpose of the universe. The argument that that is just what it took to reach the human era from the original singularity of Big Bang does not carry conviction. After all, if the end state was part of the design, why have a construction phase at all when an all-powerful Designer could go straight to the finished product at the outset? Equally however does that then mean that there is no teleological end point detectable in the nature and evolution of the universe and life on Earth? The evidence again indicates that this is highly unlikely. The staggering degree of fine-tuned calibration in the fundamental forces and particle masses within the structure of the universe, the extraordinary feedback cycles between animate and inanimate matter that have maintained the Earth in homeostasis, the symbiotic networks that have achieved the growing complexity and multiplication of life forms through cooperative dependence, the discovery that the geometry of space derives from highly interwoven networks at the funda-mental quantum level, and the (obvious, though some would argue, anti-scientific) recognition that human beings are driven by final causes and purposes as well as by mechanical and efficient causes all point towards an all-pervasive operation of purpose within the universe and on Earth.

These contrary positions need to be reconciled; but it will not be easy either logically or intellectually. From the Enlightenment onwards the search for mechanical causation has offered an enormously successful research paradigm for science in general and for biology in particular. The temptation to elevate a successful research paradigm to the level of a complete world-view may be irresistible, but it is also anti-scientific. To deny the reality of our most immediate and universal experience of purpose, because it doesn't fit the research paradigm, is radically anti-empirical. To refuse to recognise the socially destructive logical consequences that flow from the denial of purpose is profoundly anti-rational. Teleology, the causation from higher purpose, of course has its limits, but so does theorising from mechanical and efficient causation alone. Reconciling them is the task of the next chapter.

Chapter 12

The Model's Still Not Right

The shifting understanding of scientific and religious truth

The last chapter made clear that science and religion were very different disciplines, the former based squarely on evidence and the latter drawing rather on experience, though not excluding the necessity for rigorous rational assessment of such experience. Science proceeds from evidence which is publicly accessible, whereas most human experience is not. Scientific tests must be repeatable, while personal experiences are virtually by definition unrepeatable. Scientific investigation advances by seeking out general laws which can then become a basis for prediction, but the significance of personal experience lies in the interpretation put on it for the life and expectations of the person concerned. Scientific knowledge is dispassionate, objective and proceeds by measurement, while personal experience is subjective and cannot be calibrated from one experience to another. And scientific data needs to be described precisely and in detail, but describing accurately the nature of experience is often difficult, if it can be achieved at all.

As a result of these category differences, science is often seen as stable, certain and unchallengeable, whilst religion is sometimes regarded as a matter of individual opinion without any solid corpus of common ideas. The fact is however, there is finality neither in scientific statements nor in religious statements. In the case of science, it isn't so much that Ptolemy's epicycles were replaced as a means of predicting the movement of astronomical bodies by Newton's inverse square law, which was itself replaced by Einstein's theories of special and general relativity – earlier theories being not so much wrong as inade-quate predictors of certain events at the margin – but rather that the wholesale conceptualisation of the cosmos has dramatically changed over the last 400 years and continues still to change. The heliocentric view of the Earth prevailed till Copernicus' observa-tions in 1543, Newton's concept of a static and fixed universe prevailed for 200 years till it was superseded by Hubble's discovery of an expanding universe in 1929, the singularity at the origin of the universe was not hypothesized till the 1920s, the full appreciation of the gargantuan scale of the universe was not achieved till the latter 20th century, and the standard model of physics was only developed in the last 40 years. The dominant role of Ice Ages in the cycles of the Earth's history was not under-stood till the work of Agassiz in the 1840s and the age of the Earth was not realised till radiometric techniques made possible the accurate dating of rocks in the latter 19th century. The view that human beings were created was only replaced after Darwin published his theories of evolution in 1859, and even now there is no certainty about how life originally emerged on the planet. Newtonian mechanics gave way to a much more complicated system after the world of the quantum was uncovered by Max Planck in 1899. Whilst three of the fundamental forces in physics have been recently united in a single theory, the so-called Theory of Everything which would also incorporate gravity still remains elusive and will probably only be achieved after a fundamental realignment of some of today's major concepts.

Religious understanding and experience of God have similarly undergone a long and tortuous history over four millennia of shifting perceptions, from the early pagan deities of the Middle East, the insights of the Axial Age, the Christian and Islamic revelations, the passionate theological disputations within the Church, the rationalism of the Greek and Arab philosophers, the visions of the mystics, the refinements of the reformers and the European Enlightenment, through to 20th century secularization, atheism and the counter-revolution of evangelical fundamentalism. From the Old Testament triumphalism at Joshua's mass slaughter of the Canaanites to the New Testament's God of mercy and compassion, from the early Israelite storm-god YHWH living on top of the 8,000ft volcanic mountain of Sinai to a God embracing all peoples everywhere equally, from an eye-for-an-eye morality (to prevent blood feuds in an honour-killing society getting out of hand) to turning the other cheek to your enemy and forgiving not seven times but seventy times seven, from appeasement by external rituals and sacrifice to an inner morality of love and concern for others – in these ways and so many others the human understanding of God has advanced dramatically over long periods of time. Even the Qur'an containing the Word of God, and the Shariah, have undergone different interpretations over the centuries, from the Sufi influence among others, to fit more modern concepts of justice, morality and culture. The same cultural accommodation has applied to concepts of Christ through the ages: the Christ of the Byzantine mosaics – a super Emperor, the Pantocrat; the Christ of the mediaeval crucifix – a drooping, defeated victim; the Christ of liberal Protestantism – an enlightened, emancipated, successful member of the bourgeoisie; or the Christ of the liberation theologians portrayed in the likeness of Che Guevara[108]. Thus the first conclusion from comparison of science and religion is that neither is complete, and both are engaged in a ceaseless search for deeper understanding respectively of the physical universe and of the spiritual world. Within as little as a further century or two both the scientific and religious landscape may look radically different. For adherents of both science and religion, there is a constant need for each generation to explore anew and accept nothing simply on trust.

Reconciling the scientific and religious evidence

On that basis, and in this generation at this state of our

knowledge, what does the evidence point to towards understanding the role and meaning of the human condition? Several fundamental approaches have been developed, though all remain beset by difficulty.

(i) The mechanistic model

Democritus (460-367BC) first developed the atomist theory whereby a strictly materialistic world could ultimately be analysed as the mechanical activity of elementary particles. Two millennia later the Newtonian paradigm described the behaviour of a macroscopic body as reducible to the motion of its constituent atoms operating in accordance with the mechanistic laws he devised. This reductionist philosophy of breaking down physical systems into their elementary components and deriving the explanation of their behaviour at the lowest level has permeated physics and biology, especially the latter where its influence remains dominant. This concept was given elegant formulation by the French physicist Lagrange (1736-1813) who devised a mathematical procedure for generating dynamical equations to describe systems whether of particles or fields or both. This approach reaches its apogee in the search for a Theory of Everything, the theoretical ambition to unify the forces of nature and provide a complete description of all subatomic particles. Its aim would be to find the ultimate principles that operate at the lowest and simplest levels of physical description, and thus expose the fundamental elements from which the entire universe is built. Indeed the theorist Stephen Hawking concludes his book 'A Brief History of Time' with the words: "If we do discover a complete theory....it would be the ultimate triumph of human reason – for we would then know the mind of God"[123]! The implication was that if the fundamental Lagrangian of all known fields could be uncovered through the methodology known as super-gravity, then theoretical physics would have reached its climax and the world would be totally 'explained'.

However, this approach is seriously flawed by the assumption that a Lagrangian which correctly accounts for all the observed fields and particles constitutes an explanation. Defining a problem away does not explain it. It does not answer how individual atoms, whilst responding in accordance with the strict causal laws of physics only to local forces produced by adjacent atoms, can nevertheless act collectively in an organised and purposeful manner over scales hugely beyond inter-molecular distances. Physical laws cannot explain biological finalism or the teleological activities of living beings. Reductionism does not allow for the fact that at each successive level of complexity occurring in biological systems, new qualities can and often do arise which cannot be understood by processes of sub-division, but only by recognition of the effects of integration. Equally, if it is argued that both animate and inanimate matter are subject to the same physical forces and that therefore living things can be explained in terms of the laws of physics, that is to miss the whole point, namely that there is a crucial distinction between living and non-living systems. Pace Dawkins' 'Selfish Gene', life cannot be reduced to physics. And even within the realm of inanimate matter, non-linear systems can display chaotic and unpredictable behaviour that cannot be understood by breaking it down into component sub-systems and studying each separate piece.

(ii) The creative universe

If reductionism is rejected partly because it revives the now discredited concept of determinism, partly because it is blind to complex organised forms that cannot be derived from lower level laws, and partly because it denies any reality to such important phenomena as the arrow of time, an alternative model that avoids these pitfalls whilst acknowledging the centrality of the emergence of new, more complex, higher-level living forms is the idea of a continuously creative universe. The philosopher

Henri Bergson (1859-1940) postulated that wholly new things arise which are neither dependent on what went before nor constrained by any predetermined goal (since he regarded finalism as merely the inversion of the mechanistic model). The modern philosopher Karl Popper claimed that "the evolution of the universe, and especially the evolution of life on Earth, has produced new things, real novelty....the universe has never ceased to be creative or inventive"[124]. However, this uncaused creativity, which brings into existence things that are different and not necessitated, gives no explanation as to how such higher levels of organisation actually arise. What is it within the universe which produces this inherent progression towards well-ordered complexity, and why should a collection of material substances co-operate, without being prompted by any cause, to produce a novel and unexpected consequence?

One solution to this problem is to predict that there may indeed be an inbuilt tendency in nature for matter and energy to undergo spontaneous transition into new states of higher organisation which are neither dependent on lower level laws nor happen randomly or arbitrarily. The hypothesis is that organisational complexity tends to increase with time, though that presents a major difficulty for neo-Darwinianism which does not contain any means to predict a long-term increase in complexity since random shuffling merely produces haphazard drift with no coherent directionality. Now there is indeed empirical evidence of critical points at which systems move sharply into higher states of greater organisational complexity, and these processes rather than random mutation or natural selection may well determine the course of progressive biological evolution. These critical points occur when open systems are continually forced away from their usual state of dynamic equilibrium. The causal factor may be slow and incremental like the cumulative build-up of oxygen or sudden and violent like an asteroid strike. Either way, evolutionary change would be expected to occur in abrupt jumps (or saltations), and Gould and Eldredge[125] have developed a theory of punctuated equilibria along exactly these lines.

This concept has been taken further by Stuart Kauffman[126] who studied the behaviour of randomly assembled ensembles of cellular automata and found that they can manifest a wide range of emergent properties which he believes may be relevant in explaining biological evolution. He found that sufficiently complex mixes of chemicals can spontaneously crystallize into systems which can collectively catalyze the network of chemical reactions by which the molecules themselves are formed. Such collectively autocatalytic sets sustain themselves and reproduce, like a living metabolism. He thus posits that life is an emergent phenomenon which comes into being as the molecular diversity of a prebiotic chemical system increases beyond a threshold of complexity. On this basis, life is not located in the property of any particular molecule, but rather as the collective property of systems of interacting molecules. Another key implication is that on these premises the emergence of autocatalytic sets is almost inevitable, and hence life is also almost inevitable, snapping into existence as a phase transition. Even more remarkably, since orderly autocatalytic networks need to settle down into small state cycles if their behaviour is to be stable, he also found that with a system like the human genome with 100,000 genes and $10^{30,000}$ states, this colossal network rapidly settles down and cycles among merely the square root of 100,000 states, in fact just 317. This is an extraordinary discovery: in this category of open thermodynamic systems, the dynamics (from wherever they derive) push the system into an infinitesimal miniscule of its state space and keep it there – a staggering achievement of order without apparent cause.

Kauffman hypothesises that these generic self-organised properties may emerge as "biological universals, widespread in organisms not by virtue of selection or shared descent, but by virtue of their membership in a common ensemble of regulatory systems"[127]. It is an example of a local organising principle which arises for mathematical reasons independent of any detailed physical mechanisms involved in producing a particular effect. Similarly the American physicist Mitchell Feigenbaum found that many systems approach chaotic behaviour through period doubling, and that the transition to chaos in many cases displays certain universal features irrespective of the precise details of the system. Equally, Wolfram's studies of simple automata provide some expectation that new universal principles of order may be uncovered which may operate in much more complex natural systems[128]. Such logical principles will be developed further by the study of fractals, games theory, network theory, and catastrophe theory. In addition the concept of dissipative structures (i.e. those where a system is driven away from thermal equilibrium by external constraints that have exceeded certain critical values), as championed by the Italian chemist Ilya Prigogine, crucially explains how systems open to the environment can evade the degenerative effects of the second law of thermodynamics. Whilst the traditional techniques of physics and chemistry are applied to closed systems near to equilibrium, an open dissipative structure exports its entropy (or decline in the system's energy to do work) to its environment. This unravels the paradox that the universe should be dying because of the pressure exerted by the second law, yet seems continually capable of increasing its level of organisation and complexity.

However, the science of self-organisation is still in its infancy. It is given force, not only by the empirical work already described, but also by the recognition that existing physical laws cannot explain the high degree of organisational potency found in nature. But that then raises the question whether these new organising principles should be bolted on to the existing laws of physics, or whether the latter need to be re-written in some way. This can be explored at all different levels. At the cosmological level, the fact that matter and energy erupting from Big Bang in such a titanic explosion arranged itself with such incredible uniformity, as revealed by the extraordinary large-scale regularity of the cosmos, has been addressed either by the so-called cosmological principle (which is merely a statement, not an explanation), or by appealing to a special set of initial conditions (which simply transfers the problem to a metaphysics beyond science), or by the inflation scenario posited in the first second of the universe's existence (which also requires certain special conditions to operate). None of these 'explanations' is therefore satisfactory. Equally, the origin of the relatively small-scale irregularities that brought the stars and galaxies into being is unclear without questionable add-ons to the standard model. Might the same cosmological organising principles, if such exist, account for both these phenomena? At the level of the microscopic laws of physics, Prigogine has proposed that non-equilibrium is the source of order and that the basic level of physics is formed by non-equilibrium ensembles which are less well determined than wave functions and evolve in a manner to increase this indeterminism[129]. The physicist David Bohm has posited that while evolution mostly proceeds randomly, there are transitional periods of fast, non-random change in which mutations occur rapidly and are strongly directional in some ordered fashion – a process that could be continued indefinitely over long periods of time to produce an ever-developing hierarchy of higher orders of structure and function[130].

A more radical reformulation of the principles of causality has been proposed by the biologist Robert Rosen. He argues that so far from simple systems representing the norm so that complex systems should be seen as special-case extensions of the norm, the truth is actually the reverse in that the vast majority of dynamical systems found in the real world belong to the unpredictable class of chaotic phenomena, while the simple dynamical systems in physics textbooks actually form an extremely restricted class. He points out that a set of quantities describing the rates of change of different aspects of a complex system cannot be combined in a way that warrants the latter very special description[131]. This upturns the whole concept of causality which has prevailed for the last three centuries in relativistic and quantum mechanics and also in field theory and thermodynamics. In the latter case it confirms Prigogine's thesis that the textbook near-to-equilibrium closed systems are highly specialised idealizations, very different from the far-from-equilibrium open systems found overwhelmingly in nature. Rosen even doubts whether simple systems exist at all since if complex systems are those that can only be described by 'a web of informational interactions', that characterisation might seem to apply almost universally. The implications of all this are very radical indeed since it opens up again the Aristotelian set of differential causation including the concept of final causes which is absolutely forbidden within the class of simple systems. He even hypothesises that complex systems may contain subsystems which can act as predictors of future behaviour and thus be used to modulate the current change of state. Such ideas have been taken yet further by the biologist Rupert Sheldrake who reintroduces teleology in direct form by positing the idea in developmental biology of what he calls morphogenetic fields, namely fields which store information that guides the development of an organism towards its final form [132]. Whether or not these ideas survive systematic scrutiny, they still demonstrate that, despite the enormous advances in fundamental science, many (or even most) phenomena within the natural world still seem to require the invoking of some explanatory higher principle.

The resurgence of holism implied in the research and interpretative work of the last thirty years opens up a very different picture of the universe. The Newtonian paradigm viewed the universe as a clockwork machine, with deterministic forces operating irreversibly along a predetermined path to an inescapable fate. The thermodynamic paradigm, pioneered by the nineteenth century kinetic theory of gases developed by James Clark Maxwell in Britain and Ludwig Boltzmann in Austria, postulated a universe that started in high disorder and then decays. The self-organisation paradigm of a creative universe, by contrast, is built around the premise that collective and holistic properties in physical systems can generate new and unpredictable behaviour. This pattern has not only been demonstrated in physics and chemistry, but in astronomy, geology, biology, computing, and throughout the range of science. These emergent properties, which could never be generated at a lower atomic level, could only arise – most dramatically in the form of life or consciousness – when matter and energy reach higher, more complex states. But this still leaves open several unanswered questions. Do these higher-level qualities require higher-level laws to explain them? Some scientists have postulated biotonic laws for this purpose in organic systems[133], while dialectical materialism also holds that each new level in the development of matter generates its own laws which are not reducible to those at lower levels. But if there are such laws, what exactly is their nature, and from whence did they derive? Or do these organising principles flow from the special initial conditions of the universe – despite all recent attempts to avoid dragging in this metaphysical element by positing the alternative devices of inflation (Guth), a physical principle not yet identified (Penrose), or a mathematically prescribed wave function of the universe (Hawking and Hartle)? Whatever the origin of these cosmic organising principles, what is the balance entailed between predisposition (not the same as determinism) and choice, and how is this defined? Again, since it turns out that the constants of physics are peculiarly conducive to the eventual emergence of complex structures, and particularly living organisms, do the constants determine these structures or simply encourage them, and if the latter, what is the precise mechanism? What choices remain in play during the subsequent evolution of the universe, not just at the critical points of a singularity where new principles can readily arise? There are not yet definitive answers on these points, but what is perhaps most intriguing about this new developing paradigm of modern physics is the idea of a cosmic blueprint – "a pre-existing plan or project which the universe is realizing as it develops", as the theoretical physicist Paul Davies describes it[134], a revival of Aristotle's teleological concept of the universe.

The religious model

Although Paul Davies eschews resort to mystical or transcendent considerations, it is remarkable that a very similar approach has been taken in recent theological thinking. Keith Ward writes:

> ...the universe is a value-realizing emergent totality; within that totality human persons have their proper role to play in realizing such values. The urge to seek truth is not a meaningless by-product of a mechanistic process. It is an intuition of the inner tendency of the whole physical system of the cosmos to move towards the realization of conscious value, self-knowledge and self-direction. Seen in that light, religion become the quest for the meaning and purpose of the whole cosmic process, and for the role we can play within it"[135].

Though Davies would regard any idea of ultimate human purpose as beyond the scope of science, the compatibility of the physicist's creative universe paradigm with the theologian's value-realizing emergent universe is striking.

Just as science has moved over the last 300 years from the Newtonian model to the thermodynamic paradigm and now towards the holistic and creative concept of cosmological organising principles, so religion has moved over a vastly longer period from the localised tribal religions and imaginary cosmogonies, through the founding of the great scriptural traditions and the codification of revelation, to a third stage embracing a global vision, a convergent spirituality and what might be described as a Socratic faith. Ever since Galileo (1564-1642) the Western Christian Church has been forced by scientific discovery to narrow its cosmic perspective. Not only was the Earth not the centre of the universe, but its status as a tiny planet revolving round one star amongst perhaps 200 billion stars in a single galaxy among some 100,000 billion galaxies was the death-blow to anthropocentrism. Then in the miniscule portion left allotted to humans, Newtonian mechanical materialism seemed, while elevating God as the creator of a profoundly well-ordered mathematical universe, to exclude any room for God to operate in human affairs because the machine model of the physical world ruled that out. God then became superfluous except as the inventor to start the whole machine going. The final apparent coup-de-grace was supplied by Darwin's discovery that man was a descendant from the ape line and that complex organisms like hominids had evolved by chance through the accidental mutation of nucleic acids. If random mutation operated without any purposive direction at all, then any idea that God purposefully created human beings and valued them as the culmination of the divine order completely collapsed.

The religious model was thus challenged on two fronts – whether there was purpose and design in nature, and whether physics offered a complete explanation of the reality which rendered God irrelevant. However, that seemed to invoke a paradox: how can Newtonian science produce a picture of the world driven by blind and purposeless mechanical laws when mechanism implies design, and design implies purpose? Equally it seems odd (though not logically inconsistent) that a random and purposeless universe should come to be inhabited by living beings who are conscious, rational, inquiring and purposive. It is even odder that an insightful and imaginative mathematical genius like Newton should produce a world perspective which denies the consciousness, rationality, freedom and imagination of which he was himself so brilliant an example. It is this bifurcation between experimentally verifiable fact on the one hand and consciousness, feeling and value on the other – the negative legacy of Newtonian mechanics, the dehumanization which sees humans as mere parts of an impersonal machine – which has brought about the instrumentalist view of the physical world, that it is there to be exploited for human use. The concept that God created the world, and that human beings were stewards of the Earth holding it in trust – a view strongly held by ancient tribes and still maintained by many today – was effectively buried. This irreligious outlook towards the natural order then opened the way to the technological imperative and the subjection of the environment, and ultimately now to the dominance of a consumerism driven only by calculations of profit and utility.

The new 20th century physics however, with its more open, probabilistic, indeterminate, holistic picture of the universe, offered a very different world-view from the machine predictability which ejected purpose and value from nature. Humans can be seen, not as cogs within a determinist framework, but as symbols of emerging responsibility, creativity, insight and self-control within an emergent world process. God is no longer understood as the all-powerful nationalistic warrior of the ancient religions or even the watch-maker of 18th century theology, but as an empowering ideal where revelations of divine nature and purpose caught within religious experience provide a glimpse of a goal and cosmic ideal which empower efforts to achieve it. Newtonian and Neo-Darwinian materialism which sought to explain the complex in terms of the ultimate individual part is superseded by the new physics which shows that, on the contrary, the part can only be explained in terms of the whole, the process in terms of its goal, and the simplicity of underlying laws in terms of the complex ends they generate. The implications of this emergent view for religion are very great. It is a breakthrough in understanding that religious truth is no longer confined to past revelations which inspired seers and prophets in some past age, but is drawn towards an ultimate goal in the future towards which all things move. As Keith Ward notes, this insight has been incorporated into the Indian Hindu tradition by Aurobindo and into the Western Christian tradition by Teilhard de Chardin. It means that religious perspectives are no longer unyielding defences of past unrevisable truth, but can be perpetually renewed and can interact fruitfully with insights in other faiths.

The religious model has also been radically transformed by the discovery of aeons of biological evolution over some 4,000 millennia. Not only must the biblical stories of Genesis (with parallels in some of the Eastern cosmogonies) surrounding the creation of Man be seen for what they are – parables with a spiritual meaning put together in 8th century BCE Palestine, not a literal truth – but the advent of the human species itself has now to be viewed in a very different light. Just as the biological model of the smooth, linear, upward ascent of Man from the apes is now seen to be a pure anthropomorphic conceit, so the idea of Man as the final, climactic culmination of the entire evolutionary saga has to be abandoned. The incomprehensibly colossal dimensions of the universe, the inexplicably vast delay before the appearance of humans after more than 13.5 billion years had elapsed, and the massive unlikelihood of the emergence of humans at all after an exceedingly fortuitous and improbable chain of evolution amid repeated mass extinctions, all signify a very different picture from the steady growth of spirituality leading up to man at the apogee as the master of creation. Furthermore, the systematic scientific unravelling of the detailed composition and inherent laws of the physical universe raises unanswered questions about the role and nature of divine creativity. If explanation of the physical order does not require supernatural intervention, is God's role confined to the first moment of creation, which is anyway rather a slippery concept? What is the mechanism by which a non-material spirituality impacts on the material world? Does God represent an immanent presence within a created order of fantastic complexity, or transcendence with no interplay with the physical realm? If there are cosmic organising principles underpinning the evolution of the universe, what relation, if any, does God have to these fundamental formative influences? It is not enough that strict adherence to the pre-scientific beliefs of the world's scriptures is superseded. Religion will only achieve the new potential vision that scientific discovery has opened up when it fully and consciously embraces the new insights of the post-scriptural age.

Implications
Both the scientific and religious paradigms have undergone huge change over previous centuries, and will no doubt continue to do so in future. Any idea of comprehensive and conclusive finality in either sphere is chimerical, so that theories and doctrines in any generation (including this one) should be treated with considerable caution. It is very likely that both the religious and scientific landscape will look significantly, even radically, different from now. New discoveries, re-interpretation of the existing evidence, and constructions of profoundly new paradigms will continue unabated. It isn't that the fundamental reality is necessarily changing (though at the quantum level the material world is in constant flux), but rather that our scientific and spiritual understanding of that reality is continually altering and deepening. The traditional religions, which have always relied on ultimate authority and even infallibility, are seriously challenged by the modern rise of critical consciousness and the

insistence that no truth be accepted without question and analysis. A religion that clings to outdated dogma, which reflected the thinking, customs and mores of a long defunct society, will lose its dynamism because of its perceived irrelevance. The key spiritual dimension in human society will only survive if its fundamental truths are wholly renewed in a manner intelligible and inspirational within the cultural patterns, intellectual thinking and scientific understanding of each successive generation.

Attempts at reconciliation of the scientific and religious world-views remain problematic. Each of the main paradigms provide powerful explanations at different levels of reality, but are found to be flawed if pressed as universal principles. Reductionist materialism does not account for emergent complex structures, non-local connections in the quantum world, biological finalism, or non-linear chaotic systems. The more recent concept of a creative universe, reflecting a constant in-built spontaneous transition to higher complex states driven by underlying cosmological organising principles, opens up a holistic and teleological understanding of reality, though the derivation of such organisational forces remains unclear. Whilst it would be tempting but unwise for the religious model to seize on these latest postulates as evidence of overriding divine intervention guiding the cosmos (the latest example of the 'God of the Gaps' fallacy), it is still very striking how closely the thinking of some physicists and some theologians have converged on the idea of a cosmic blueprint which the universe is self-realising as it develops. Crucially this new emergent view of religion is no longer backward-looking to the ancient revelation of the ideal, but drawn towards a future higher-level goal in the light of which fundamental religious insights can be perpetually renewed and reinvigorated. But this requires a profound re-formulation of the religious concept of Man and it leaves many key questions unanswered. The next chapter will seek to bind together these latest scientific, religious and philosophical developments into a new coherent, integrated whole.

Chapter 13

Who Then Are We?

A New Theory
So what is this long complex saga of the history of the universe and its living beings actually telling us? This chapter selects the dominant themes which characterise the nature of the development of reality in order to draw together within a coherent framework the key dimensions of existence as they are so far understood. It ends by exploring the likely future of the human race and Humanity's place within the universe.

(a) The universe is designed
The arguments against an infinite 'steady state' universe without beginning or end, a finite universe without a beginning, a universe originating either by chance or by necessity, and a universe arising ex nihilo out of a quantum fluctuation are set out above. The prevailing standard model of physics posits the universe as originating from a singularity, but the model is so dependent on a whole set of adjustable parameters retrospectively fitted to align the theory to observations that alternative theories have been postulated which dispense with these hypothetical constructs and thus with the Big Bang scenario itself, including a plasma cosmology and a modified Newtonian dynamics (relativistic MOND). There can be little doubt that theories of the origin of the universe have still to undergo substantial revision. But whatever further conclusions are reached about the precise process of the universe's birth, or of that of pre-existing versions in a genealogical reductio ad infinitum of past universes, there still inevitably remains the question of what agency beyond time and space set off the whole

process in the first place. This supernatural agency is conventionally given the name 'God', the uncaused cause, but the semantics is in reality a philosophical device to describe the indescribable and the utterly unknowable. A metaphysical causal entity does not readily equate with the personalised loving God of the world's great religions.

What however is clearly known, and requires explanation, is the 'Goldilocks' nature (neither too much, nor too little, but just right) of this current universe. The fine-tuning to a staggering degree of all its central components – the almost incredible balancing between the original centrifugal and centripetal forces at Big Bang, the particle masses, the force strengths, the fundamental constants, all interacting with mind-boggling precision to produce a universe conducive to life – has been addressed in various ways. One is to cite the anthropic principle as the physicist Steven Weinberg did in 1987, when he argued that we shouldn't be surprised to find ourselves in such an unlikely place because it is only here that life could exist. But that is a statement of fact, not an explanation. Another approach is to regard it as a lucky accident. But Penrose has dismissed this as virtually inconceivable since, without initial conditions guaranteeing a smooth beginning (which would itself require further explanation), the accuracy required for selecting this extremely highly ordered universe from the range of physically possible ones would be of the order of one part in 10^{123} (i.e. a chance of one in 100000000000000000000000000000000000000000000000000000000000 000000000000000000000000000000000000000000000000000000000000 0000000000)! Yet another approach has been to hypothesise the existence of a vast ensemble of universes, perhaps almost infinite in number, whether contemporaneously or serially, within which it is surmised will in the end be found a universe which demonstrates the special physical laws for life. The arguments against this however are conclusive. Firstly, this is a purely speculative construct for which there is no independent empirical evidence at all. Secondly, the number of universes needed to satisfy all the conditions of such an exceptionally fine-tuned universe rises exponentially to mega-astronomic levels (i.e. this theory is merely a variant of the fortuitousness model rejected above). And thirdly, all the proposals made to explain how such a colossal, almost infinite, array of universes ever came into existence are forced either to introduce even more extreme metaphysical appendages or to fall back on ultimate premises which require the very same degree of exquisite fine-tuning that their hypotheses are designed to avoid. Even Smolin's ingenious proposal of cosmological natural selection, whereby successive universes over aeons of time randomly try out large sets of parameters until a highly improbable set with fantastically extreme values is finally generated, does not escape the counter-arguments just deployed against multiverse theory.

The only other explanation for a universe so exceptionally fine-tuned with such incredible precision as to be conducive to life seems to be that it was designed for this purpose. This runs contrary to the whole thrust of scientific inquiry since the Enlightenment 300 years ago which has consistently sought to explain reality in a manner which avoids any hint of super-natural agency and has focused on efficient causation to the exclusion of any teleological basis to the laws of physics. However, even an agnostic scientist with the reputation of Fred Hoyle has felt obliged to conclude that it appears that "the laws of nuclear physics have been deliberately designed with regard to the consequences they produce inside the stars" and hence ultimately the creation of life. Nevertheless there are clear caveats to be drawn. First, there are many instances in the history of science where a gap in explanation is attributed to super-natural intervention (the notorious 'God of the Gaps'), only to be superseded later by new empirical evidence or revised scientific theorising which adequately fills the gap. In this case, however, the category of explanation is of an entirely different order – not supplying new data, but providing a structural or conceptual overview of the entire process of universe creation which, given the huge set of extraordinary improbabilities of breathtaking precision on which it is based, is highly unlikely to be superseded. Second, there is no automatic read-across from a designed universe to a designer God, at least in the conventional religious sense. Some philosophers have posited an abstract Neoplatonist divine creative principle (though this concept remains obscure), while some modern theoretical physicists have perceived the operation of certain cosmological organising principles. At the very least, the link between the cosmological generation of the universe (or universes) and the personal, loving message of the God-revealing messiah or prophet figures of the great religions remains uncertain. Third, there is no inconsistency between the design of the current universe and the idea of multiple universes. If the present universe did indeed originate from a singularity and if, as is widely believed, the counterpart to a singularity is the implosion of a massive dying star into a black hole from another universe, there may well exist a number of other universes outside our own (though it is likely that a very high proportion of them collapsed shortly after they were generated).

(b) The paradox of design: the free play of natural forces

A designed universe does not imply that its operation is deterministic. Indeed the saga of the universe strongly suggests that one of its key characteristics is that it is designed to allow maximum variation in both atmospheric and terrestrial ecologies and in an immense range of life forms. There are several trends that illustrate this. First, within an underlying framework of order, chance and unpredictability still play a central role in evolution at all levels. Though its underlying forces and particle masses were seemingly engineered with phenomenal precision to create the conditions for the emergence of life, the dynamism of the cosmos is still driven by a continuing cataclysmic violence of destruction (and consequential recycling) at all levels, the effects and long-term impacts of which are unforeseeable and chaotic. At the cosmic level, the enormous supernova explosion of super-massive stars in their death throes, the swallowing of everything and even major stars within large regions of space within black holes, the colossal release of energy across the universe in gamma-ray bursts, and the ripping apart of whole galaxies in collision reconstruct the fabric and composition of the universe unpredictably with unimaginable violence. In the solar system alone, the minutest speck within the universe, massive bombard-ments from space by asteroids, comets or other planets especially about four billion years ago have wrought catastrophic havoc rendering the Earth inhospitable to life for 200,000 millennia or more. And extreme environmental conditions have brought about at least ten mass extinctions on Earth in the last billion years. There is clearly no settled preconceived plan either for the cosmos or for its smallest elements. Rather it is an endless cycle of renewal by violence of the most intense ferocity, though not all the violence was negative in its effects. Most notably, within some 100 million years after the solar system was formed, a huge asteroid the size of Mars crashed into the Earth at about 25,000 mph, creating an explosion fifty thousand trillion times more violent than the Hiroshima bomb, and then bounced back into space and gradually evolved as Earth's only moon. This turned out to be a critical condition for intelligent life on Earth for several reasons. The lunar gravity held the Earth's axial tilt between 22º and 25º, thus modulating the climate; it slowed the Earth's rotation, thus preventing terrestrial winds of 200 mph or more; and the lunar tidal drag was also a key factor in producing Earth's very powerful magnetic field which protects its surface from lethal cosmic rays from space[137].

Another illustration of the free, undirected play of natural forces given full rein lies in the indiscriminate explosion of life forms in Earth's history. The weird animals found in the Middle

Cambrian Burgess Shale in Canada dating from 520 million years ago, and so painstakingly analysed by Stephen Jay Gould – creatures as bizarre as Opabinia, Wiwaxia, Laggania and Anomalocaris – reveal Nature's unfettered experimentation with life forms in the extreme conditions of that period. After each mass extinction the abandonment of habitats by devastated species opened up environmental niches for Nature to explore wholly new varieties of life forms, and these reveal no overall long-term plan of development, but rather short-term expedients to exploit new ecosystem opportunities driven by continental drift, huge volcanic eruptions, enormous swings in sea levels, and climactic change, then further winnowed over time by natural selection. There is no smooth upward path of progress from micro-organisms to large creatures and ultimately to humans, rather the reverse – virtual immobile stasis in biota for tens of millions of years, abruptly halted by catastrophes of overwhelming violence (the 'punctuated equilibrium' theory of Gould and Eldredge), often disrupting whatever progressive advances may be detectable. The elimination in the cataclysm sixty-five million years ago of the dinosaur specimen, Stenonychosaurus, which appeared headed towards human-like intelligence and manoeuvrability, illustrates this well. Even within those constraints, life would still not have proceeded even from its simplest forms without a whole series of unpredictable environmental conditions being satisfied, most notably the development of photosynthesis, an enormous increase in oxygen levels, an increase in nitrogen as an ocean nutrient, and the evolution from prokaryotic to eukaryotic cells. And at later stages of evolution, the line of development is haphazard, oscillating forwards and backwards, non-directional. Proto-mammals, the ancestors of humans, which dominated the world for twenty million years till struck down by the mega-catastrophe at the end of the Permian era 251 million years ago, only just recovered, but then lost out to their semi-reptilian competitors which were themselves replaced some 215 million year ago by the dinosaurs, confining the surviving mammals to eke out an existence by evolving into small, mouse-like creatures not meriting the attention of dinosaur predators, and only able to emerge again when the dinosaur ascendancy was destroyed 150 million years later. The line from the early mammal Probainognathus through Kuehneotherid, the ancestor of all mammals alive today, and thence ultimately to humans was precarious in the extreme. So far from being the chosen goal, humans were only reached as the perilously threatened twig at the end of a branch leading to many boughs in a once luxuriant tree where over 99% of the species that have once lived have now died. Chance and unpredictable contingency has played a dominant role throughout.

All this still probably substantially under-states the degree to which the universe has generated an endless cascade of life forms in almost unimaginable profusion. A third dimension of life's prolificity, experimenting with every design, shape and size with almost reckless abandon ('let a million flowers bloom'), may well be discoverable on planets currently beyond our reach across the universe. Astronomers calculate that there may be as many as 10^{20} planets suitable for life forms of one kind or another, and since the components of organic life are already seen almost everywhere we look in the universe, the chances are that many of these 100,000,000,000,000,000,000 planets actually are carriers of some kind of life. It would be foolish to suppose, as science fiction sometimes does, that it necessarily in any way resembles humans or indeed any other creatures currently on Earth, since the environmental conditions on other planets and moons are known in many cases to be vastly different from Earth's. Even in the case of the single nearest planet, Mars, it is known that the gravitational tug of Jupiter pulls it right over on its side roughly every ten million years[136], producing a distinctly different ecological history and hence the likelihood of quite different life forms. Although the nearest star is over twenty-two trillion miles from Earth, dozens of planets circling stars have already been identified, and if significant unexpected differences were found in their geological or climactic history, their life forms (where they exist) could well be extremely diverse and unusual. This view might be seen as reinforced further when string theory suggests that our universe could be just one of 10^{500} variants, i.e. the potential for variation between universes or between unexplored regions in this universe is almost infinite.

(c) The universe is not purposeless

The universe is therefore designed yet, paradoxically, displays no apparent plan determining its evolution. The Earth's history is pitted with an irregular series of gargantuan upheavals which episodically utterly transform the ecological landscape and its life forms, reflecting no detectable logical pattern but rather the unfettered operation of blind chance and unpredictability. Moreover, there is no reason to doubt that the free play of natural forces, sometimes awesome in their magnitude, has had similar impacts on planetary systems throughout the universe. But, again paradoxically, this does not mean that the universe is purposeless or meaningless. On the contrary, it displays a deep level of self-organisation and order at almost every scale.

There is strong evidence of a natural process whereby at certain thresholds of growing complexity matter and energy are spontaneously transposed into new higher organisational states which are not derived from lower level laws. This happens particularly where open systems are continually forced away from their usual equilibrium state (Prigogine's dissipative structures, found ubiquitously in nature). It is sharply discrepant from neo-Darwinian theory which does not predict increased complexity but only gene reshuffling on the basis of blind and directionless chance. The evidence for these transitions to a qualitatively different order of organisation have been drawn both from biological and cosmological systems and has even been cited as an explanation for the origin of life itself. Thus Stuart Kauffman has hypothesised that a chemical mix of sufficient complexity can collectively catalyze the framework of chemical reactions to form molecules which are then capable of reproduction. Life is then vested, not in any molecular property, but in the relational network of molecules interacting with each other beyond a certain complex level. Kauffman has also postulated that these generic self-organised properties may be a biological universal, and that these new principles of order may operate widely in natural systems at varying degrees of complexity. He found that highly complex open thermodynamic systems with a colossal number of potential states, like the human genome, quickly settle down within the tiniest miniscule of its state space – a very significant discovery since that is a necessary condition for their operational stability. And there is evidence that this applies at the cosmological level too. Smolin has concluded that "there can be no doubt that the system of a spiral galaxy is characterised by autocatalytic cycles of energy and material, of the same general kind that underlie the ecology of the biosphere"[138]. Yet another facet of inbuilt self-organising principles which produce progression towards well-ordered complexity lies in Simon Conway Morris' elucidation of convergence in biological systems. He notes hundreds of examples of multiple paths leading to similar functional outcomes, of parallel evolution whereby different species when confronted by similar environmental challenges on different continents adapt in the same (optimal) way, and of the variety of paths leading towards intelligence. The potential development of the humanoid-like dinosaur towards human characteristics was stymied by mass extinction, but through other distorted routes human intelligence was still achieved forty million years later.

Other mechanisms indicating the operation of purposeful dynamics within nature include the Gaian thesis of the biosphere as an adaptive control system holding the Earth within equilibrium. It posits a variety of feedback loops at global level, including between living creatures and the non-living environment, which have kept the Earth habitable in the face of shocks and disturbances both from outer space and internally from within the Earth's biosphere itself. In addition, the symbiotic network theory advanced by Margulis and Lovelock argues that the growing complexity of life forms is driven, less by Darwinian selection operating blindly by mutations, than by systematic co-operation and strong mutual dependence. Perhaps the most striking example is one of the first in the history of the Earth when prokaryotes, cells without a nucleus, achieved the staggering feat three billion years ago of inventing all the key miniaturised chemical systems controlling life – an accomplishment that has never been equalled since and which natural selection could scarcely ever have brought about. A key aspect of this achievement is that symbiosis enabled all the world's bacteria potentially to have access to each others' genes and thus to the adaptive mechanisms of the whole bacterial domain. This cross-communicating and mutually co-operating global network of bacteria propelled the biosphere towards fertility, steadily providing a habitat for larger life forms. And by systematically creating organisms whose parts were permutations of all possible bacterial components, symbiotic alliances pushed evolving creatures into new and higher levels of complexity.

Our understanding of these underlying strategic organising principles and the forces driving them, leading endlessly towards new patterns of complexity and hence to novel emergent properties, is in its infancy. There are good reasons for rejecting a mechanistic model of the universe (paras. 12.5-12.7), but a relational, as opposed to reductionist, view of the universe is still only fragmentarily understood. The phenomenon of quantum entanglement (para. 11.19), for example – whereby subatomic particles which interact locally and then move enormous distances across the universe must still be treated as an indivisible whole because measurement of one will still partly depend on the state of the other and information about either will lie only in their joint properties – bizarrely appears to be distorting the laws of cause and effect. Even weirder are recent experiments which seem to show that moments of time can themselves become entangled so that measuring a photon polarisation again affects the earlier polarisation. But whatever the full explanation, which may be opening up as profound a rewriting of the laws of classical physics as Planck's original discovery of the quantum in 1899, it strongly indicates a model of the universe which is subjective, holistic and purposeful rather than analytic, reductionist and arbitrary. Just as Margulis' theory of a worldwide symbiotic network opened up a new biological paradigm which is collective, co-operative, and innovative, implying underlying purpose, so the fuller understanding of quantum geometry – especially if string theory were reformulated in terms of pure relations – may present a picture of the universe which is not as pointlessly capricious, but driven by tightly interwoven organisational networks with some inbuilt sense of purpose. In the biological sphere Rosen has postulated that complex systems, defined as a web of informational interactions, may contain mechanisms to anticipate future behaviour and thus to moderate their change of state, while Sheldrake (para. 12.13) has even hypothesized that such information stores (which he calls morphogenetic fields) may guide the organism towards its final form – a full-blown re-introduction after two millennia of Aristotelian teleology.

(d) But God cannot be left out of the equation

That then raises the obvious question: does this re-discovery of final causes, self-organisation and holistic properties in astronomy, biology, computing (as illustrated by Poundstone's study of recursion in mathematics, physics and self-reproduction[139] and elsewhere in science imply that organising principles underpinning the operation of the natural world are governed by higher-level laws, and if so, what are they, and from whence do they come? Do they derive from the special initial conditions of the universe, a sort of overarching blueprint that the universe brings into reality as it develops, or from God (which some might see as another, more personalised way of expressing the same abstract proposition)? It is tempting to reach such a metaphysical conclusion, but it should be firmly resisted. At the overall systemic level there are two critical areas where science has (as yet) achieved no adequate explanation. One concerns the origin of the universe – not the character and conditions of the initial singularity (though even that remains disputed), nor an alternative interpretation if the inconsistencies in the Big Bang theory cannot be resolved or the standard model of particle physics is superseded, but rather the question of what caused the original singularity in the first place and why there is a universe at all. These matters lie outside the purview of science, but they are not inadmissible questions. Equally, the nature and derivation of the universe's organising principles as delineated, both at the macroscopic cosmological level and the microscopic sub-atomic level, remain obscure, at this point at least. On the other hand, to apply a semantic label of God to resolve these problems is less an explanation than an admission (as with similar attributions of the anthropic principle) that no proper explanation exists. God is not a concept conveniently invented to solve scientific puzzles.

This is not to suggest that the invocation of God (if God exists) in this context is necessarily irrelevant. God's existence is predicated, not on scientific evidence (on that basis it is wholly unprovable), but solely on revelation and personal non-scientific (i.e. spiritual) experience. Apart from that, God is systematically unknowable. The record of revelation and personal experience of God contains no authoritative reference to God's role as architect, designer, creator of the universe other than the attribution that a

Being shown in revelation to be so extraordinarily far beyond human comprehension in omnipotence and omniscience must possess these overriding capabilities. To make such a claim therefore that God created the universe is not a scientific statement, but rather an acknowledgement of God's supremacy and transcendence based on overwhelming personal experience. That is not to say that it is wrong, rather that it is the elision of two entirely different concepts. Just as Cartesian dualism posited the separateness of mind and body, though they remain intimately intermingled, so science and religion are quite separate modalities of human experience, even though they are both valid interpretations of the same indivisible reality and for that reason must be in some sense ultimately reconcilable. But to subject statements drawn from one paradigm of experience to the tests of validation of the other (as many scientists propounding atheism have done in the present fashionably anti-religious intellectual culture) is simply to make a category mistake.

It does however raise the question, if religious statements cannot be judged by scientific criteria and cannot conveniently infill gaps in scientific knowledge, then what fundamental validity do they have at all? That depends on the assessment of the revelation of the founders and prophets of the world's great religions, the witness of the most profound mystics (especially Spanish, German and English from C14-16th Europe), the almost universal sense of overawing numinous power in human society, and above all the authenticity of deeply-felt personal experience whether sudden and overwhelming (as par excellence in the case of St. Paul) or, much more commonly, through contemplation and insight into the deeper meaning of events in ordinary lives. Revelation never offered direct access to divine reality – Jesus never claimed to be God, Muhammad acted as messenger for the transmission of the dense and mesmerising power of the Qur'an, and Buddha taught abandonment of the concept of self to transcend the selfishness of the ego rather than any concept of God. But in the case of Christianity, Jesus' intense awareness of God as depicted in the Gospels, the disciples' transformation from fearful despair to life-risking proclamation at Pentecost, and the post-crucifixion revelations of the resurrected Jesus are powerful, though indirect, evidence of the religious reality, whilst in the case of Islam, Muhammad's overwhelming experience of God palpably pervades the whole Qur'an. And all the world's religions, from their Axial roots onward, unite in jointly sharing the centrality of divine love as the message at the heart of all of them.

The witness of the mystics is shrouded in indescribable experience incommunicable in human language, but the mystical tradition has powerfully suffused all the great religions for the last three millennia from the avatars of Hinduism and Buddhism, kenosis (the self-emptying ecstasy of God) prominent in Judaism and Islam, to the late flowering in Christian northern Europe. Nor were the great mystics over-emotional visionaries given to hypnoid states of ecstasy, but intensely practical and energetic organisers and reformers. Yet the mystics' experience of God is bewildering. They encountered, not an objective reality at all, but, variously, transcendental union and an incomparable transport of joy, a vast and profound solitude, darkness and no-thing-ness, and an overwhelming and terrifying holiness. None of this can be externally verified, though those who have experi-enced it vehemently attest to its certitude, not only in mediaeval Europe but in contemporary society including such penetrating rationalists as Jung. Yet all such affirmations should be questioned, and only those that pass the highest bar of spiritual reality – that such experiences are utterly life-transforming – deserve to be accepted. But subject to that stricture those cases, few or otherwise, must be enough on any objective balancing of the evidence to be judged to be opening up at least a glimpse of an inaccessible and ineffable spiritual reality. There is no other route: there is no authority for God's existence outside the inward conviction born of personal experience, mystical or meditative.

But that route cannot be ignored. It reveals an existential reality as profound and meaningful, indeed much more so, than human love or artistic sensibility, though these equally cannot be proven, only understood in the fullness of experience. Its power has prevailed throughout recorded history, though its impact has continually fluctuated in the face of political, social and cultural forces. On these grounds its influence in the West over the last half-century has waned against a background of scientific reductionist materialism combined with rampant consumerism. As so often before, such pressures have begun to seed a strong countervailing reaction, whether in the rise of militant fundamentalism (both in Christianity, Islam and Judaism) or in a revival of evangelical and eschatological sects, as well as more pervasively in a nagging disenchantment with an unsatisfying acquisitiveness, weakened moral order and sense of loss of ultimate meaning in their lives. It is also true that whilst religious observance has reduced in the West – though it is growing in much of the Southern world – surveys have shown that this is not because people's belief in God (however that is articulated) has declined, but partly because the predominance of the current mechanistic model in science has undermined credence in any other experience than that which can be communicated by the five senses, partly because religion is perceived too often to be associated with intolerance and suppression in religious wars and persecution, and partly because the message of the Churches is seen to be based too much on past revelation and not sufficiently attuned to a modern globalised, high tech, internet world. This is a serious critique of the current religious order which deserves to be comprehensively addressed, by challenging the narrow exclusiveness of the current scientific paradigm, by focussing more determinedly on relieving poverty and deprivation wherever it is found and contesting the political domination that generates it, and by adopting a much more forward-looking message that resonates in today's world and embraces a wider ecumenism – if the Christian message were being composed today, it would be radically different from the Nicene creed which addressed internal church disputes of the 4th and 5th centuries CE. It is indeed noteworthy that the critique centres on the authorities' presentation of religion, not on the essence of religion in people's experience of a spiritual reality. Conditions may well be right, not for the death of religion now so confidently being predicted in some quarters, but for its renaissance, though only via a radically different exposition that speaks to today's world.

(e) The universe was not made for Man

If religion is a key part of existential reality and we live in a designed universe where science has detected cosmic principles of self-organisation, holistic structures and progressive development towards realising some kind of cosmic blueprint, and if within that pattern Earth is exquisitely finely tuned for life, does that place Man as the culmination of this whole process? The religious message has indeed often proclaimed just that – that God made the world in order to produce creatures that would respond to his love and that the history of human religious experience has been one of summoning his people to recognise and respond to their relationship with him, calling them back whenever they strayed because they remain the focus and purpose of his world. Again it is tempting to embrace this picture which puts humans at the centre of the universe, spiritually if not physically. But again it should be resisted because it doesn't fit the facts.

If the advent of the human species were the teleological end point of the universe, it seems inconceivable that the stage set for this role should be a universe of almost incomprehensible magnitude, with humans located on a tiny planet in the solar system of a single star amongst 100 billion other stars in a single galaxy amongst 100-200 billion other galaxies, leaving aside the postulated existence of other universes. It also seems inconceivable, if the human race were the objective, that such a stupendous period of time should be spent reaching that point, no less than 99.9993% of the 13.7 billion year lifetime of the universe, and that even on Earth itself more than three billion years should elapse, four-fifths of its entire history of life, before single-cell organisms were superseded by multi-cellular creatures. And it seems scarcely credible, if the emergence of humans were the goal, that the enormously long, hazardous and precarious lineage to homo sapiens should be made subject to recurring mass extinctions which repeatedly wiped out a very high proportion of total global species, such that the odds against survival in the face of such cataclysm were perilously high in the extreme. As a palaeontologist Gould has referred to the "awesome improbability of human evolution"[52], and several critical contingencies can be identified in that evolutionary history when life could easily have taken a very different turn due to chains of unpredictable and fortuitous factors. Even that short period of history, roughly the last 600 million years, leaves out the previous three billion years where the vicissitudes to life remain largely unknown. Against all that background it is difficult to credit that the emergence of humans was preordained or planned for.

Another facet of this argument is: just how unique and special are humans anyway? Such differentiation is focussed not on DNA (shared almost entirely with chimpanzees), but on the staggering complexity of the human brain containing 100 billion interconnected neurons which opens up unprecedented capacities in areas of intelligence, consciousness, aesthetics and spirituality. Even in some of these fields however human uniqueness is not as clear-cut as is sometimes imagined. Experiments have shown that various animals have achieved skills and insight in culture, mind-reading, emotions, tool use, morality, personality, and communication, though only the human brain (so far) has attained more sophisticated versions and the application of abstract reasoning. The nature of human consciousness is still much disputed, but it is likely that at certain levels of complexity, which some have estimated at a critical mass of 500 million inter-connected neurons in the brain, new emergent properties arise which humans have exploited to achieve their own dominance. Even cranial size however is not per se sufficient explanation when Neanderthals had bigger brains than homo sapiens and elephants today have a larger brain, though in terms of brain-body ratio and therefore flexibility and speed of response humans are obviously superior. But what is perhaps most striking is the deeply embedded human belief that this superi-ority marks out the human race, not as a fortuitous contingency in life's lottery nor as a temporary episode in the ever-changing kaleidoscope of the constant climactic-geological-biological interplay on Earth, but as the unique and final pinnacle in the development of life.

Further evolution may soon lay bare that belief for the anthro-pocentric conceit it is. Quite apart from the total unknown of the nature of life forms on any life-bearing planets among the ten thousand trillion estimated to be spread across the universe, on Earth itself the process of novel self-organisation at critical thresholds of complexity yielding new emergent properties is never-ending. The development of a new higher intelligence can only be conjectural, though concepts of the mind as a computer and the mind as an algorithm suggest it might be silicon-based and machine-engineered. What is clear from past experience is that the process is non-linear, unpredictable, ceaseless, and sometimes attended by overwhelming violence and cataclysm. Whilst in the past the latter involved global glaciation and asteroid strikes, both of which will continue to threaten to overwhelm life on Earth at long and irregular intervals, Man's own technological ingenuity has now added the threats of worldwide resource depletion and climate catastrophe as well as the potential for global destruction by nuclear war. Against the perspective of geological time, the human ascendancy is short and precarious. Whilst the dinosaurs dominated Earth for 160 million years, the human supremacy has lasted scarcely 0.1% of that period and yet in such short time is threatening through an unsustainable economy and civilisation to push the planet so far from homeostasis that its ecological elasticities will be overwhelmed, leading to an abrupt and violent tipping over to a radically new equilibrium. So far from the universe being made for Man, it is this grotesque conceit of human beings about the centrality of their role which is primed to destroy the very foundation of their existence.

Destination of the species Conclusion

The phenomenal rise of science in the last four centuries has profoundly changed the checks and balances that previously held the Earth broadly in equilibrium. It has unleashed a techno-logical, industrial and cybernetic power in the hands of the dominant species unparalleled in the history of the planet, which has steadily transformed the modality of stewardship of the Earth to one of ruthless exploitation. The human race has almost become its own geophysical cycle. Its biological carbon produc-tivity is outpaced only by krill in the oceans. Its civil engineering works shift more soil each year than all the world's rivers bring to the seas. Its industrial emissions now eclipse the emissions from all the world's volcanoes. It is now bringing about a species loss in biodiversity on a scale of some of the mass extinctions of palaeohistory. It is transforming the nitrogen cycle, adding more to rainfall even than that added by agriculture. And it is dissem-inating pollution across the globe so that even in the remotest parts of the world such as the Arctic trace contaminants like lead and DDT are now appearing in the natural food chain. This unprecedented mastery over nature has now been exacerbated by two further factors. One is the rise in the human population. It took 150,000 years from the time when homo sapiens moved out of Africa to conquer the world before the human race reached one billion in number, but just 123 years to reach two billion, then only fourteen years to reach three billion, another fourteen years to reach four billion, thirteen years to reach five billion, and just twelve years to reach six billion. UN estimates believe it will reach nine or ten billion by 2050, with 99% of the projected growth in population by that date taking place in the developing world. This would represent a staggering quintupling of the global human population in just a century and a half. The second factor is gross over-exploitation of the Earth's resources, astonishingly bountiful though they are. Half of the world's 2 5 trillion barrels of oil have been utilised since oil was first discovered 150 years ago, but given the demands on oil from worldwide industrialisation and the frenetic growth rate in India and China which alone contain two-fifths of the global population, the oil supply will be exhausted in some forty years. Even more critical is the growing water shortage where global consumption of freshwater is doubling every twenty years. Already 1.2 billion people lack access to clean water, but the UN estimates that by 2025 the numbers living in areas of severe water stress will have risen to a staggering three billion. Fish, a key source of protein, are being hunted to extinction. Nearly half of all fish stocks are fully exploited, 20% are over-exploited, and only 2% are recovering. These examples can be multiplied. The ravaging of the Earth is utterly unsustainable.

The net impact of all these trends on the Earth's carrying capacity has been measured by a technique called ecological footprinting. The charity WWF[140] has calculated that the human race is currently overshooting the planet's biocapacity by 20% and that, on conservative estimates, this will grow to 130% by 2050, so that we will then need 2.3 Earths to sustain its population. A later Footprint of Nations study put the overshoot in 2006 at 40%. Many other attempts at measuring planetary carrying capacity have arrived at similar figures, and agree that a sustainable population for the Earth is around 2.2 billion. What is most alarming about these trends and future predictions is the exponential rate of increase within such a brief period. Set against the 4.5 billion year age of the Earth, these accelerating rates of growth in population, energy consumption, minerals extraction, food and water scarcity, and pollution within a mere half-century, scarcely the batting of an eyelid, are wildly out of proportion both with past experience and future durability. The consequences are entirely predictable. The end of oil, which is a sine qua non for industry, industrialised agriculture, car and plane transportation systems, and for fighting wars, will bring about an economic, social and political dislocation without precedent in human history, and will severely narrow the parameters within which economies, civilisations and individual quality of life operate. Sharp reductions in water availability will generate wars which, given the spread of nuclear weapons, could prove unprecedentedly destructive. The colossal growth of population in the poorer developing world will produce a crisis of massive environmental refugee flight to the more prosperous (and cooler) northern regions of the Earth which will bring the smouldering rich-poor divide into prolonged and violent conflict. The predictions of Malthus (1766-1834) that population excess is kept in check by natural causes such as war, pestilence and famine were disproved by the sharp increase in productivity brought about by the Industrial Revolution and later by oil, but this time it is highly unlikely that any innovation on the necessary scale can stall a huge economic and population crash.

This grim scenario is now exacerbated by the intensifying onset of climate change. Though this phenomenon is not universally accepted (mainly not by those with a vested interest in denial – the oil companies and OPEC), the evidence is very strong that sharply rising greenhouse gas concentrations in the atmosphere, caused largely by fossil fuel burning, are linked (over and above the normal variability of the climate) with increasing average global temperatures and thence with the increasing frequency and ferocity of hurricanes, floods and rising sea levels as well as in other areas with drought, desertification and almost unstoppable forest fires. The greenhouse gas levels have risen from 280 ppm (parts per million) before the Industrial Revolution to 387 ppm today. The great majority of the world's scientists believe that this blanket should be curbed for safety at below 450 ppm, or certainly no more than 550 ppm if runaway climate change is not to devastate the world. Even this scenario may well be too risky since global climate change is not a linear process where warming grows smoothly and predictably, but rather is beset by feedback mechanisms which abruptly, and maybe uncontrollably, magnify the climate change with unpredictable consequences. Scientists are still uncertain whether some of the known mass extinctions in the Earth's history may have happened for these reasons. Such mechanism might include the melting of the Antarctic and Greenland ice-sheets, the die-back of the world's rainforests like the Amazon, and the mass release of billions of tonnes of methane hydrates from the ocean sea-bed.

In the face of such an enormous global risk, a precautionary policy is the only sensible course. The failure of governments and peoples across the world to take any such meaningful action – the Kyoto Protocol of 1997 being limited to only thirty industrialised countries out of 185 and excluding the US, China and India, as well as falling well short of its very modest targets and ending in 2012 with no sign yet of its replacement – says a great deal, if not about man's place in the universe, then certainly about the current state of the human condition. It reveals climate change concerns being sidelined both by the major economic powers determined to maintain their wealth, dominance and competitive edge and by the poorer nations prioritising economic growth over all other considerations to escape poverty and enjoy Western living standards. It reveals a very widespread human commitment to short-term gain over long-term precaution, even though the risk could be incalculably vast. It reveals, for all of man's intelligence and scientific knowledge, a reckless preference for postponing action if it might prove uncomfortable until quite likely too late. If the universe was made for man as some assert, man has comprehensively disappointed – in ruthlessly pursuing economic and military dominance over shared global governance, in ratcheting up grotesque wealth inequalities across the world, and in putting the whole planet at serious risk of climate change convulsion.

So where then is this saga of the human race heading? The optimists have no doubt about man's capacity ultimately to take over the universe. Barrow and Tipler put it thus:

> Once space travel begins, there are in principle no further physical barriers to prevent homo sapiens (or our descendants) from eventually expanding to colonise a substantial portion, if not all, of the visible cosmos. Once this has occurred, it becomes quite reasonable to speculate that the operations of all these intelligent beings could begin to affect the large-scale evolution of the universe"[141].

This hubristic notion complacently assumes that the Earth remains stable and viable as a base for cosmic space travel into the indefinite future. The evidence is mounting strongly that this is not so even in the tiny fraction of time immediately ahead. The pessimists take a very different view. Leslie, in his exploration of Brandon Carter's doomsday argument[142], exhaustively lists both risks already well recognised and risks often unrecognised, as well as specific man-made disasters, and argues powerfully that the likelihood of human extinction is real and quite high, unless strenuous efforts (of which there is as yet little sign) are made to avert it. Lovelock, enunciator of Gaia theory which propounds the idea of a cybernetic network interconnecting the animate and inanimate components of Earth into a living planet, regards the regulatory Gaian mechanisms as powerful enough to dispose of alien elements that threaten its own survival[143], including humankind as the virus if humans continue drastically to undermine its integrity. As an illustration he notes that whilst carbon dioxide has remained fairly constant in the air at below a concentration of 0.03% since the end of the last Ice Age 11,000 years ago, its rapid increase by a quarter in the last century largely as a result of human activity will, if it continues gradually to accelerate, compromise the survival of all living creatures, leading if unchecked to a mass extinction destroying up to 90% of global human populations, a greater cataclysm than any in the recorded history of the Earth.

Upsetting the natural self-regulatory processes that safeguard the Earth's viability could thus terminate a human ascendancy which has lasted a mere 40,000 years, scarcely a flicker of geological time. Humans are not the pinnacle of evolution, simply one stage along the way in a ceaseless process, just one species among many, with intelligence too little matched by wisdom and self-restraint for our own good. The current political and economic governance structures place too much emphasis on competitiveness, aggrandizement, greed and self-interest for humans to achieve their real destiny of living, creatively and co-operatively, within the minutely balanced systems of the cosmos. We are increasingly uncovering the rules that govern these systems, but are not willing to abide within them. Our destiny is still defined in terms of our power, our technological mastery over the whole natural world, our capacity to conquer and colonise the cosmos. We neglect the emergent property of our spirituality, the single most important attribute of human uniqueness, and our capability now in a globalised world to universalise human welfare we subordinate to our primitive drive to dominate. The challenge now for humans is not to transform the world, but to transform themselves.

Glossary for destination of the Species

algorithm	a method of solving a problem involving a finite series of steps
allopatric	relating to groups of similar organisms that could interbreed but don't because they are geographically separated
amino acid	any of a group of 20 water-soluble organic compounds that possess both a carboxyl and an animo group attached to the same carbon atom
amniote	a vertebrate whose embryos are totally enclosed in a fluid-filled sac
arthropoda	invertebrate animals comprising over a million species possessing an outer body layer that functions as a rigid protective exoskeletonand with a body usually forming distinct specialised body regions like head, thorax and abdomen (e.g. crustacea, centipedes)
asteroid	a number of small bodies that revolve round the sum between the orbits of Mars and Jupiter
autocatalysis	catalysis in which one of the products of the reaction is a catalystfor the reaction
axon	the long thread-like part of a nerve-cell (neurone) that carries the nerve impulsetowards either an effector organ or the brain
bacteria	a diverse group of ubiquitous micro-organisms all of which consistof only a single cell that lacks a distinct nuclear membrane

Big Bang	the cosmological theory that all the matter and energy in the universe originated from a state of enormous density and temperature that exploded at a finite moment in the past
bilaterian	animals, including humans, whose body is divided into two halvesthat are mirror images of each other along one plane only
biomass	the total mass of all the organisms of a given type and/or in a given area
black hole	an object in space that has collapsed under its own gravitational forces to such an extent that its escape velocity is equal to the speed of light (186,325 miles per second)
catalytic	the capacity of a substance to increase the rate of a chemical reaction without itself undergoing any permanent chemical change
chert	very hard flints of microcrystalline quartz and chalcedony found inchalk and limestone
chloroplasts	chlorophyll-containing organelles that are found in large numbersin those plants undergoing photosynthesis
chordates	animals characterised by a hollow dorsal nerve cord and later a flexible skeletal rod and gill slits opening from the pharynx (e.g.sea squirts)
cnidaria	a phylum of aquatic invertebrates that include jellyfish, seaanemones and corals
comet	a small body consisting mainly of gas,

	dust and ice that travels round the sun in an eccentric orbit
constant	a term which does not change its value
cortex	the outermost layer of tissue of various organs
cosmological constant	an entity independent of space and time put forward by Einstein to allow for the possibility of a static universe
cyanobacteria	a phylum of photosynthetic bacteria formerly classified as blue-green algae
cyclotron	a cyclic particle accelerator which accelerates charged particles in an outward spiral path inside two hollow conductors
cytochrome	proteins that form part of the electron transport chain inmitochondria and chloroplasts
dark matter	matter that is posited to exist to explain the discrepancy between the actual mass of the universe and that estimated by observations from radio-telescopes
deuteron	a nucleus of a deuterium atom, consisting of a proton and a neutron bound together
dinoflagellate	single-celled organisms that have two flagella for locomotion and usually a rigid cell wall of cellulose encrusted with silica
DNA	deoxyribonucleic acid, the genetic material of most living organisms, which is a major constituent of the chromosomes within the cell nucleus and controls protein synthesis in cells
Doppler effect	the apparent change in the observed

	frequency of a wave as a result of relative motion between the source and the observer
echinoderms	marine invertebrates that include sea urchins and starfish
echolocation	a method used by some animals, such as bats and dolphins, to detect objects in the dark
entropy	a measure of the unavailability of a system's energy to do work
enzyme	a protein that acts as a catalyst in biochemical reactions
epicycle	a small circle whose centre rolls around the circumference of a larger fixed circle
escape velocity	the minimum speed needed by a space vehicle to escape from the gravitational field of a celestial body
eukaryote	an organism consisting of cells in which the genetic material is contained within a distinct nucleus
fractal	a curve or surface generated by a process involving successive subdivision
fractionation	the separation of a mixture of liquids by distillation
function	any operation or procedure which relates one variable to one or more variables
ganglion	a mass of nervous tissue containing many cell bodies and synapses, usually enclosed in a connective-tissue sheath
gauge symmetries	a set of symmetries in quantum fields put forward to explain fundamental interactions

general relativity	Extends Einstein's Special Relativity proposing 4D space-time continuum where space is curved by massive objects.
genome	all the genes contained in a single set of chromosomes
glia	cells of the nervous system that support the neurones
Hamiltonian	a function which expresses the energy of a system in terms of its momentum and positional coordinates
heuristic	a method of solving a problem for which no algorithm exists, i.e.it involves trial and error
Hilbert spaces	a linear vector space that can have an infinite number of dimensions
Hubble constant	the rate at which the velocity of recession of the galaxies increases with distance as determined by the redshift
hydrate	substance formed by the combination of a substance with water
imaginary number	a number that is a multiple of the square root of munus 1
inflation	the idea that the vacuum state gave rise, after Big Bang, to an exponential expansion of the universe
inverse square law	a law in which the magnitude of a physical quantity is proportional to the reciprocal of the square of the distance from the source of that property
isotope	one of two or more atoms of the same element that have the same number of protons in their nucleus, but different numbers of neutrons

isotropic	a medium whose properties are independent of direction
marsupials	mammals where the female bears an abdominal pouch into which the newly born young in a very immature state move to complete their development
mass	a measure of a body's inertia or its resistance to acceleration (often used synonymously with weight)
mechanics	the study of the interactions between matter and the forces acting on it
metabolism	the sum of the chemical reactions that occur within living organisms
metazoa	a sub-kingdom comprising all multicellular animals
microbe	very small creatures (micro-organisms) including bacteria, virusesand fungi
mitochondria	structures within the cytoplasm of plant and animal cells that carry out aerobic respiration
molecule	the smallest part of a chemical compound that can take part in a chemical reaction
mollusc	soft-bodied invertebrates characterised by an unsegmented body
morphogenesis	the development, through growth and differentiation, of form and structure in an organism
nebula	an extended and somewhat fuzzy white haze (as observed with atelescope) consisting largely of interstellar dust and gas
neoteny	the retention of the juvenile body form, or particular features of it, in a mature

animal

neutrino an elementary particle with no charge, thought to have zero rest mass and to travel at the speed of light

nucleosynthesis the synthesis of chemical elements by nuclear processes

nucleotide an organic compound consisting of a nitrogen-containing purine or pyrimidine base linked to a sugar and a phosphate group

organelle a minute structure within a plant or animal cell that has a particular function

phase space a system in which each point represents a state of the system

phase transition a change in a feature that characterises a system

photosynthesis the chemical process by which green plants synthesize organiccompounds from carbon dioxide and water in the presence of sunlight

phylogeny the evolutionary history of an organism or group of related organisms

pituitary a pea-sized endocrine gland attached by a thin stalk to the hypothalamus at the base of the brain

prokaryote an organism in which the genetic material is not enclosed in a cellnucleus

protein any of a large group of organic compounds found in all living organisms, comprising carbon, hydrogen, oxygen and nitrogen, and most also contain sulphur

protists/protoctista a kingdom consisting of unicellular or simple multicellular organisms that

	possess nuclei and cannot be classified as animals, plants or fungi
protozoa	a group of unicellular or acellular, usually microscopic, organismsvery widely disctributed in marine and moist terrestrial habitats
pulsar	a celestial source of radiation emitted in brief (0.03 second to 4seconds) regular pulses
quantum	the minimum amount by which certain properties, such as energy or angular momentum, of a system can change
quasars	a class of astronomical objects that appear on optical photographs as starlike, but have large redshifts quite unlike those of stars
radiometric dating	the use of some measurable change that occurs at a known rate
redshift	a displacement of the lines in the spectra of certain galaxies towards the red end of the visible spectrum
ribosome	a small spherical body within a living cell that is the site of proteinsynthesis
RNA	ribonucleic acid, a complex organic compound in living cells thatis concerned with protein synthesis
scalar quantity	a quantity in which direction is either not applicable (as in temperature) or not specified (as in speed)
singularity	a point of infinite density subject to infinite compression where the laws of physics break down
special relativity	Einstein's theory (1905) that the speed of light is constant and independent of

	the speed of the observer
spectrometer	an instrument for producing a spectrum and measuring the wavelengths, energies, etc. involved
spin	the part of the total angular momentum of a particle that can continue to exist even when the particle is apparently at rest
stromatolite	a rocky cushion-like mass formed by the unchecked growth of millions of lime-secreting blue-green bacteria
supernova	an explosive brightening of a star in which the energy radiated by it increases by an exponential factor of 10s by 10000000000000000 times
superstring theory	a unified theory of the fundamental interactions involving supersymmetry in which the basic objects are one-dimensionalobjects (superstrings)
symbiosis	an interaction between individuals of different species in which both species benefit
synapse	the junction between two adjacent neurones (nerve cells)
taxa	groups of any rank in the hierarchical classification of organisms
tetrapods	jawed chordates comprising all verte-brate animals with four limbs
topology	the branch of geometry concerned with the properties of geometrical objects that are unchanged by continuous deformations such as twisting or stretching
trilobite	an extinct marine arthropod that flour-

ished 590-280 million years ago

vector   a quantity in which both the magnitude and the direction must be stated

vector space   a set of vectors of which the sum, when added together, is also a the vector

References

Chapter 1

SJ Gould, Ever Since Darwin, p.44

P Atkins, Creation Revisited, Harmondsworth, Penguin, 1994

R Penrose, The Emperor's New Mind, OUP, 1994, p.445

Chapter 2

Statement co-signed by Eric Lerner and 33 other scientists from 10 countries at www.cosmologystatement.org

Riccardo Scarpa, of the European Southern Observatory in Santiago, Chile

Mordechai Milgrom, of the Weizmann Institute in Rehovot, Israel, in a paper in 1985

K Ward, God, Chance and Necessity, Oneworld Publications, 1996, p.48

Chapter 3

JD Barrow and FJ Tipler, The Anthropic Cosmological Principle, Oxford, Clarendon Press, 1986;

PCW Davies, The Accidental Universe, CUP, 1982;

J Leslie, Universes, Routledge, 1996;

IL Rozenthal, 'Physical Laws and the Numerical Values of Fundamental Constants', Soviet Physics: Uspekhi, 1980, vol.23, p.293-305

R Penrose, in CJ Isham, R Penrose and DW Sciama, eds., Quantum Gravity, 2, 1981, OUP, p.248-9

RH Dicke and PJE Peebles, in SW Hawking and W Israel, eds., General Relativity, CUP, 1979, p.514

JD Barrow and FJ Tipler, op. cit., 1986, p.358-9

P Ehrenfest, Proceedings of the Amsterdam Academy, vol.20, 1917, p.200

GFR Ellis and GB Brundrit, 'Life in the Infinite Universe', Quarterly Journal of the Royal Astronomical Society, vol.20,

1979, p.37-41

AD Linde, 'The Universe: Inflation out of Chaos', New Scientist, 1985, 7 March, p.14-18

AH Guth, in GW Gibbons, SW Hawking and W Israel, eds., The Very Early Universe, CUP, 1983

DV Nanopoulos and others in CERN Preprints of 1984

TWB Kibble, in MJ Duff and CJ Isham, eds., Quantum Structure of Space and Time, Cambridge, 1982, p.395

E Guzig, J Gehenian and I Prigogine, Nature, 17 December 1987, p.621-4

EP Tryon, 'Is the universe a vacuum fluctuation?', Nature, 14 December 1973, p.396-7

JA Wheeler, in CW Misner, KS Thorne and JA Wheeler, 'Gravitation', WH Freeman, San Francisco, 1973

K Sato, H Kodoma, M Sasaki and K Maeda, Physics Letters, vol.108B, 14 January 1982, p.103-7

A Linds, in GW Gibbons, SW Hawking and STC Siklos, eds., The Very Early Universe, CUP, 1983

Chapter 4

R Brandenberger and C Vafa, in B Greene, The Elegant Universe, Vintage, 2000, p.358

L Smolin, The Life of the Cosmos, Phoenix, 1977, especially chapter 7

Chapter 5

Nature, 7 November 1996

S Kauffman, At Home in the Universe: the Serrch for Laws of Complexity, Viking, 1995

J Parkes, in The Evolution of Hydrothermal Ecosystems on Earth, eds. G Bock and J Goode, p.37

E Shock, 'High Temperature Life Without Photosynthesis as a Model for Mars', in Journal of Geophysical Research – Planets, 102, 1997, 23687

P Davies, The Fifth Miracle: the Search for the Origin of Life, Allen Lane (Penguin Press), 1998, p.149

B Gladman et al., 'The Exchange of Impact Ejecta Between Terrestrial Planets', Science, 271, 1996, 1387

P Weber and M Greenberg, 'Can Spores Survive in Inter-Stellar Space?', Nature 316, 1985, p.403

CM Kay, 'Promethean Ice', Mercury, 25, 1996, p.15

F Hoyle and C Wickramasinghe, Or Place in the Cosmos, Phoenix, 1993, p.99

C Woese, 'Evolution of the Genetic Code', Naturwissenschaften 60, 1973, p.447

P Davies, The Fifth Miracle, p.82-4

Chapter 6

35A AH Knoll, Life on a Young Planet, Princeton University Press, 2003

PE Cloud, A Working Model of the Primitive Earth, American Journal of Science, 272, 1968, p.537-48

DC Catling, KJ Zahule and CP McKay, Biogenic Methane, Hydrogen Escape, and the Irreversible Oxidation of the Early Earth, Science, 293, 2001, p.839-43

DJ Des Marais, Isotopic Evolution of the Biogeochemical Carbon Cycle during the Proterozoic Eon, Organic Chemistry, 27, 1997, p.185-93

W Martin and M Muller, The Hydrogen Hypothesis for the First Eukaryote, Nature, 392, 1998, p.37-41

WB Harland and MS Rudwick, The Great Infra-Cambrian Ice Age, Scientific American, 211 (2), 1964, p.28-36

40A AH Knoll, ibid., p.208

J Kirschvink, Late Proterozoic Low Latitude Glaciation: the Snowball Earth, 1992, p.51-2, in JW Schopf and C Klein, eds., The Proterozoic Biosphere: A Multidisciplinary Study, CUP, 1992

PF Hoffman and DP Schrag, The Snowball Earth Hypothesis:

Testing the Limits of Global Change, Terra Nova 2002, 14, p.129-55

SJ Gould, Wonderful Life: the Burgess Shale and the Nature of History, Norton, New York, 1989

JR Nursall, Oxygen as a Pre-requisite to the Origin of the Metazoa, Nature, 1959, 183, p.1170-2

DE Canfield and A Teske, Late Proterozoic Rise in Atmospheric Oxygen Concentration Inferred from Phylogenetic and Sulphur-Isotope Studies, Nature, 1996, 382, p.127-32

SJ Gould and NE Eldredge, Punctuated Equilibrium Comes of Age, Nature, 1993, 366, p.223-7

Chapter 7

R Bakker, The Dinosaur Heresies, Longmans, 1987

C Sagan, Dragons of Eden, Coronet, 1978, p.135

M and J Gribbin, Being Human, Phoenix, 1993, p.94

M and J Gribbin, ibid., p.137

DC Johanson and MA Edey, Lucy, Granada, 1981

SJ Gould, Wonderful Life, Penguin, 1989, p.24

SC Morris, Life's Solution: Inevitable Humans in a Lonely Universe, CUP, p.127

JD McIver and G Stonedahl, in Annual Review of Entomology, 38, 1993. p.353-79

SC Morris, ibid., p.236

L Marino, Convergence and Complex Cognitive Abilities in Cetaceans and Primates, in Brain Behaviour and Evolution, 59, 2002, p.28

R Foley, Commentary on RR Skelton and HM McHenry, in Trends in Evolution and Ecology, 8, 1993, p.196-7

Chapter 8

M-C King and AC Wilson, in Science, 11 April 1975

SJ Gould, Ever Since Darwin, Penguin, 1977, p.63-8

59A J Trefil, Are We Unique?, New York, John Wiley, 1997

SJ Gould, The Panda's Thumb, WW Norton, 1982

WH Calvin, The Cerebral Code, MIT Press, Cambridge, Massachusetts, 1996

R Penrose, The Emperor's New Mind, New York, OUP, 1989; and Shadows of the Mind, , New York, OUP, 1994

DC Dennett, Consciousness Explained, Boston: Little, Brown, 1991

DJ Chalmers, The Conscious Mind, New York, OUP, 1996

F Crick, The Astonishing Hypothesis, Simon and Schuster, 1994

J Cohen and I Stewart, The Collapse of Chaos: Discovering Simplicity in a Complex World, Penguin Books, 1994

A Damasio, Descartes' Error: Emotion, Reason and the Laws of Physics, New York, Avon Books, 1994

F Crick, op. cit., 1994

Chapter 9

As recounted in The Babylonian Genesis, ed. A Heidel, University of Chicago Press, 1963

J Campbell, Primitive Mythology, London, Penguin, 1969

K Jaspers, The Origin and Goal of History, New Haven, Yale University Press, 1953

K Armstrong, The Great Transformation, London, Atlantic Books, 2006

K Armstrong, ibid., p.39-40

K Ward, The Case for Religion, Oxford, Oneworld Publications, 2004, p.124 and passim

D Hume, Natural History of Religion, in Dialogues and Natural History of Religion, ed. JCA Gaskin, 1757; and OUP, 1993, p.176

J. Frazer, The Golden Bough, 1922; and Harmondsworth, Penguin, 1996

E Durkheim, The Elementary Forms of Religious Life, trans. J. Swain, Allen and Unwin, 1963

M Epstein, A Genis and S Vladiv-Glover, Russian Post-

Modernism: New Perspectives in Post-Soviet Culture, New York, Berghahn Books, 1999

Quoted in C Taylor, A Secular Age, Harvard University Press, Cambridge, Massachusetts, 2007

J Hick, An Interpretation of Religion, London, Macmillan, 1989, p.23

K Ward, op. cit., p.232

K Armstrong, A History of God, Heinemann, London, 1993, p.456

Chapter 10

Teresa of Avila, The Interior Castle, Fifth Abode, Ch.1, in Oeuvres, trans. Bonix 3, p.421-4

St. Johnof the Cross, The Dark Night of the Soul, bk.2, ch.17, in Vie et Oeuvres, 3rd edition, Paris, 1893, 3, p.428-32

St. Augustine, Confessions, 9, 24, trans. H Chadwick, Oxford, 1991, p.171

Gregory, Morals on Job, 24, 11

L Weatherhead, The Christian Agnostic, Hodder and Stoughton, 1965, p.40

Meister Eckhart, in Dominican Spirituality, by S Tugwell, in L Dupre and D Saliers, eds., Christian Spirituality III, New York and London, 1989, p.28

Meister Eckhart, The Essential Sermons, Commentaries, Treatises, and Defence, E Coledge and B McGinn, London, 1981, p.87

W James, The Varieties of Religious Experience, Viking Penguin Inc., 1982, p.409

M Furlong, in the Daily Mail, 24 December 1962

R Otto, The Idea of the Holy, 1917

Josephus, Antiquities, 18, 3

W Barclay, The Gospel of Luke, St. Andrews Press, 1957, p.7

Luke's Gospel, ch.1, verses 39-40 and 56

Luke's Gospel, ch.22, verse 15

Matthew's Gospel, ch.20, verse 22

Luke's Gospel, ch.22, verse 18

L Weatherhead, op. cit., p.75-6

John's Gospel, ch.20, verses 1-20

J Huxley, The Observer, 31 March 1963

John's Gospel, ch.16, verse 16

Paul's First Letter to the Corinthians, ch.15, verse

R Bell, Introduction to the Qur'an

John's Gospel, ch.16, verses 12-13

K Ward op. cit., 2004, p.88-9

K Ward, op. cit, 2004, p.98

Chapter 11

L Newbiggin, Foolishness to the Greeks, SPCK, 1986, p.8

SJ Gould, Wonderful Life, Penguin, 1989, p.25

SC Morris, op.cit., p.xii

HJ Jerison, The Evolution of the Brain and Intelligence, New York, Academy Press, 1973

SJ Gould, Ever Since Darwin: Reflections in Natural History, Penguin Books, 1977, p.61

E Laszlo, The Creative Cosmos, Floris Books, Edinburgh, 1993, p.85-6; MK Munitz, Cosmic Understanding: Philosophy and Science of the Universe, Princeton, 1986, p.239-40; S Hawking, A Brief History of Time, Bantam Books, London, p.131-40; P Davies and J Gribbin, The Matter Myth, Touchstone Books, New York, 1992, p.284-6

J Gribbin and MRees, Cosmic Coincidences, Bantam Books, New York and London, 1989, p.269

F Hoyle, The Intelligent Universe, Michael Joseph, London, 1983, p.218

J Lovelock and L Margulis, Tellus, 1974

J Lovelock, Gaia: A New Look at Life on Earth, 1979

N Eldredge and SJ Gould, Punctuated Equilibria: An Alternative to Phyletic Gradualism

E Mayr, Systematics and the Origin of Species, New York, Columbia University Press, 1942

L Margulis and D Sagan, Microcosmos: Four Billion Years of Microbial Evolution

S Ghosh, Nature,vol.425, 2003, p.48

L Newbiggin, op. cit., p.36

Chapter 12

123 S Hawking A Brief History of Time, Bantam Press, 1988, p.175

Popper and J Eccles, The Self and Its Brain, Berlin, Springer International, 1977, p.14

SJ Gould and N Eldredge, Palaeobiology, 3, 1977, p.115

SA Kauffman, At Home in the Universe: the Search for Laws of Complexity, Viking, 1995

SA Kauffman, Emergent Properties in Random Complex Automata, Physica, 10D, 1984, p.145

S Wolfram, 'Statistical Mechanics of Cellular Automata', Reviews of Modern Physics, 55, 1983, p.601

I Prigogine, From Being to Becoming: Time and Complexity in the Physical Sciences, Freeman, San Francisco, 1980, p.23

D Bohm, 'Some Remarks on the Notion of Order', in CH Waddington

R Rosen, 'Some Epistemological Issues in Physics and Biology', in BJ Hiley and FD Peat, eds., Quantum Implications: Essays in Honour of David Bohm, Routledge and Kegan Paul, London, 1987

R Sheldrake, A New Science of Life, Blond and Briggs, London, 1981

G Montalenti, 'From Aristotle to Democritus via Darwin', in FJ Ayala and T Dobzhansky, eds., Studies in the Philosophy of Biology, Macmillan, London, 1974, p.13

P Davies, The Cosmic Blueprint, Penguin Books, London, 1987, p.200

K Ward, A Vision to Pursue: Beyond the Crisis in Christianity, SCM Press, 1991, p.147

S Clark, New Scientist, 24 May 2008, p.37

Chapter 13

A Berry, The Next 500 Years, Headline Book Publishing, 1995, p.186-7

L Smolin, The Life of the Cosmos, Phoenix, 1997, p.162

W Poundstone, The Recursive Universe, OUP, 1987, p.122-32

World Wildlife Fund, Living Planet Report, 2005

JD Barrow and FJ Tipler, The Anthropic Cosmological Principle, OUP, 1986, p.614

J Leslie, The End of the World, Routledge, 1996

J Lovelock, The Ages of Gaia, Norton, New York, and OUP, London, 1988.

BOOKS

O is a symbol of the world, of oneness and unity. In different cultures it also means the "eye," symbolizing knowledge and insight. We aim to publish books that are accessible, constructive and that challenge accepted opinion, both that of academia and the "moral majority."

Our books are available in all good English language bookstores worldwide. If you don't see the book on the shelves ask the bookstore to order it for you, quoting the ISBN number and title. Alternatively you can order online (all major online retail sites carry our titles) or contact the distributor in the relevant country, listed on the copyright page.

See our website www.o-books.net for a full list of over 500 titles, growing by 100 a year.

And tune in to myspiritradio.com for our book review radio show, hosted by June-Elleni Laine, where you can listen to the authors discussing their books.

MySpiritRadio